SHAPING THE FUTURE
Girls and Our Destiny

SHAPING THE FUTURE
Girls and Our Destiny

PHYLLIS KILBOURN, EDITOR

WILLIAM CAREY
LIBRARY

together for children
EQUIP

Viva and Fuller Theological Seminary are working together to equip Christians working for and with children worldwide.

Shaping the Future: Girls and Our Destiny
Copyright © 2008 by Phyllis Kilbourn and Viva Equip Resources

Cover and Text Design: Hugh Pindur
Copyediting: Jennifer Orona
Editorial Manager: Naomi Bradley

Published by William Carey Library
1605 E. Elizabeth Street
Pasadena, CA 91104
www.missionbooks.org

William Carey Library is a ministry of the U.S. Center for World Mission, Pasadena, CA.
www.uscwm.org

Unless otherwise noted, all scripture is taken from the HOLY BIBLE, NEW INTERNATIONAL VERSION®. Copyright © 1973, 1978, 1984 International Bible Society. Used by permission of Zondervan. All rights reserved. The "NIV" and "New International Version" trademarks are registered in the United States Patent and Trademark Office by International Bible Society. Use of either trademark requires the permission of International Bible Society.

Library of Congress Cataloging-in-Publication Data

Shaping the Future : Girls and Our Destiny / Phyllis Kilbourn, editor.
     p. cm.
  ISBN 978-0-87808-002-1 (pbk.)
1. Missions. 2. Church work with children. 3. Girls--Social conditions.
4. Girls--Religious life. 5. Self-esteem. 6. Self-actualization
(Psychology) I. Kilbourn, Phyllis.
  BV2616.S53 2008
  259'.22--dc22
                          2008015668

CONTENTS

Contributing Authors

Sue Bates passed away in 2007. During her life, she worked in Romania with the mission group *Inasmuch*, a mission focused on working with the poorest of the poor. One of Sue's prime concerns was for street girls, especially those coming out of state-run orphanages totally unprepared for life outside these residences and with no home offered other than the streets. She and her husband started several homes for young girls and their babies.

Renita Boyle has a B.A. (Hons) degree in theology and is the former associate editor of *Reaching Children at Risk*. Boyle has worked extensively with children and youth and recently completed a project for the Toybox Charity, which works with street children in Guatemala.

Snowden Albright Howe is a graduate of the University of North Carolina at Chapel Hill. She received a master's degree in theological studies at Gordon-Conwell Theological Seminary and is a licensed professional counselor in North Carolina, USA. She is employed by Agapé Christian Counseling, Inc., where she works with adults and children.

Phyllis Kilbourn has a Ph.D. from Trinity International University, Deerfield, Illinois. She has served with WEC International since 1967, serving in Kenya and Liberia, and she founded both Rainbows of Hope, a ministry to children in crisis worldwide, and Crisis Care Training International. She has researched the needs of the girl child in many countries in Africa, Asia, and Latin America. Kilbourn is the editor of five other handbooks in this series.

David D. Kupp earned his Ph.D. from the University of Durham in England. He has recently moved from Kenya to Canada, where he is special programs director for World Vision Canada. David is passionate about building strategic servant leadership and innovative learning around participatory community development. He works through the windows of teaching, facilitation, strategic planning, and writing, built on the touchstones of biblical theology, peace, and justice.

Nancy LaDue, a registered nurse, has an associate of science in nursing degree (ASB) and an associate in general studies degree (AGS) from Indiana University. Nancy serves with Rainbows of Hope as a volunteer nurse to the 180 children in Casa Bernabe, a home for street and abandoned children in Guatemala.

Marjorie McDermid, formerly a missionary to Equatorial Guinea, West Africa, with WEC International, has worked in various children's ministries and currently serves as a child advocate and writer for Rainbows of Hope. She is the former editor of Worldwide Thrust, WEC's communiqué in the USA, and co-editor of *Sexually Exploited Children: Working to Protect and Heal,* a book in this series.

Vongai Nzenza works for World Vision Mozambique as a program officer. Part of that time she also works as the gender coordinator for the Southern African region. She graduated in Zimbabwe as a teacher and furthered her studies in Australia, where she graduated with a B.A. in town planning and a master's degree in development studies. She worked for World Vision Australia for five years before moving back to Africa.

Thirza Schneider, while working with Rainbows of Hope, traveled to South America, Africa, and Asia to work with and conduct research into the lives of children in crisis. She has now moved to Central Asia with Oasis, where she founded a project among street children. Schneider has a B.A. in journalism and sociology from City University in London and an M.A. in children's and family ministry from Bethel Seminary in St. Paul, Minnesota, USA.

Desiree Segura-April earned her Ph.D. in intercultural studies from Asbury Theological Seminary E. Stanley Jones School of World Mission, Kentucky, USA. Her dissertation focused on the missiological theories and praxis of missionaries working with girl children in Latin America. She currently teaches as the assistant professor of children at risk at Fuller Theological Seminary in Pasadena, California.

FOREWORD

Saturday, August 6, 1966, in a modern Middle Eastern city, began as an ordinary day. By late afternoon, however, my husband, Will, and I were looking at our very premature, newborn twin sons. In the hours that followed, the nurses hurried up and down the hall bringing visitors by my room to see this "American woman who was so rich to have birthed four sons." Our two older sons and our one very precious daughter were waiting at home, but that little daughter did not appear worthy to be counted in our riches.

Timothy went to be with Jesus after a few hours, and Todd followed him ten days later. Heaven came closer and we rested in God's goodness but the continued, determined remarks of those nurses left an imprint on my young mother-heart. Early in the years of our service overseas, we discovered that daughters were a big disappointment to many families; to some, girls were symbols of shame.

Many years later, we heard Dr. Phyllis Kilbourn speak on "Children in Crisis" at Cornerstone, the WEC Bible College in Holland. Along with the student body, we were stunned by her presentation of children from so many parts of God's world. To wrap our minds around the issue of the suffering of millions of children was overwhelming. To understand the plight of girl children was even more astounding.

Millions of female babies never survive nine months in the womb. Gender-selected abortion is abortion of the fetus simply because it is a female. Female infanticide is also defined as deliberate murder of the girl child or death as a result of neglect. Although several governments outlaw the use of ultrasound for gender-selected abortions, physicians still choose this technology to assist the women who choose abortion rather than give birth to a girl child. Female infanticide and gender-selected abortions are forms of violence that devalue the girl child and all females in society. In many countries, laws and constitutions guarantee legal protection of females. Nevertheless, it is never hard to find loopholes to deny females their rights. The ease with which this violence is carried out opens the door to continued violence throughout the lives of girl children and on into adulthood.

A daughter is viewed as a liability. She understands very early in her life that she is inferior and subordinate to males. Sons are celebrated and highly valued. This is evident at almost every level of society. United Nations studies done by non-governmental organizations show that girls have a much lower level of literacy, consistently receive less medical care, have a higher incidence of malnutrition, work longer hours, and are generally poorer than boys. Child marriages hold young girls captive throughout life. These marriages further contribute to poverty, high illiteracy, early childbirth, malnourished infants, high infant mortality, and low life expectancy.[1] Many governments state that child marriages are illegal but laws have little effect on the actual lives of child brides.

Many parents are reluctant to educate their daughters, believing that the education of girls brings no returns. You do not need education for reproducing, cooking, carrying water, collecting firewood, milking cows, or performing other farm labor. When a daughter marries, she becomes the property of her husband's family, her major function being to produce sons for the following generation. Even if girls are sent to school, they are very likely to be pulled out to help at home or pulled out in their teenage years for fear of verbal and sexual abuse by fellow students or male faculty members. Rape, pregnancy, and HIV infections are prevalent among school dropouts. Most of the time, the girls stand little chance of finding a listening ear or a caring heart.

In Psalm 11:4, we are reminded: "The Lord is in his holy temple, the Lord is on his heavenly throne. He observes everyone on earth; his eyes examine them." What a comfort to know that he is watching and working on behalf of girl children in our world.

---

1 UNICEF, *The State of the World's Children 2007: Women and Children: The Double Dividend of Gender Equality* (New York: UNICEF, 2007).

Phyllis, we are grateful that you have written this book. Thank you for taking us into the troubled world of girl children around the globe and leading us along the path toward practical strategies and purpose to elevate their lives. You bring us through to the glorious hope of God's intervention for the girl child through the loving hands of his servants and through training community leaders. We rejoice that he is increasing the voices of precious girls along with their loving leaders, who will together happily sing the words,

When He cometh, when He cometh
To make up His jewels,
All His jewels, precious jewels,
His loved and His own.

Like the stars of the morning,
His bright crown adorning.
They shall shine in their beauty,
Bright gems for His crown.

Rhoda Longnecker
Missionary in Asia and the Middle East

ACKNOWLEDGEMENTS

The Psalmist declares that children, including the girl child, have been given to us as a heritage, a gift from God. Children also are a sign of God's favor (Psalm 127:3–5). The authors in this book highly esteem girl children as Jesus did when he opened his arms to receive, welcome, and bestow a healing touch upon them. Because they value the girl child, the authors are actively engaged in various aspects of protecting and caring for these special God-given gifts. They count it an honor to give their time and expertise to becoming a voice on behalf of girl children, making a significant investment in their lives.

Along with the listed book authors, we must not forget the true authors behind these pages. Countless project workers from several countries and the children in their care, while not feeling capable or having the time to put their thoughts on paper, have nevertheless shared reams of information with us verbally. They freely opened their hearts to share their concerns and problems, their pains and joys, their desires and wishes, and, above all, their dreams and aspirations for a better world for the girl child. Their input has guided the development of this book.

Those of us who have been privileged to blend our voices with theirs through the pages of this book want nothing more than to inform, educate, and encourage ministry with the girl child, wherever she is found and in whatever situation. The task at hand is certainly overwhelming, often discouraging, and seldom successful numerically. However, Naaman's slave girl is an example of what heaven proves over and over again—that rejoicing is the reward of each single soul redeemed. Let us indeed pray together that more and more belong to little girls.

PREFACE

Children were an integral part of my life during the many years I spent in a rural village in Liberia. The drums rolled as jubilant moms and friends gathered on the local airstrip next to the maternity clinic to joyously participate in the traditional dances that welcomed the newborn babies into their world. Living near the clinic, I had countless opportunities to join in the welcoming celebrations for these brand-new village citizens.

Part of their and every babies' birthright is the gift of childhood—that special God-given time for them to grow and develop in safe, nurturing, and happy environments. Childhood is also the time when families and societies recognize the dignity and worth of children, doing everything possible to ensure that they enjoy a protected childhood and are provided with opportunities that enable them to develop their full God-given potential. Careful attention and happy childhoods, however, are often denied the girl child. From birth onwards, her life can be full of denials that squelch her joy, her sense of dignity and self-worth, and the development of her God-endowed gifts and potential.

In the 1980s, UNICEF India recognized the deprivation of girls as a gender concern. The issue was seen as having global relevance, and "The Girl Child" was incorporated in the UNICEF presentation at the Nairobi Conference on Women and Development in 1985. The 1990 South Asian Association for Regional Cooperation summit declared the 1990s to be the Decade of the Girl Child. Since then, support for girl child issues has continued to acquire momentum.

Before discussing the girl child, a clear distinction needs to be made between the terms sex and gender. Biological characteristics identify the sex of an individual as male or female. Gender, on the other hand, is a social construct. Gender is what it means in a particular society to be male or female. Gender attributes include codes of behavior considered appropriate to each gender, along with a division of labor between the two genders.

A recent World Vision report stated why it is crucial to support girl child issues: "Girls are the world's most squandered gift. They are precious human beings with enormous potential, but across the world, they are generally the last to have their basic needs met and the first to have their basic rights denied."[2] The girl child quickly learns there is a high price to pay for being born a girl.

An ingrained bias against women and girls, exhibited in a culture's attitudes, treatment, and valuing of the girl child, is the culprit behind the "world's most squandered gift." These biases imply that the girl child is inferior to the boy child, worthy of drowning, aborting, and being denied the basic rights of childhood—simply because she had the misfortune to be born a girl.

From a Christian perspective, we know that all children are equally important and precious to God. To believe differently denies God's justice and character. It rejects the truth that all children are created in the image of God. Advocates also recognize that today's girls are tomorrow's women, and that for a girl to reach her full potential in all stages of life, she needs to be nurtured in an empowering environment, where her needs for survival, protection, and development are met and her equal rights safeguarded.

An investment in the girl child is not meant to be an exclusion of the boy child. However, as many educators and child rights workers point out, the rightful treatment and status of girls will enhance the "lives of boy children." As we create a more just world for girls, we will experience vast social, cultural, economic, political, and spiritual advancement. An investment in girl children is an investment for all people and for the future of our world.

This book is meant to be a tool for helping you make an investment in the lives of the girl children you encounter. The first step in responding to the needs of the girl child is to become informed of the root issues causing her troubles. The more I worked on this book, the clearer it became that this would at best be a primer in facilitating a deeper

---

2   World Vision, *Every Girl Counts: Development, Justice, and Gender* (Monrovia, CA: World Vision Canada, 2001), 6.

understanding of the complex, multi-faceted issues confronting her. Volumes would be required to plumb the depths of the cultural and other concerns shaping the girl child's world.

The first section provides a global overview of girl child issues stemming from gender discrimination. We begin by laying the theological foundation for valuing, treating, and ministering to the girl child by examining how her heavenly Father considers her. Next, we look at the root causes of girl child issues in a historical overview.

The overview continues with several stories of life as a girl child in various cultural contexts. These stories reveal that though having different cultural expressions, girl child issues thrive in many settings.

The third section depicts some of the barriers that prevent the girl child from experiencing a normal, happy, healthy childhood. These barriers are not presented to criticize cultures or to simply present a litany of woes inflicted on the girl child. Rather, this section is meant to help workers gain an understanding of needed interventions; these are real experiences that girl children confront on a daily basis.

Section four provides strategies to help girl children everywhere surmount these barriers and experience the joys, security, self-esteem, and other God-given rights and privileges accorded to every child. A general overview of strategies for ministry sets the tone for a more in-depth look at the strategies of education, advocacy, and spiritual healing. Also included are some specific strategies being conducted by government and community leaders who are paving the way for change in their societies.

In conclusion, through a historical fictional retelling of the story of Naaman's young servant girl, we are given opportunity to reflect on "the emotional truth of her life" as a captive girl child in a foreign land. As an exile, a captive, and a slave, she loses her former status as a valued family member. Though in need of a miracle of her own, she allows God to use her in the healing of another. Her act of forgiveness and grace changed history, and her story demonstrates that there is healing for the deep emotional wounds inflicted on the girl child.

At the Fourth World Conference on Women held in Beijing, a rosebud symbolized the life of the girl child. Will the rosebud remain just a forgotten symbol? Or will we have the joy of watching the buds bloom into beautiful roses? Every girl has childhood dreams and aspirations. Her Creator has also endowed her with the potential to realize her goals. With your help, and God enabling you, many rosebuds will open and bloom fully, causing girls, like Naaman's servant girl, to realize their full God-given potential.

Phyllis Kilbourn
June 2008

INTRODUCTION

Girls face the double challenge of being female and being young, which can result in them having little opportunity to make decisions about their lives. Discrimination against girls is grounded in a series of traditions and norms, based on the assumption that biological differences between females and males justify that girls are denied access to rights, opportunity and voice.

PLAN UK, "EXECUTIVE SUMMARY," *BECAUSE I AM A GIRL: THE STATE OF THE WORLD'S GIRLS 2007*, 2

CHAPTER 1

BORN A GIRL: A WORLDWIDE CHALLENGE

Thirza Schneider

On a recent trip to Zambia, I had the privilege of visiting the premature babies' ward at the University Teaching Hospital in Lusaka. Lying in an old incubator was a set of triplets. Frail and tiny as they were, they had a mother to look after and feed them, unlike many of the other babies in that ward. However, after a few days it came to our attention that the mother always first checked the sex of the baby she was about to feed. Soon after, the little baby girl died. Her two brothers were alive and doing better every day. The little girl child was literally starved to death by her own mother. Questions flooded my mind. Why had the mother allowed her sweet, innocent daughter to die? What was it about this girl that had robbed her of the chance to live?

While doing research for this chapter, I gained an extensive overview of the worldwide discrimination against the girl child. I read many insightful statistics, learned about the various issues involved, and was even offered a variety of explanations, yet I received no real answers. Why do the cultures in so many countries around the world regard the female as less valuable than the male? When and how did this belief system come into our world, bringing with it such evil consequences? How does our rebellion against God and everything He created us to be contribute to this great downfall in our God-given morals, beliefs, and consciences?

Many girls all over the world are forced to overcome incredible odds to make it in life. If they are allowed to be born, they stand the chance of death in infancy, either through murder, abuse, neglect, or sickness. If they survive to the age of five, they face a life of servitude, submission, child-bearing, brokenness, exploitation, violence, sexual abuse, and discrimination. All of this takes place only because they are female.

In this book, the term "girl child" describes a female child up to the age of eighteen. Usually, the term carries with it negative images of discrimination and abusive treatment prevalent in many developing countries. As you will read in the following chapters, however, a female child faces challenges unique to her even in the developed world.

Discrimination against the girl child is with her from the womb to the tomb:

- Pre-birth: Ultrasound and amniocentesis test results are used to abort unwanted baby girls.
- Infancy: Female infants experience infanticide and discriminatory neglect; girls are also breastfed less and weaned earlier.
- Childhood: Girls receive less nourishing food, are immunized less and taken for medical care later and in worse condition than boys; girls get much less education and have to work up to twice as many hours in the home as boys.
- Pre-adolescence: Girls are married off much earlier than boys.
- Adolescence: As child brides, many girls get pregnant in their teenage years, facing great health risks for themselves and their babies.[3]

---

3   UNICEF, *State of the World's Children 2007: The Double Dividend of Gender Equality* (New York: UNICEF, 2006), 4–5; Plan UK, *Because I am a Girl: The State of the World's Girls 2007* (London: Plan International, 2007), 14, 17, http://www.plan-uk. org/pdfs/plan_uk-girls_report2007.pdf.

FORMS OF DISCRIMINATION & ABUSE TOWARD GIRL CHILDREN

During his years as president of World Vision, Robert Seiple said: "The most disposable human commodity—and these should be repulsive words to us—in the world today is the girl child, the little girl."[4]

As you read this volume, several important and interrelated themes will be examined from a variety of different angles. These themes, described in Parts One, Two, and Three, provide a backdrop for Part Four's discussion of effective ways to empower girl children through ministry.

GENDER EQUALITY

Customs, traditions, beliefs, practices, social norms, and values develop over centuries. Because these are steeped in history, change is often resisted aggressively. Where lineage and inheritance are traced through the man, the inevitable result is the devaluation of the woman.

"Because she is of no value, she is a burden to the family; and because she is a burden, she is of no value," says Radha Paul (World Vision's vice president for people).[5]

Girls face and experience discrimination, sexual stereotypes, rejection, devaluation, and even violence, often at the hands of the people whom the girls should most be able to trust and love.

In certain cultures, a baby girl's birth is met with mourning rather than with celebration. If the baby is the second or third daughter, her mother becomes an object of pity in her community. Her husband is likely to leave her for another woman, hoping that this one will bear him a male heir.

---

4   Robert A. Seiple, "A Rent in the Garment," in *The Girl Child: Enhancing Life, Sustaining Hope 1998 Washington Forum,* ed. World Vision (Federal Way, WA: The Institute for Global Engagement, World Vision Inc., 1998), 9.
5   Radha Paul, "What About the Girl Child?," *Together* (January-March 2000): 13.

Although in western culture this bias against the baby girl is perhaps not as obvious, pink or blue clothes and dolls or guns for toys reinforce the gender distinctions in our society and make us acutely aware of our male/female consciousness. In the United States of America, surveys have revealed a clear preference for male babies as the first child. Western society also puts enormous pressure on young girls to keep their bodies strikingly thin, leading to potentially fatal eating disorders such as anorexia and bulimia, along with emotional and psychological problems, including extremely low self-esteem, depression, and suicidal tendencies.

In many societies, the patriarchal social structure, along with long-practiced customs, taboos, and superstitions, catch the girl child in a web of prejudices that wraps around and chokes her individuality and slowly but surely molds her into the "ideal wife"—quiet, submissive, self-effacing, self-sacrificing, long-suffering, devout, obedient without protest, and silently suffering a multitude of humiliations and violence.

Not respected as a child, the girl child in many cultures is forced into the roles of a woman, a wife, a mother, the sole food producer, and an illiterate homemaker before she turns sixteen.

HEALTH & NUTRITION

Not only do girl children have less access to nutritious foods and health care, but they also undergo many cultural (and sometimes violent) experiences specifically because of their gender. As has already been mentioned, media and self-image contribute to eating disorders, emotional and psychological challenges, and other health-related issues for girls. Female genital mutilation (FGM), forced early marriage, and teenage pregnancy also have serious health consequences.

ACCESS

Neglect is the greatest cause of sickness and death among girls between two and five years old worldwide.[6]

For infants and toddlers, differential feeding practices have been documented.[7] Boys are breastfed for up to two and a half years and then provided with more high-protein solid food. Girls are often weaned after only one year, in hopes that the mother becomes fertile more quickly to bear a son. Where there is not enough food to go around for everyone, the girl usually has to sacrifice in favor of her brother(s). These practices can cause severe malnutrition and ultimately stunting or even death in girls.

FEMALE GENITAL MUTILATION[8]

All of my cousins had their genitals mutilated. The elders of our community think that women need to be circumcised because a woman's clitoris is impure and being operated on purifies you. Our ancestors practiced it so they want us to, but there are no advantages and only problems from it. It causes infections, makes it difficult to urinate, menstruate and give birth. If my relatives knew I had not been mutilated, I would be treated as impure. I would be an outcast. I've really tried my best to understand why we're still practicing this. I think it's a tradition that should be eradicated."[9]

—A Girl in Senegal

---

6   UNICEF, "Domestic Violence against Women and Girls," *Innocenti Digest,* no. 6 (June 2000): 6.

7   See, for example, WHO Statistical Information System (WHOSIS), "Mortality Database, Table 1: 'Numbers of registered deaths,' Ecuador 2000, Peru 2000, El Salvador 1999, Mexico 2001, Uruguay 2000," http://www3.who.int/whosis/mort/table1.cfm?path=whosis,mort,mort_table1&language=english. See also Plan UK, *Because I am a Girl,* 17, 19, 30.

8   Sometimes called "female genital cutting" or "female circumcision," we will primarily be using the term "female genital mutilation" to emphasize the harm that this practice causes to girl children.

9   World Vision Canada, *Girls! Stories Worth Telling: Report and Conference Manual* (Toronto: World Vision Canada, 1998), 20.

In many African countries, as well as in some regions in Asia and the Middle East, female circumcision is considered a traditional rite of passage from girlhood to womanhood, and a way to ensure girls' virginity until marriage. Performed usually on girls between four and eight years old, up to 130 million girls and women (and 3 million more per year) in more than thirty countries of the world suffer the consequences of this harmful procedure.[10]

CHILD MARRIAGE

Mulugojam[11] is from Ethiopia, and her story is typical:

I got married at the age of nine. I lived with my in-laws until I was 11. Then they told me to sleep with [my husband]. He was very big, and I found it very difficult but I soon got pregnant. I gave birth when I was 13. My in-laws didn't really look after me. I had to gather wood for the fire, do the farm work, cook, everything. They didn't care at all. I worked hard all day and struggled with him at night. I didn't know how to feed the baby when I was so busy doing all the housework. The baby suffocated and died. After this I ran away. My mother used to tell me I was lucky. She still had her baby teeth when she was married.[12]

In many developing countries, the girl is recognized as a transitory member of her family from birth. Her sole purpose in life is to be with her husband and his family. Marriage controls the girl child's life from the cradle to the grave. Early marriage for girls is encouraged because it alleviates the problem of protecting the girl's virginity and relieves

---

10 UNICEF, *State of the World's Children 2007*, 4; D'Vera Cohn, "The Campaign Against Female Genital Cutting: New Hope, New Challenges," Population Reference Bureau, http://www.prb.org/Articles/2007/CampaignAgainstFemaleGenital Cutting.aspx; World Health Organization, "Female Genital Mutilation," WHO June 2000, http://www.who.int/ mediacentre/factsheets/fs241/en/.

11 Throughout this volume, names have been changed to protect the identities of the children.

12 Ellen Mocria, *Child Brides*. London: Channel 4, Documentary, 1999.

poor families from having to take care of her. Although families lose their daughter's labor, they have one less mouth to feed.

In parts of Africa, the *lobola*, or bride price, provides welcome income for the bride's family. In Asia, the bride's family has to pay a price to the husband and his family as a condition for the marriage. Dowries are not only given at the time of marriage but also frequently continue afterwards. The illegal dowry system can cause financial ruin for many families with girls. However, whether money is given or received, the girl bride is reduced to a commodity to be sold and bought. All of the arrangements go completely around her. Sometimes the girl even pays with her life, when the girl's family cannot keep the promises made at the time of their daughter's wedding arrangements.

There are many problems associated with child marriage:

- Girls hoping to finish school like their brothers are suddenly uprooted and forced to become virtual slaves of their husbands. They usually do not return to school.
- A daughter is forcibly removed from the security of her home, required to live with a family she does not know, and embark on what can be a terrifying first sexual relationship for which she is unprepared and with a man she has hardly met.
- Early sex often results in serious injuries, including rips and tears, lacerations, and fistulae (tears in the wall between the vagina and bladder or bowel, which causes incontinence). All these can cause long-term medical problems and separation from her husband and loved ones.
- Girls giving birth under the age of fifteen have a much higher risk of death than women in their twenties.
- Babies of teenage mothers are often born too early and too small, which leads to increased chances of infant death.

- Early marriage becomes cyclical and does not provide a way out of poverty.
- Child marriage brings with it enormous responsibilities too heavy for pre-pubescent girls to carry. They are overloaded with domestic tasks, become pregnant young, and often suffer abuse at the hands of their husbands or their in-laws. Child marriage is characterized by intimidation, rape, and a life of servitude.[13]

Even though laws do exist prohibiting marriage under the age of eighteen in many regions of Africa and Asia, cultural beliefs and norms frequently lead to the marriage of girls fifteen years and younger.

Soldiers' "Wives"

Says Grace, a former child soldier in Uganda:

> *I was only fifteen when I was abducted by rebels. I lived in captivity for almost three years. Three days after my abduction I was given to a man to be his fourth wife. He was quite old and was a bad man who was harsh and rude. Twice he beat me and I almost died. [When] I had a baby girl, I was given a gun and sent to the war front to fight with my baby strapped to my back.*[14]

In wars all over the world, children suffer horrendously. However, girls suffer violations unique to them because they are female. About one-third of the child soldiers in the Lord's Resistance Army in Uganda are girls. Most of these are forced into marriages with soldiers and

---

13 UNICEF, "Child Marriage," Child Protection from Violence, Exploitation and Abuse, http://www.unicef.org/protection/index_earlymarriage.html; UNICEF, *Early Marriage: A Harmful Traditional Practice, A Statistical Exploration* (UNICEF, 2005), http://www.unicef.org/sowc06/pdfs/Early_Marriage_12.lo.pdf.

14 Melanie Gow, "Assisting Children in Especially Difficult Circumstances," *Together* (January–March 2000): 4.

officers. Girls with "firm, young breasts" are abducted in northern Uganda to become wives, while those with "flat and less firm breasts" are abused, flogged, and chased off naked to go back to their homes since they are considered "useless harlots." If the "husband" dies at the war front or of sickness, the young "wife" is married off to another rebel. Joseph Kony, the rebel leader, has more than thirty "wives" at the same time.[15]

When the girls are rescued or manage to escape, they talk of shame, humiliation, and fear of rejection by their relatives and possible future husbands. In addition, the girls are often diagnosed with a variety of sexually transmitted infections, and sometimes they have gun or knife wounds, broken bones, lice, bruises, and other infections.

Temple "Wives"

In some countries, young virgin girls are given over to the religious temples to serve the priests as "wives" and thereby appease the gods for wrongdoings committed by the girls' relatives. These shrine "prostitutes" or "wives" lose all their rights and become modern-day slaves.

In Ghana, the Tro Kosi system forces hundreds of women to become the concubines of the fetish priests, bear their children, work on their farms, and perform ceremonial duties. Many of these girls are as young as thirteen or fourteen years old.[16] In southern India, young women and girls *(devadasis)* are "donated" to serve a temple and very often end up being prostituted.[17]

---

15   World Vision, "The Effects of Armed Conflict on Girls," *World Vision* (July 1996): 18, 25; World Vision, ed., *The Girl Child: Enhancing Life Sustaining Hope 1998 Washington Forum* (Federal Way, WA: The Institute for Global Engagement, World Vision, Inc., 1998), 17.

16   See Commission on Human Rights, "Report of the Special Rapporteur on the Sale of Children, Child Prostitution and Child Pornography, Ms. Ofelia Calcetas-Santos," Human Rights Internet, para. 20, http://www.hri.ca/fortherecord1999/documentation/commission/e-cn4-1999-71.htm#chii.

17   Karen C. Tumlin, "Trafficking in Children and Women: A Regional Overview" (paper presented at the Asian Regional High-Level Meeting on Child Labour, Jakarta, Indonesia, March 8–10, 2000), 13, http://www.ilo.org/public/english/region/asro/bangkok/download/yr2000/child/trafficking.pdf.

EDUCATION

> *"To educate a girl is like watering the neighbor's garden!"*
>
> —*Indian Saying*

"How can I go to school? I should finish all the household work. My parents go to work early in the morning and come back at about seven in the evening. Who doesn't like to go to school? But who will do all this work?" says Sabita Nepali, thirteen years old, from Nepal. Asked why she doesn't send her daughter to school, her mother replies, "What do I feed them in the evening if she goes to school?"[18]

In many countries around the world, the issues surrounding a girl's education are very real: Where do parents get the money for school fees, books, and uniforms? And why should they pay for the girl's education, if only her future husband's family benefits? Who is going to do the girl's work at home or in the field while she is at school? How can she do her schoolwork when she has many tasks to do around the house after school? Who is going to find a husband and pay the higher dowry price for an educated girl?

There are many reasons given to explain why girls worldwide don't attend school:

- The family is too poor to pay school fees or needs their daughter's labor to supplement family income.
- School is too far away, and it is not safe for the girl to walk such a distance alone.
- The quality of education is too low to be worth the investment.

---

18   Kanti Khadka, "Learning from Experience: Girls Rights" (presented at the Save the Children Listen to Girls Forum, December 1998).

- There are not enough female teachers, and the general atmosphere at school is very much boy-oriented.
- Educational investments in a girl will never be recouped because she will one day belong to her husband's family.
- A girl doesn't need an education to be a wife and mother; she is dependent on her husband anyway.
- Men want to marry young, uneducated girls, before they have opinions of their own.
- The girl has to work in the house so her mother and father can work for payment.
- When the mother dies, the girl becomes the surrogate mother for her younger siblings and has to drop out of school.

Illiteracy is also a powerful shackle for those who would like to keep girls in submission. Denying girls an education is an effective way of silencing them. Currently, out of 115 million children worldwide who are not attending primary school, more than 61 million are girls. And, as UNICEF states, "nearly 1 of every 5 girls who enroll in primary school in developing countries does not complete a primary education," but "evidence indicates that the under-five mortality rate falls by about half for mothers with primary school education." In other words, ensuring that girls receive a formal education will have multiplied benefits for years to come.[19]

EXPLOITATION

Around the world, girls are more vulnerable to exploitation. They are more likely to perform informal work both in their own homes and in the homes of others, which can lead to increased chances of physical, emotional, and sexual abuse. Girl children who work in the public sphere also experience specific risks because of their gender. In addition, far more girls are vulnerable to and actually experience sexual exploitation.

---

[19]   UNICEF, *State of the World's Children 2007*, 4, 7.

GIRL CHILD LABOR

Pausing long enough to wipe beads of perspiration from her brow, Undina Kogoya bends down once again, shoves her calloused fingers below the dirt, feels for the tuberous sweet potato and plucks it from the ground. She occasionally prods the soil with a sharp stick to loosen the hardened earth around the root. It is part of the back-breaking work Undina performs five to seven hours a day. One might expect better for the oldest daughter of an Indonesian village chief. Undina attended school when she was younger but dropped out shortly before her youngest sibling was born. Undina's father, Lepinus, admits that without Undina's help at home the family could not function. Undina wants to be a nurse. Now, however, her life as a 12-year-old is spent being a surrogate mother to her four younger siblings. Undina cooks, cleans, washes, collects water, helps in the field and carries goods from field to home and home to market. Her dreams of being a nurse are far from fulfilled.[20]

Child labor data are not gender neutral. While boys tend to work in the formal sector that shows up in a nation's census or gross national product, girls' work is mostly hidden, uncounted, unpaid, and unseen: it is almost completely invisible in the informal sector of society. This is why it looks like more boys work than girls when the reality is far from that. According to the International Labour Organization, girls would outnumber boys as child laborers if the unregistered work of domestic servanthood or working at home could or would be measured.[21]

---

[20] World Vision, ed., *The Girl Child*, 2.
[21] ILO-IPEC, "Multilateral Programme of Technical Cooperation," International Labour Organization, 3, 5, http://white.oit. org.pe/ipec/documentos/docproying.pdf. See also Plan UK, *Because I Am a Girl*, 4.

If the boys in a family need to work in the formal sector, their sisters wake up before them to cook, heat their bath water, and get their brothers ready for work. In many cases, the girl child has to stay behind to watch younger siblings so that both her mother and father can go to work. Her brothers may be able to go to school because of the girl child's sacrifice. At other times, the girl is handed over to another family to work as their domestic servant and thereby supplement her family's income.

Domestic labor is one of the most hidden, abusive, and exploitative forms of work in the world. Millions of children, 90 percent of them girls and some as young as seven, are trapped in this practice that closely resembles slavery. They take on heavy burdens, work extremely long hours, have no private or public lives, are at high risk of physical and sexual abuse, and live away from their own families. Many of the girls do not even earn a salary, but work in return for simple room and board.

CHILD SEXUAL EXPLOITATION

Cham Watey, a fifteen year old trapped in the sex industry of Cambodia, talks about her ordeal:

> *Although I didn't want to service men, the brothel owner warned me every time. She would shock me with an electric wire if I refused. I was so frightened, I never refused. I hosted five to ten men each day. Some nights I had bad dreams of people hurting me. I tried to commit suicide three times, but I was caught each time. The brothel owner hit me and warned me not to do it again. All I wanted was to escape.*[22]

---

[22] Linda Dorman, "Trafficking Women and Girls in Asia," *Together* (April–June 2000): 7.

Cham, who comes from a rural village, was sold to a brothel by a woman who offered to help Cham find a job in the city.

Millions of girls in developing countries are forced into prostitution to supplement their families' income. At times, they are lured by promises of good jobs in the city. Being illiterate and naïve, most of these girls have no idea what they are getting into and are easy targets of exploitation, oppression, and abuse. Some girls are knowingly sold into the commercial sex business by their parents, who see prostitution as a source of easy income. Older daughters especially are expected to take on the responsibility and sacrifice to provide for their families. With the widespread belief that having sex with a young virgin girl will cure AIDS, the industry's entry age and retirement age are getting lower and lower. Many girls now start their lives as prostitutes at the age of nine, and too many of them are hopelessly diseased or dead before they turn sixteen. At age twenty-one, they become "second-class" prostitutes who try to make a living in the most run-down brothels and quarters of a city.

About 1.2 million children are trafficked each year.[23] In Cambodia, many of the girl prostitutes are not even paid for their labor. The one-time payment to the trafficker is considered enough for subsequent services. In fact, many girls are even told that they are in debt for this payment and for meals and clothing. The girls find out in painful ways that they have no rights, and if they resist sexual intercourse, they are beaten, raped, and/or punished by electric shock. Most customers do not use condoms, and many girls are rightfully fearful of the sexually transmitted diseases they are exposed to.

With the authorities increasingly clamping down on child prostitution in Asia, the industry has started to boom in Latin America as well as in Eastern Europe. Dysfunctional societies, economic

---

23   UNICEF, "Children in Unconditional Worst Forms of Child Labour and Exploitation," *State of the World's Children 2006*, http://www.unicef.org/sowc06/pdfs/figure3_7.pdf.

depression, migration, and conflict all contribute to the growing numbers of children involved in prostitution across Africa, the Middle East, Australasia, Western Europe, and the world.[24]

Says Janet K. Museveni, the first lady of Uganda: "Something has gone extremely wrong with the human race that little girls should be included in sex tour packages to entice tourists in order to boost national economies. Is it not odd that human beings should sexually violate their young when even animals know better than to do that?"[25]

Sexual Abuse in War Situations

Even the slight protections afforded women and girls by society are torn away in times of war. Not only do they face bombs and bullets, starvation and sickness like everyone else, increasingly, girls are treated as spoils of war and mass rape is common, particularly in ethnic conflicts.

During the war in Bosnia, it was a deliberate policy to rape women and girls so as to force them to bear "the enemy's" children. In Rwanda, rape was systematically used as a weapon of ethnic cleansing to destroy family and community ties.

Even when girls are not physically forced to have sex, they may be forced to trade sex for food or protection from soldiers. Refugee camps are also known for their widespread sexual promiscuity. Pregnant girls often become ostracized by their families and communities, then abandon their babies or commit suicide.

VIOLENCE

Violence against the girl child comes in many destructive ways to further violate girls.

---

[24] ILO-IPEC, "Combat the Trafficking of Children," International Labour Office 2002, http://www.ilo.org/ipecinfo/product/viewProduct.do?productId=767.

[25] Janet K. Museveni, "Cultural, Political and Social Empowerment of Girl Children," in *The Girl Child: Enhancing Life Sustaining Hope 1998 Washington Forum*, ed. World Vision (Federal Way, WA: The Institute for Global Engagement, World Vision, Inc., 1998), 23.

Sex-selective Abortion

It is illegal to determine the sex of a fetus in India. Yet around the country, some 4,000 clinics with ultrasound machines are booming in business. Tests are conducted openly, and subsequent abortion results show the vast extermination of baby girls. Across the globe, estimates "of the number of 'missing' girls and women due to such practices vary, but some are as high as 100 million."[26]

Female Infanticide

Even if a girl child is born, she may face death at the hands of her own mother by means of poisoning, drowning, strangling, induced choking, or neglect.

In China, considerable pressure is exerted on couples to have only one child. With girls seen as a liability and sons as the parents' caregivers in old age, most Chinese couples desperately long for a son as their only child. Though sex determination tests and sex-selective abortion are illegal, conservative estimates suggest that more than 100 million babies have been destroyed after birth in China since the one-child policy was implemented. The overwhelming majority of these deaths were baby girls. The *South China Morning Post* reported that 6 million little girls in China are named "Lai Di," meaning "a son follows quickly."[27]

Domestic Violence

Not even in the home are girls and women always safe from abuse. Though each country differs, between 20 and 50 percent of women in any given country have experienced physical violence at the hands of a family member or intimate partner.

Regardless of region or culture, worldwide about half of all sexual assaults within the home are committed against girls fifteen years and younger.[28]

---

26 Plan UK, *Because I am a Girl*, 24.
27 Seiple, "A Rent in the Garment," 9.
28 UNICEF, "Domestic Violence against Women and Girls," *Innocenti Digest*, no. 6 (June 2000): 6.

CONCLUSION

This chapter was an overwhelming one to research, write, and read. You may be wondering what you can do to help alleviate the problem of discrimination against girls.[29] I could encourage you to value your own daughters, to adopt abandoned baby girls, to raise awareness about the girl child, to support projects and workers reaching out to girls worldwide, and to campaign against obvious abuses such as female genital mutilation and domestic violence. This would certainly be a good place to begin. However, as I mentioned in the beginning of this chapter, discrimination against the girl child is a cultural issue that is difficult to change. What it comes down to is that only Christ has and is the answer. As people come to know Jesus Christ as their Savior and Lord, their attitude has to change, including their view of girls and women. In that respect, if there is one thing I would like you to take away from reading this chapter, it is a burden to pray. Pray for God to change the nations, to soften the hearts of the abusers, to empower the girls to stand up for their God-given rights, and to provide for those who reach out to these girls. Christ is the only answer to all the needs of this world, and prayer is how we can take an active part in the work God is doing around the world.

---

29   For more on empowerment and other solutions, please see Part Four of this volume.

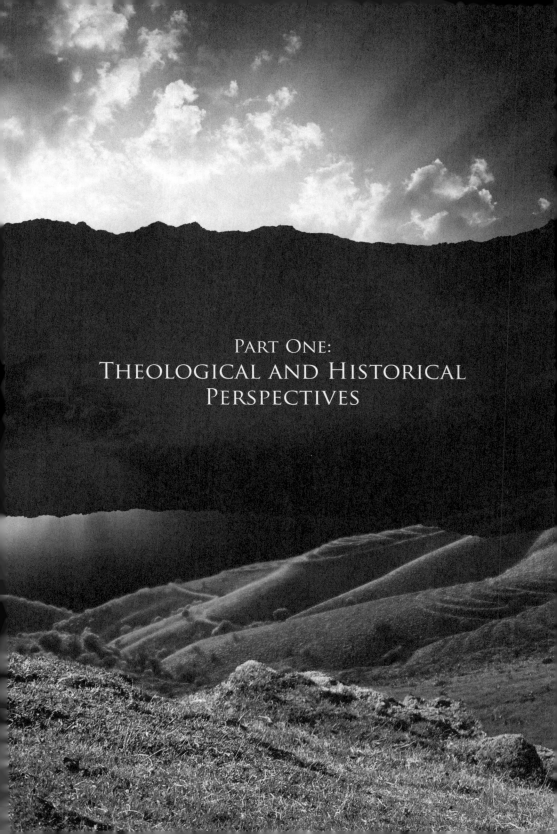

PART ONE:
THEOLOGICAL AND HISTORICAL
PERSPECTIVES

For God so loved the world
that he gave his one and only Son, that whoever believes in
him shall not perish but have eternal life.

JOHN 3:16

But Jesus called the children to him and said,
"Let the little children come to me, and do not hinder them,
for the kingdom of God belongs to such as these."

LUKE 18:16

CHAPTER 2

GOD SO LOVED THE GIRL CHILD

Marjorie McDermid

O, Divine Father—
restorer of past losses,
sustainer of the present,
hope of the future—
I am your child,
your girl child.
I may call you Father,
know your compassion,
experience your love—
love as of a mother,
friend,
redeemer.
O, Divine Father,
thank you.

Contemplating intervention for the girl child in today's world creates one all-important question for every Christian: Does God, the heavenly Father, care about her and take action to respond to her need?

Most, if not all, Christians would give an affirmative answer to that question immediately. The query becomes important to Christian caregivers, however, because most of the rest of the world, even in the twenty-first century, would answer that a girl child is not worthy of God's notice, let alone his attention, care, and protection. Reasonably then, they think, "We humans don't need to bother with her either."

Knowing God's value of the girl child will:

- govern the way we personally treat her.
- reinforce our appeals as advocates.
- strengthen our supplications to God for her.
- empower us to teach her how the heavenly Father views her.
- give her hope for her future both in this world andthe next.

One of the greatest losses to a girl child who has been traumatized by family or societal abandonment is the sense of belonging. Now unable to love or accept love, she needs to know her worth in the caregiver's sight, but more importantly, she needs to know how God values her. She may have committed sins that make being loved by a pure, holy, righteous God seem impossible. If so, imagine the impact on her life when she is convinced that she can belong to such a Father, such a family.

How does God plan to defend, protect, and care for the girl children of this world in our generation? Through his hands, feet, and voice: through his people, the family of God. With this conviction firmly in our minds and hearts, knowing God's view about and attitude toward girl children becomes consequential for us.

As we look at girl children from the perspective of Scripture (as in other realms also), we need to keep in mind that girl children grow up to be called women. God's view of women relates closely to what he thinks of the girl child.

GIRLS IN GOD'S PLAN

A study of references to God's dealing with the girl child in both the Old and New Testaments of the Bible throws light not only on God's role for her in the past, but also on her place in his kingdom today.

God appraised females as equals with males in the creation, fall, and redemption of humankind as well as the opportunity and responsibility of service in God's kingdom. That some of their roles differ is immediately obvious, such as in child bearing, but study of Scripture makes clear the equality shown by God in these four areas.

Equality of Females in Creation

The generic term for humankind at creation was "man" (Genesis 5:2). The female is pictured, along with the male, as made in God's image (Genesis 1:27; 5:2). Together, with no hierarchy noted, man and woman were given dominion or authority over the earth and its creatures (Genesis 1:26, 28).

God records his purpose for creating another human in Genesis 2:18, where he says, "It is not good for the man to be alone. I will make a helper suitable for him." "Helper" or "help" as used in this verse is also used in speaking of Almighty God as a help or helper and expresses strength (as in Exodus 18:4; Deuteronomy 33:7, 26, 29; Psalm 33:20). Rather than connoting a person of lesser value or a subordinate, this word exemplifies God's view of the female helper as one of strength and equality with man, both made in God's image.

Adam looked the scene over and liked what he saw. He acknowledged his total oneness with woman in his now celebrated words: "This is now bone of my bones and flesh of my flesh; she shall be called 'woman' for she was taken out of man." We see no indication here, either in God's mind or Adam's, of a creation of lesser quality or esteem. Instead we see two humans, one unit, gloriously beautiful and the crown of God's creation.

The Fall

How painful to think of what follows! The first girl child born suffered because of her parents' sin—particularly her mother's—and all girls who followed her to this day are affected by that disobedience. The first girl born inherited sorrow upon sorrow, became a victim of pain in bearing children, longed for the equal authority her mother once enjoyed as a bride with her bridegroom, and came under the rule of her husband (Genesis 3:16).

History, early, medieval, and late, documents the sorrow with which the majority of Eve's daughters live: some of them in unimaginable suffering all their lives. Women, some as young as pre-teen, bring forth children with more pain than almost any other creature.

According to New Testament Scripture, God still requires that a woman be subject to her husband in the home. We should notice, however, that Eve's sentence of submission, passed on to all her daughters, was only with regard to her husband, Adam. Since that time, however, women—especially young girls—are most often looked on as subservient to men in general and therefore considered of less value. We should be careful not to read such a verdict into what God said to Eve. Nowhere do we read that God gave authority to brothers or other male members of the family to require acquiescence of females. Females, as well as males, are commanded by God to respect their fathers and obey them, but grandfathers or uncles, to say nothing of males outside the family, were not given permission by God to demean or sexually abuse the girls of the home. Fathers were and are commanded to protect their children, including the girls (Isaiah 38:19; Colossians 3:21).

Scripture makes it clear that females' sorrow, pain, and subjection to their husbands directly relate to the fall of humankind. The New Testament gives abundant evidence that girls and women are now, with their male counterparts, equal recipients of God's gracious redemption.

Redemption

A brighter day dawned for us all, both male and female, when God kept his promise to the serpent (Genesis 3:15) and sent his son, Jesus, to redeem humankind who were and are so hopelessly caught in the web of sin. Jesus found both sexes equally sinful but also with equal access to God's forgiveness and redemption.

The Scripture declares that the whole world is a prisoner of sin, so that what was promised, being given through faith in Jesus Christ, might be given to those who believe (Galatians 3:22).

> *For God so loved the world [including the girl child] that he gave his one and only son that whoever [girl child included] believes in him might have eternal life.*
>
> *John 3:16*

The splendid entrance of God's redemptive plan granted forgiveness for sins from all the way back to that original transgression. The girl child, in God's sight, may now be an heir to the righteousness of God and to freedom in Christ.

Her mother Eve's original state at creation may now be the girl child's experience through faith in her Redeemer. Guilt need no longer enslave her. The Holy Scriptures further tell us:

> *So in Christ Jesus you [all who believe] are all children of God through faith.... There is neither Jew nor Gentile, neither slave nor free, neither male nor female, for you are all one in Christ Jesus.*
>
> *Galatians 3:26, 28*

God's Kingdom

Females of all ages and all nations are included in all God's glorious promises as well as his terrifying judgments. All that God purposes to do for his human male creation he purposes also for the female. When his Word says, "Precious in the sight of the Lord" (Psalm 116:15), "Beloved of the Lord" (Deuteronomy 33:12), "All have sinned" (Romans 3:23), "Come to me" (Matthew 11:28), "Accepted in the beloved" (Ephesians 1:6), "Never will I leave you, never will I forsake you" (Hebrews 13:5), and myriad other declarations, it refers to both female and male.

For reasons connected mostly with the fall of humankind and resulting male dominance, in many cultures even to this day, girls and women suffer as if the Almighty cared only for males. Perhaps that is why God occasionally makes special mention of his care for the female, as we shall see.

GIRLS VIEWED FROM OLD TESTAMENT SCRIPTURE

From the beginning of the human race, woman is valued equally as man in procreation (Genesis 1:28; 3:20; 7:7). When Abraham prayed, God answered by healing Abimelech, his wife, and his slave girls so they could have children again (Genesis 20:17). The offerings required at the birth of a male or female child were the same (Leviticus 12:6–7). Although a longer period of purification was required for the girl child (Leviticus 12:2–5), we note that the uncleanness was on the part of the mother, not the child.

God, under the old covenant, shows himself as protector, defender, advocate, and redeemer of the marginal and the downtrodden, whether male or female (Deuteronomy 22:23–38). He exemplified this principle in his command to Lot in Genesis 19 when Lot was running for his life to escape God's judgment. He asked, "Do you have anyone else here—sons-in-law, sons or daughters, or anyone else in the city who belongs to you? Get them out of here!"

God's law also prohibited making girls prostitutes because God said that making their daughters prostitutes would fill the land with wickedness. He told parents, "Do not *degrade* your children by *making them* prostitutes" (Leviticus 19:29, emphasis mine). Yes, the heavenly Father was and is concerned about the welfare of the nations, but he is also intimately concerned about those tender, innocent little girls and teenagers. God considers sexual abuse of a girl in the same category as profaning his name (Amos 2:7b).

Challenging the Religious/Occult World

God's care and protection for the girl child reached into the religious world and protected her from sacrifice to idols. When the people made idols and began to worship Baal, they also offered human sacrifices by making their sons and daughters pass through a fire. This sin, combined with others, made God so angry that he wiped the people "out of his sight" into exile and slavery (2 Kings 17:16–18). King Josiah of Judah knew God considered the sacrifice of girls and boys as serious as defiling his sanctuary and defaming the name of God (Leviticus 3:20; 18:21). These strong words were followed by equally strong measures of punishment. Anyone—Israelite or foreigner—who destroyed children in this way, God said, should be put to death by stoning (Leviticus 20:2).

At a place called Topheth, Jewish children were passed through fire as a sacrifice to the Ammonite god, Molech. Josiah violently tore down and completely destroyed Topheth so that "no one could use it to sacrifice his son or daughter in the fire to Molech" (2 Kings 23:10). It is noteworthy that daughters are mentioned as well as sons, leaving no room for saving boys and exploiting girls. Many years later, God listed this sin, among many others, to the prophet Jeremiah and said, "I never commanded, nor did it enter my mind, that they should do such a detestable thing" (Jeremiah 32:34).

God explicitly mentions female members of the family in some areas:

- He expected the same obedience from girls as from boys (Exodus 20:1; Deuteronomy 5:14; Nehemiah 10:28).
- He allowed them to participate in the blessing of the offerings (Leviticus 10:14; Numbers 18:19; Deuteronomy 12:18).

God Valued Slave Girls and Saw That They Had Rights

Slavery as we know it seems to have begun as paid servanthood. The sinful abuse of this arrangement led to indentured slaves. People began to be bought and sold and children made to work off parents' debts. The laws God gave about slaves were given not only for the protection of the master but also for the protection and good of the slaves, including the children and especially girl children (Exodus 21:4–11).[30]

All the way back to Old Testament times, wages for work outside the home favored the male. The female always received considerably less wages, though the rates varied with the age groups (Leviticus 27:2–7). But when Zelophehad died leaving no male heirs, his daughters petitioned Moses for an inheritance and got it (Numbers 27). Moses, apparently confronted with a new idea, brought the matter to the Lord, who said the girls were right in their request. The Lord proceeded to make a legal requirement for girls who had no brothers, and therefore no family finances to draw on, to receive the father's inheritance at his death.

Treatment by Those Who Feared God

Throughout the biblical account, righteous, God-fearing men always personified God's esteem for women by treating them with integrity and respect. Boaz found Ruth, a young emigrant from Moab, picking up leftovers in his fields behind his servant-girl harvesters. Greeted by their boss and owner with a friendly "The Lord be with

---

30   For more on the topic of girls and slavery, please see the final chapter of this volume.

you," the girls replied, "The Lord bless you." After inquiring about the stranger in his field, Boaz went to Ruth and said respectfully, "My daughter, listen to me. Don't go and glean in another field...stay here with my servant girls." He promised her—a foreign young woman with no rights—all the daily provisions and protection that he graciously gave to his female servants (Ruth 2:8–9).

When Jesus, in his famous Sermon on the Mount, told his audience, "Anyone who looks at a woman lustfully has already committed adultery with her in his heart," he did not suggest any minimal age limits. His searing words echoed Job's understanding of God millennia earlier. "What shall I say in my defense when I stand before a just God?" Job wanted to know. If I have looked lustfully at a girl. If I've allowed myself to be enticed by a woman, or if I've snuck around my neighbor's door looking for a chance to seduce his wife, and if I allow my heart to follow my eyes and temptation leads to deed, what can I expect from a righteous God? (cf. Job 31:1–12.)

Jesus' conclusions as the Son of God and Job's conclusions as a servant of God match quite well and show God's respect for women of all ages:

- Adultery should (and probably will) cost the loss of everything dear to you, including your family and your wealth.
- Failure to keep a covenant of chastity deserves the loss of the eyes that destroyed the girl's innocence and the limbs that degraded her.

King Abimelech, realizing he had inadvertently offended Abraham's wife Sarah and following the custom of the day, gave Abraham a thousand shekels of silver. "This is to cover the offense against you before all who are with you; you are completely vindicated," he told her (Genesis 20:16).

Laban seemed to understand how precious his daughters and granddaughters were in God's sight. When his son-in-law, Jacob, fled secretly with his family, Laban realized he had little power to protect his now-adult daughters or their daughters. But he warned Jacob firmly, "If you mistreat my daughters..., even though no one is with us, remember that God is a witness between you and me" (Genesis 31:50).

God Loves Happy Childhood Scenes

According to the prophet Zechariah, a truly happy scene to God has both girls and boys playing together in the streets (Zechariah 8:5). He pictures them as "our sons in their youth...like well-nurtured plants, and our daughters...like pillars carved to adorn a palace" (Psalm 144:12). What beautiful words to describe the world's children: created by God, loved by God, protected and nurtured by God!

JESUS & THE GIRL CHILD

Jesus seems not to have preferred boys to girls. We note that in both Matthew's and Mark's accounts of Jesus blessing the children, he referred to the creation of both male and female and gave a discourse on divorce and marriage.

"Then," Matthew says, "little children were brought to Jesus for him to place his hands on them and pray for them" (Matthew 19). Sisters were of little account in a family and sometimes seen as burdens in the cultural attitude of Jesus' day. It is remarkable, then, that Mark records Jesus' inclusion of "sisters" in the list of those loved ones to be sacrificed for the privilege of following Jesus (Mark 10:29–30).

We witness his value of females, both young and old, in the way he healed the crippled woman on the Sabbath and called her a "daughter of Abraham" (Luke 13:16). He talked with and ministered to "sinful" women (John 4 and 8), admitted women to the group of those who traveled with him (Mark 15:16), and had women among his closest friends (Luke 10), treating them all with respect.

When Jesus raised Jairus' daughter, about twelve years old, from the dead (Mark 5), he took her by the hand and said to her, "*Talitha koum*!" (which means, "Little girl, I say to you, get up!"). Her spirit returned to her, and as she stood up, Jesus told those around her to give her something to eat. He knows when children are hungry!

A Canaanite woman came to Jesus (Matthew 15) crying out, "Lord, Son of David, have mercy on me! My daughter is suffering terribly from demon-possession." Jesus, showing compassion to this "foreign" woman and her child, gave his healing touch, and the child became well.

THE GIRL CHILD IN THE NEW TESTAMENT CHURCH

God's respect for and attitude toward the girl child are reflected in accounts from the New Testament church. His offer of opportunities and responsibilities become particularly important in the light of treatment of girls today.

The account in Acts 16 of the slave girl tells us more than a story of a frustrated Apostle Paul and his evangelizing band. Let Luke, author of the Book of Acts, tell us the story.

Once when we were going to the place of prayer, a slave met a girl who had a spirit by which she predicted the future. She earned a great deal of money for her owners by fortune-telling. This girl followed Paul and the rest of us, shouting, "These men are servants of the Most High God, who are telling you the way to be saved." She kept this up for many days. Finally Paul became so troubled that he turned around and said to the spirit, "In the name of Jesus Christ I command you to come out of her!" At that moment the spirit left her. When the owners of the slave girl realized that their hope of making money was gone, they seized Paul and Silas and dragged them into the marketplace to face the authorities.

Acts 16:16–19

If the apostles were only out to get this girl off their backs, the result of their initiative caused them a lot of pain and time in jail. I believe Paul's concern was not so much for them as for the tormented girl. He knew the power of God would be as effective for her as it was for the adults to whom he ministered. He was not afraid of the consequences, and he brought deliverance to the suffering child.

SERVICE IN GOD'S KINGDOM

After what we call the fall of humankind, patterns of subordination of women began to develop. We find in both the Old and New Testaments that, generally speaking, no public office or significant roles in society were offered to women. Rule of husband over wife soon became rule of man over woman. Gilbert Bilezikian says, "It took only six generations from Adam to Lamech for hierarchy to disintegrate into polygamy."[31] This ungodly legacy continues to be handed down in much of the world today.

So, with women and girls being looked on as not only unequal to their male counterparts, but also of little value except as at best procreators and at the least playthings, the Prophet Joel had a lot of courage to announce women among the recipients of the Spirit and its effect on them as well as on men:

> *And afterward, I will pour out my Spirit on all people. Your sons and daughters will prophesy, your old men will dream dreams, your young men will see visions. Even on my servants, both men and women, I will pour out my Spirit in those days.*
>
> *Joel 2:28–29*

---

31   Gilbert Bilezikian, *Beyond Sex Roles* (Grand Rapids: Baker Book House Company, 1985), 57.

Whatever your interpretation of the word 'prophecy,' in the New Testament context, women were allowed to do it (1 Corinthians 11:5). And Paul considered women worthy to be trained to love their husbands and their children (Titus 2:4).

Some have written books on what the Bible says about how God used women. We have touched on just a few of these incidences, endeavoring only to show in general terms God's esteemed place for his girl children.

CONCLUSION

To say that all God's promises, his benefits, his rebukes, and his discipline apply equally to the girl child as to any other human may seem easy to accept in the Christian world. But let's apply it to little orphan girls thrown onto the streets from state orphanages with no recourse but prostitution for survival. Consider its implications for the countless girls sold to be shrine slaves and prostitutes. Think of it in terms of very young girls forced to be child brides for enemy soldiers or wealthy old men. Are these as valuable to God as girl children from affluent western homes?

Most of the world turns a deaf ear to these children: little girls who have no opportunities; no education; no health care; little or no food, clothing or shelter; many of them overworked, abused, sold; their lives destroyed. Divine intervention is the only solution for them. How will it come about?

I submit that it will happen as we pray according to Scripture for:

- you and me to have Jeremiah's deep empathy with their needs (Lamentations 2:11–13);
- God to fulfill his promises to the fatherless (Psalm 10:12–14; 68:1–6) and those sold into other countries (Deuteronomy 10:18);

- these children to hear and understand how Jesus values them (Matthew 19:14–15) and died to redeem them (John 3:16);
- restoration of their emotional losses (Psalm 6:2; 80:3; 126:4; Matthew 13:15; 1 Peter 5:9–10);
- and a sense of belonging and ability to receive and give love (Jeremiah 30:17).

Gender discrimination is not a consciously practiced science or discipline. Yet it surrounds us.
Meeting human obligations to childhood is a universal responsibility. All components of human society...have to lend their committed energy, time, and resources to restore childhood and dignity to girlhood.

NEERA KUCKREJA SOHONI, *THE BURDEN OF GIRLHOOD*, vii, 205

Promote gender equality and empower women.

UNITED NATIONS, MILLENNIUM DEVELOPMENT GOAL 3

CHAPTER 3

"BOYS ONLY": EXPOSING THE ROOTS OF GIRL CHILD TROUBLES

David D. Kupp

Let's play Mothers and Fathers.
You go find food
and water
and cook it
and tend the
animals
and have the
babies
while I make up a song
about it

Chris Radley

INTRODUCTION

We have grown up these past few years. Difficult stories of childhood from around the world no longer surprise us: children caught in wars, minefields, sweatshops, brothels, and refugee camps. Not too many years ago, perhaps as part of our inheritance of post-World War II "boomer" attitudes, we still held as attainable the myth of childhood as a time filled with carefree innocence. Wiser now, we have adjusted the myth: we know that virtually everywhere in the world, growing up as a girl or boy has its tough times. Despite every child's need for joy, security, and love, carefree innocence often meets a different reality. That reality arrives for many simply in the daily hard scramble for food, shelter, and clothing. For some, it arrives in the trauma of physical, emotional, or social abuse or deprivation. And for every child, that reality certainly involves the everyday pain and pleasure of discovering and growing up within the boundaries of community traditions and family expectations.

Although we may be re-balancing our mythologies of childhood bliss, there are stories that can still catch us by surprise: stories about girls that are radically different from stories about boys. Too often the stories of girl children are jaded with discrimination, and laced with abuse and exploitation, practiced under the rubric of "traditional cultural practices."

As spelled out by the United Nations High Commissioner for Human Rights (UNHCHR), these traditional cultural practices arise out of generations-old values and beliefs specific to every community.[32] Some traditional cultural practices are beneficial to all community members. Others are harmful to particular sectors of a community, such as women. These harmful traditional practices may include female genital mutilation (FGM), early marriage, taboos, and practices that prevent women from controlling their own fertility, nutritional taboos and forced feeding of women, and son preference with its negative implications for girl children, such as female infanticide, early

---

[32]   See http://www.ohchr.org/EN/Pages/WelcomePage.aspx.

pregnancy, and bride dowry. These harmful practices persist in many communities unquestioned because they have taken on an aura of necessary morality among their practitioners and supporters.[33]

As you will read in many of the other chapters of this volume, girl children often experience discrimination, abuse, and exploitation. Yet gaining an accurate picture of the situation of the girl child is difficult. Girls are often not visible in statistical profiles. Only in the mid-1980s did the differential health and nurture of the young girl in many parts of the world begin to attract the attention of those who study the well-being of children. They began to document the patterns and impact of girl child discrimination, painting a picture of cumulative disadvantage inherited at birth, cycling through the generations from parents to daughter, and from her to her offspring.[34]

What has emerged provides at one level a simple history of the girl child issue. Most basically explained, the dilemma of the girl child arises out of a widespread and longstanding preference for male children: *parents want baby boys.* So although we may be surprised by the depth and detail of this emerging picture of girl neglect, we have long and almost universally known without speaking it, that many of our cultures worldwide simply take for granted within their traditional codes and practices the valuing of sons over daughters.

The attempt to answer why, where, and how our cultures express and practice boy preference prevents the girl child from remaining a simple story. This chapter highlights a single seminal strand of that more complex fabric, leaving the other chapters in this publication to further weave their parts of the girl child tapestry. This chapter focuses on the roots of gender inequality, reviewing some of the historical and cultural beliefs and behaviors at the heart of the phenomenon we call "the girl child issue."

---

33 For more on harmful traditional practices, please see chapter 7 of this volume.
34 UNICEF, *Sex Differences in Child Survival and Development* (Amman: UNICEF Regional Office for the Middle East and North Africa, 1990).

JUST A MOMENT...

I begin this chapter with a caveat, and with a caution. As a review of the cultural causes of girl neglect, this essay could become a profoundly negative treatise, filled with condemnations of various people groups and their harmful practices. But this impression needs to be qualified: very few activists working on behalf of girl–boy equity are arrogant pessimists. At least not the ones I meet, whose passion for change is more than skin-deep. Those dedicated to re-balancing cultures in favor of equity for girls and boys, and for women and men, are "possibility people." The best girl child advocates work out of a presumption of hope, and from a standpoint of humility.

Why is this important? In exploring the root causes of the girl child dilemma, none of us can afford to cast judgment, or to impose some "ethically superior worldview" over such a complex construct as gender culturalization. All of us, to one degree or another, wear the limitations and blinders of our own cultures, whether we write computer code in a post-industrial valley of the silicon type or milk camels in a pastoralist valley of the herding type. Scratch the surface of even the most "objective" academic anthropologist, and she or he quickly reveals her or his biases. Every culture "eats its own children" to some extent—a perverse statement perhaps, but uttered from the standpoint of assessing comparatively harmful practices.

In a world of cross-cultural complexity such as ours, who is able to declare unequivocally that one society's treatment of girls or boys is more harmful than another's? As one example, is the relegation of millions of children to endless hours of television, video games, and inactivity more or less harmful than the daily requirement that millions of children spend endless hours toiling in collecting water, gathering firewood, and producing food for the survival of their families? Who becomes the better adult out of the experience? There begins our dilemma, and hence my caveat: there are undeniably harmful cultural practices we work to eradicate, including numerous traditions around son preference and daughter neglect, but none of us stands above the call for always deeper analysis and conscientization around our own culture's beneficial and harmful practices.

And so humility (and at times even a sense of humor) about the foibles of our own cultural traditions and gender practices is an essential starting point for anyone venturing into this important debate of the girl child. If a foundation of cultural humility is my opening caveat, avoiding leaps in logic between politics, religion, and rights is my opening caution. This caution centers on an assumed compatibility between human rights and the Christian and Jewish scriptures and belief systems. Any review of the global roots of traditional girl–boy inequity butts squarely into a wide number of religious traditions, and an even wider range of devoted adherents' beliefs and practices within those traditions.

In the past fifty years, the religious ground has shifted with the introduction globally of a "Rights Revolution," embodied in the Universal Declaration of Human Rights.[35] And since 1989, the United Nations' Convention on the Rights of the Child (CRC) has provided another benchmark for measuring progress: the girl child (and boy) has the birthright to be loved and nurtured, to learn, to play, to discover her community and world, and her rights and responsibilities within it. And above all to be herself, to grow into her unique and full human potential, free from coercion, exploitation, and abuse.

But to what degree are Christian scriptures, faith, and practice supportive of and compatible with the Rights Revolution as understood in the twenty-first century? This is a topic far larger than we can adequately address here, but my caution is simply to point to the existence of some debate around these issues. The debate is both political and religious, involving at least two overlapping circles of critics, from within and outside western society, and from within and outside Christian theology and belief.[36] It provokes us on the one

---

35   See Michael Ignatieff, *The Rights Revolution: The 2000 Massey Lectures* (Toronto: House of Anansi, 2000).

36   For more on this topic, please see Paul Brink, "Debating International Human Rights: The 'Middle Ground' for Religious Participants," *The Brandywine Review of Faith and International Affairs* (Fall 2003); Judith Ennew and Paul Stephenson, eds., *Questioning the Basis of Our Work: Christianity, Children's Rights, and Development* (London: Tearfund, 2004); Dave Scott, "Theological Dignity and Human Rights for Children," in *Understanding God's Heart for Children: Toward a Biblical Framework*, eds. Douglas McConnell, Jennifer Orona, and Paul Stockley (Federal Way, WA: Authentic, 2007), 23–31.

hand to reassess the political and cultural agendas behind the Rights Revolution, and asks whether human rights have *de facto* become the handmaiden of western hegemony, bent on standardizing all cultures and imposing a single model for economic, political, and civil society development. Although human rights proclaim a gospel of freedom and tolerance, does it in fact reduce the options available for development, and is it in fact deeply intolerant of cultural difference?

When we add the dimensions of Christianity and other faiths, the debate challenges us to re-examine the interplay of human rights, religion, and culture. The issue here is not to doubt the powerful good wrought by human rights movements throughout human communities everywhere, but to revisit the ancient and modern faith traditions within the context of the Rights Revolution as to where they support, challenge, or even strain each other's tenets and practices. Hence, my opening caution is for us to remember that much work remains to be done in looking at all major religious traditions in light of the human rights movement in different parts of the world. On the one hand, many social and political scientists and cultural commentators underplay or forget the critical importance of religious traditions in the girl child issue, or ascribe to religion a generally negative role. On the other hand, faith-based commentators on the issue can assume polarized viewpoints: on one side, some conservatives refuse entirely to countenance human rights within their religious worldviews; on the other side sits a too-easy conjoining of Scripture and human rights.[37]

AT ISSUE:
THE ROOTS OF GIRL-BOY DISPARITY

The tradition that girls are worth less than boys emerges from a complex web of biology, history, beliefs, and practices. There are numerous examples.

---

[37] See the comprehensive human rights surveys of Evans, *Human Rights Fifty Years On: A Reappraisal* and Steiner and Alston, *International Human Rights in Context: Law, Politics, Morals* and recent publications by Michael Ignatieff.

- **Culture:** Father–son family lines: almost all cultures inherit a patriarchal social structure in which males exercise authority in a closed, hierarchical structure.
- **Tradition:** Long-practiced customs, taboos, and superstitions, which denigrate women and girls, are entrenched in many communities. Practices such as bride dowry can make daughters an economic burden to their families.
- **Politics:** Their participation viewed as unnecessary, women and girls have long been unconsulted about policy decisions at family, community, regional, and federal government levels.
- **Religion:** Sacred writings from all major faith traditions are sometimes interpreted as being opposed to female–male equality; and some long-held religious sayings and beliefs contradict respect for woman and girls.
- **Sexuality:** A girl's sexuality is seen as needing male control. A new bride may be required to prove her virginity, but not the groom.
- **Laws:** The underclass status of girls and women frequently gives them few or no legal rights in such areas as inheritance, property ownership, court testimony, and divorce.
- **Economics:** People in poverty frequently look to sons for their earning potential. Women are often disadvantaged when seeking credit, equal pay, leadership positions, and recognition for labor in the home.
- **Media Images:** Around the world, girls and women are often stereotyped by the media and advertising in traditional, maternal roles, or as sexual objects.

Over generations and cultures, and across various countries, ethnic groups and religions, a wide variation of practices that are harmful to girls have been produced by this web of history and beliefs. These harmful practices by a girl's community and family stem from the basic belief that this girl and all females are inferior, that she does not benefit the family into which she was born, and that she must be controlled as well as prepared for her main roles as wife and mother, essentially her only source of earned respect and status.

In many countries, measurable indicators are now revealing this discrimination against the girl child right from birth, following through childhood and into adulthood. The impact of these age-old harmful practices is startling, and increasingly evident: fewer girls than boys are surviving into adulthood, so that men outnumber women by five in every hundred in some areas of the world.[38] Underneath these statistics sit the real practices surrounding cultural preference for sons, including lesser quantity and quality of food for daughters, female genital mutilation, lesser access for girls to medical treatment and education, and early marriage and childbearing by daughters. As a result, many girls enter adulthood in poor health, with limited energy and no spare time, barring them from real participation in the development of their communities and from developing themselves through education and training.

Centuries of such practices have also built cultural self-reinforcement into communities' perpetual re-enactment of these traditions, and psychologically into generations of girls and women's self-understanding. "Girls are often treated as inferior and socialized to put themselves last, thus undermining their self-esteem. Discrimination and neglect in childhood can initiate a lifelong downward spiral of deprivation and exclusion from the social mainstream."[39] There is a cumulative impact—that a girl is socialized from an early age to put herself last culminates in her disadvantage as an adult woman,

---

38 See, for example, Plan UK, *Because I am a Girl: The State of the World's Girls 2007* (London: Plan International, 2007), 24, http://www.plan-uk.org/pdfs/plan_uk_girls_report2007.pdf.

39 United Nations, "The United Nations Fourth World Conference on Women," Division for the Advancement of Women, http://www.un.org/womenwatch/daw/beijing/platform/girl.htm.

when she is discriminated against or otherwise has fewer rights and opportunities compared with men. This often produces a final fatalism within her and her community that immobilizes them, and freezes the cycle in perpetuity.

DEFINING GIRLS & FIGHTING FATALISM

The 1990s really brought full definition to this issue, essentially as a product of the numerous previous global discussions on human rights, which recognized and highlighted the inalienable nature of human rights for women and girls. The 1995 Fourth World Conference on Women in Beijing provided additional recent momentum toward addressing constraints faced by the girl child, defined by the CRC as any female below the age of eighteen. Throughout these debates and declarations, the gender dimension of human rights has gained new prominence in application to girls. Gender "refers to the ways in which roles, attitudes, values and relationships regarding women and men, boys and girls are constructed by societies all over the world."[40]

Bloem asserts, "These roles and relationships are therefore shaped not by nature (biology) but by social, economic, political and cultural factors." This statement is agreeable, but needs two modifications: (1) biology is not entirely divorced from shaping these roles and relationships, but remains in basic interplay with the social nurturing of boy–girl characteristics; and (2) religious traditions must be identified as another factor distinct from those normally listed as shaping forces, and not simply subsumed within categories of culture and tradition. The social creation of gender distinctions (what it means to be male or female) varies across cultures and changes over time. However, as gender critics note, most societies have historically constructed themselves in favor of the male's enduring enjoyment of his rights and privileges, with the resulting distortion that girls' and women's full access to and experience of their personal, social, and economic potential have been both visibly and invisibly diminished. There is no question that distinct

---

40   Renate Bloem, "Child Labour: A Gender Perspective," *Women's Watch,* United Nations, November 16, 1999.

social constructions of male and female roles and relationships will always exist, but at issue is moving toward constructions that are fairer to both sexes, and toward the elimination of any harmful traditional practices, which express those social constructions.

Why are so many girls born into discrimination, undervalued in comparison to their brothers, exploited as temporary, transitory members of their own birth families, and compelled as helpers to their overburdened mothers? Why does girls' sexuality increase their vulnerability to violence and abuse? Why are these harmful attitudes and practices often so rooted in seemingly complacent societies that remain apparently content not to challenge the status quo?

UNHCHR's summary provides one perspective:

> *Most women in developing countries are unaware of their basic human rights. It is this state of ignorance that ensures their acceptance—and, consequently, the perpetuation of harmful traditional practices affecting their well-being and that of their children. Even when women acquire a degree of economic and political awareness, they often feel powerless to bring about the change necessary to eliminate gender inequality. Empowering women is vital to any process of change and to the elimination of these harmful traditional practices.[41]*

Many practices harmful to girls are perpetuated due to people's ignorance of the short- and long-term harm such practices actually cause. Women themselves can end up socializing their own children to these cultural norms, without necessarily being sensitized to what is at stake. Where the harmfulness of the practices is recognized, fear of the severe consequences of social ostracism from one's group through isolation, humiliation, and rejection keeps the practices alive.

---

[41]   United Nations, "Fact Sheet No. 23, Harmful Traditional Practices Affecting the Health of Women and Children," Office of the High Commissioner for Human Rights, http://www.unhchr.ch/html/menu6/2/fs23.htm.

In many cases, violence emerges as a form of control. Since girls already begin life within an imbalance of power, and with low social and economic status, this enables males to continue operating on the other side of the power balance, exploiting and abusing their inherited position with varying degrees of awareness. In many of these environments, the underlying causes of male–female power differentials remain unassessed and unanalyzed, and male dominance stands generally accepted. Control of women is often culturally prescribed, and this violence is easy to maintain when it has long been encouraged as normal, like when a man beating his wife is seen as a healthy form of control. Within this system of control, girls and women are repeatedly and permanently socialized to be undervalued, with little recognition for their work, and few opportunities for change and improvement. All this rests on a foundation of limited or eroded confidence and self-esteem. A fundamental fatalism rears its head here, providing an almost insurmountable inertia and disbelief in possibility and change. When the seeds of this fatalism are planted in the hearts of girls and boys, they themselves become the bearers of the next generation of unchangeable traditions and harmful practices.

Within the larger movement for gender equity, it has become clear that the girl child provides the best window of opportunity to break through this cycle of fatalism and harmful practices. She is the key to a shared and lasting solution for girls and women, through a slow and early shifting of her generation's attitudes and behaviors. When her rights, privileges, and future are comprehensively promoted and protected by one or two champions within her world, a fresh opening appears, and together with her younger generation, she can create a movement for awareness and advocacy, generating skills and opportunities to prepare girls to participate actively in decisions and activities affecting them. Such an approach must be built on the sacrosanct principle of the divine spark of God's image in every girl and boy, and on the recognition of human rights as appropriate and applicable to every environment and community. The call here is for fundamental change in people's worldviews, always a slow process, involving a community's reassessment of the true value of its traditions, via skillful facilitation and leadership with a great deal of sensitivity.

MANIFESTATIONS OF HARMFUL TRADITIONAL PRACTICES

Among those traditional practices harmful to girls and women, a number deserve mention here as most in need of targeting for change along with brief assessments of the culture and belief systems that continue to promote such practices.[42]

SON PREFERENCE & HEALTH, EDUCATION, & WORK FOR GIRLS

An important starting place for understanding this issue is the preference given to the boy child over the girl child. Although more rooted and explicit in some traditional cultures, son preference is an almost universal phenomenon, as a common reflection of the values, economics, and culture of the patriarchal systems in most societies. Son preference incorporates a broad spectrum of beliefs and traditions that accord a higher status to the male child. Where the phenomenon is most prevalent, it frequently results in neglect of the female child. In these settings, son preference amounts to daughter disadvantage. The extent of that disadvantage for the female child is dependent on numerous factors within the family and community, including availability of resources. But in some cases, son preference promotes behavior as extreme as selective abortion or female infanticide through increasingly sophisticated methods of sex detection in amniocentesis tests, sonography, and other means.

Son preference amounts to daughter disadvantage.

---

[42] For more on this topic, see chapter 7 of this volume.

Patrilineage is often a key factor in son preference. Where the family line and name are carried only through the son(s), where only the sons can usher in peace for their parents in the next world by personally performing their burial rites, where religious ceremonies are carried out only by male priests, pastors, and sheikhs—that is where parents wish first and foremost for a son. A girl drops her family's name and takes her husband's family name. A girl remains without status until she joins another household to become a wife and give birth to a son. A girl cannot bury her parents properly. A girl cannot gain the status of a priest, pastor, or sheikh, and perform important religious ceremonies.

In communities with settled agriculture, where land is owned and protected in continuity by men and their sons, the son is considered to be the family pillar. He is the immediate and extended family's income source, the old-age pension for his parents, the political leader, and the keeper of rituals and religious teaching. And so in many of these settings the birth of a son is welcomed and celebrated, and the birth of a daughter is lamented as an impending economic drain. As the Asian proverb says, "bringing up girls is like watering the neighbor's garden."

Girls are exploited in terms of unequal household and agricultural workload compared to male siblings, and later in comparison to their spouses. For many girls living in rural settings, this often includes a great deal of time and physical energy caring for younger siblings, carrying very heavy loads of firewood and water, and producing, processing, and preparing food. In return, girls often receive less nutritious food, get less rest and fewer opportunities. For example, "in South Asia, women and girls spend three to five hours more than men in a week on activities such as fetching wood and carrying water, and between 20 and 30 hours a week more on housework."[43]

As noted above, scientific evidence of the negative consequences of son preference on the health of girl children is beginning to accumulate, as evident in abnormal sex ratios, in mortality rates for infant and

---

[43] Plan UK, *Because I am a Girl*, 34.

young girls, and in nutritional indicators of at least twenty-six countries. The fact that even mortality rates reflect this discrimination against girls points to the severe consequences of the practice of son preference.

In the field of education, the content and orientation of primary and secondary curricula in many countries continue to express explicit and implicit biases toward traditional son preference. Even with problematic curricula, however, increased access of girl children to education at least increases their opportunities on two key fronts: literacy and economic potential. Differential rates for boy and girl enrollment in primary school are still very significant in a number of countries, and are even more disproportionate for girls where overall enrollment is very low. The higher dropout rates for schoolgirls, often due to early marriage, schooling costs, and required household and farm work, continue to reflect the priority given to sons.

A healthy balance of work and recreation also continues to most elude the girl child in rural and poor urban settings, in the midst of her extraordinary burdens of domestic work and sibling care—a direct reflection on the role and status of her mother. As these girls grow older, the legal, training, credit, and employment barriers they face continue to evidence the major inequalities they began life with. They are often relegated to the landless, informal, and invisible sector of developing countries' labor forces, beyond the reach of much social and labor legislation and benefits.

EARLY MARRIAGE & DOWRY

The tradition of marrying off girls at the age of eleven, twelve, or thirteen years old is prevalent among certain ethnic groups in Asia, Africa, and elsewhere. Parents and communities most often cite the importance of girls' virginity and maintaining a premium price for the bride dowry as reasons for the practice. If girls have been protected from sexual contact and are believed (and sometimes verified by the in-laws) to be virgins at marriage, then the family's and girl's good standing can compel the highest dowry to be paid by the husband.

The physical and psychological stresses of child marriage are obvious, created by removal of the girl from her parents' home to that of her husband and in-laws, by marriage to a man not her age-mate but often many years her senior, who requires an intimate emotional and physical relationship before she may be fully developed. It is increasingly recognized that early marriage devalues women and that the practice continues as a result of son preference. Girls may be promised to male suitors even before birth, or (for example, in Burkina Faso and Mauritania) fattened up with forced feeding of milk and cereals, and groomed and adorned with jewels to make them look older and more appealing to a prospective spouse.

The economic underpinnings of dowry can also perpetuate both early marriage and FGM. The dowry or bride price of a woman is an agreed value in cash or in kind exchanged between the bride's family and her future in-laws, seen as beneficial to both families. The woman's future in-laws want the extra labor she and her children will provide, and her own family wants the greater security provided by the dowry. FGM is seen to help preserve the girl's higher dowry price by maintaining her virginity.[44]

On the other hand, some societies in South Asia require that the girl's parents pay a marriage dowry to the husband's parents in compensation for her low status. Catastrophe can follow if her parents do not complete the dowry payments. There are regular reports of a wife being starved, raped, tortured, or burned alive by her husband and/or in-laws in such cases.[45]

In assessing the circumstances surrounding girls being married off too early in some cultures, there is an interplay of numerous obligations and traditions at work. Almost inevitably, that interplay involves social and economic structures that create pressures and incentives for a specific marriage timing. One United Nations study analyzed a number of traditional factors that proved to have variable effects on the timing of marriage among women fifteen to nineteen years old.

---

44 See further in United Nations, "Fact Sheet No. 23." Please also see chapter 7 in this volume.
45 See, for example, http://en.wikipedia.org/wiki/Bride_burning.

These factors can include the following:

- food production systems (agricultural, pastoral, aquaculture),
- patrilineage as opposed to matrilineage,
- inheritance of property and land through males or females,
- political and social stratification, and /or
- literacy.

The study's most critical conclusion was that literacy has the greatest impact in delaying women's marriage age, as a factor of modernization that produces high proportions of singles.[46]

Literacy has the greatest impact in delaying women's marriage age.

In societies where a girl's main role is to become a wife and a mother, with her primary marriage value based on virginity and fertility, early marriage is often preferred, so that she can establish herself and achieve this means of recognition in the community. A bride price is then set according to whether the woman is a virgin, has been married before, and has children or not. Where property can be passed through women, in Islamic agricultural societies, for example, girls are often married off very early. However, in Islamic pastoralist societies, with caste endogamy and preferential parallel cousin marriage, property transmission produces exceptionally late age at marriage for women. In some societies that carry a system of matriarchal lineage, women tend to marry later.[47]

Frequently, parents promoting early marriage of girls are working from a perceived need to protect girls from being sexually violated (even if such restrictive measures are not taken to control males), and are acting in their social role as the primary decision-makers regarding

---

46 United Nations, *Patterns of First Marriage: Timing and Prevalence* (New York: United Nations, 1990).
47 UNICEF, "Rights of Girls," *UNICEF Staff Working Papers: Evaluation, Policy and Planning Series* (New York: UNICEF, 1999).

marriage timing and the choice of their daughter's spouse. These roles, plus expectations for a large family, and extended family assistance in establishing the new household, have a major influence on the pattern of early marriage. Conversely, where marriages are "free-choice," they tend to be associated with later marriage of females.[48]

Ultimately, when girls come from within traditional, subsistence agriculture family systems with high illiteracy, fewer employment opportunities for girls in the modern sector make them more narrowly dependent on their households, which reinforces early marriage. When these rural families are struggling economically, early marriage of girls can be an opportunity to increase economic security through the labor of additional children.

FEMALE GENITAL MUTILATION

Female genital mutilation involves cutting away parts or all of a girl's most sensitive genital organs. It is sometimes erroneously called "female circumcision." It has been a customary practice for centuries in many communities around the world. For many, this practice serves within an important rite of passage ceremony for the coming of age of the female child. For some communities, mutilating the female's genital organs is also seen as a means to control her sexuality and thus ensure her virginity before marriage. The age ranges for mutilation vary widely, from infancy to pre-adolescence to adolescence and even adulthood.[49]

FGM violates numerous international and national laws, and directly contravenes the right of the child to the "enjoyment of the highest attainable standard of health."[50] FGM brings with it a host of health complications for girls and women, and an equally imposing list of psychological problems—these will be fully addressed in other chapters.

---

48 United Nations, *Patterns of First Marriage.*
49 See fuller explanations of FGM in Efua Dorkenoo, *Cutting the Rose: Female Genital Mutilation—The Practice and Its Prevention*; Fran P. Hosken, *The Hosken Report: Genital and Sexual Mutilation of Females*; and United Nations, "Fact Sheet No. 23." Also, please see chapter 9 for a discussion of the health ramifications of FGM.
50 United Nations, "Convention on the Rights of the Child," Geneva: Office of the High Commissioner for Human Rights, 1989. Article 24, paras.1 and 3.

The historical roots of FGM have not been fully uncovered, but the practice appears to predate the arrival of Christianity and Islam in communities that practice FGM today. The practice of "Pharaonic circumcision" in ancient Egypt is apparent where mummified bodies bear evidence of both excision and infibulation. Records show that in ancient Rome measures to prevent procreation by female slaves were attempted by fastening metal rings through their labia minora. Husbands about to travel far from home had metal chastity belts fastened about their wives in medieval England to prevent promiscuity. Records in nineteenth-century England, France, America, and Tsarist Russia show the practice of clitoridectomy, with FGM sometimes performed as a "cure" for numerous psychological ailments.[51]

Practitioners of the custom of FGM—women, girls, and men alike—cite a broad range of reasons for maintaining the ritual. Upholding traditional and religious duty is probably the most common rationale, with such expressed needs as to preserve and defend culture and spirituality, or sometimes to be clean and fit for marriage. As already noted, supporters often refer to physical and sexual reasons, for example, the perceived need to maintain the girl's virginity, decrease her sexual desire, increase the male's sexual enjoyment, improve the girl's hygiene, improve the looks of her genitalia, increase her fertility, or remove her "male part" (clitoris). FGM is often seen as a panacea for all mental and physical ailments, and even as a means of preventing contamination of food (passed through the woman's "dirty" sexual secretions). Social identity frequently is raised in, for example, the need for a girl to fully identify with and belong to her ethnic group, to successfully pass from girl to woman, to become eligible for marriage, or to learn how to be a good wife. For the girls undergoing FGM in some cultures, the attractive gifts of clothing and jewelry, and being surrounded by guests, singing, and dancing explain the girls' own willingness to proceed.[52]

---

51 United Nations, "Fact Sheet No. 23."

52 See further in Asma El Dareer, *Women, Why Do You Weep? Circumcision and Its Consequences* (London: Zed Press, 1982).

FGM is thus a custom or tradition drawing from a hybrid rationale, synthesized over various places and times from numerous values and traditions. Both women and men within practicing cultures are often passively compliant with ongoing FGM, keeping it alive through tacit approval. Men may be removed from the actual practice, thinking FGM to be a "woman's matter."

Today, the ritual is challenged by marked improvement in women's education, large migrations from rural areas to cities, and the increased exposure of women to new female role models and patterns of female fulfillment, sexuality, and independence. In some societies, the traditions and customs of body and facial scarification and lip tattooing for women have decreased or disappeared in the face of education and modernization, but FGM has continued. This may be due to the lack of discussion about FGM because of the parts of the body involved.[53] According to the UNHCHR, the international community has remained wary about pushing this harmful practice to a level requiring international and national scrutiny and action, since FGM has been a sensitive cultural issue falling within the private sphere of women and the family. Governments and the international community, however, are increasingly challenging the implications of FGM, as a practice that violates the rights to health, life, dignity, and personal integrity.

Ultimately, the strongest forces around FGM focus on the integrity and alignment of family with culture—we all want our children to grow up as valued members of our communities, with all the privileges of belonging, making friends, and being fully accepted.

---

[53]   UNICEF, "Rights of Girls."

> *In some communities, circumcision is the ritual which confers this full social acceptability and integration upon the females. Without it they become estranged from their own kith and kin and may lose their right to contribute to, or participate in, the community life of their homeland, to own property, to vote, or to be voted for. The loss of such rights and privileges may even extend to a male head of a family in which the daughters and wives are not circumcised.[54]*

EARLY PREGNANCY & NUTRITION

In many traditional communities where a husband and sons provide a woman with her primary social status, the practices of early marriage and early pregnancy shortly after puberty remain strong, despite the raising of legal marriage age in many countries. International health organizations have long contended that girls should not bear children before the age of eighteen. The bodies of girls younger than this simply are not ready for pregnancy and giving birth. The health risks for these young mothers and their children substantially increase. According to UNICEF's *State of the World's Children 2007*,

> *Girls under 15 are five times more likely to die during pregnancy and childbirth than women in their twenties. If a mother is under 18, her baby's chance of dying in the first year of life is 60 percent greater than that of a baby born to a mother older than 19. Even if the child survives, he or she is more likely to suffer from low birthweight, undernutrition and late physical and cognitive development.[55]*

---

54 Olayinka Koso-Thomas, *The Circumcision of Women: A Strategy for Its Eradication* (London: Zed Press, 1987).
55 UNICEF, *State of the World's Children 2007: The Double Dividend of Gender Equality* (New York: UNICEF, 2006), 4.

As we will see, research shows that increased education goes hand in hand with delayed childbearing and decreased health risks for mothers and children.[56]

Because of poor resources, religious beliefs, cultural practices, and their status, many girls, pregnant women, and lactating mothers also endure dietary imbalances and micronutrient deficiencies. When these are the result of local taboos placed on certain foods, a disproportionate, unnecessary burden is added to girls and women. Many communities throughout Africa withhold essential nutrients through taboos that dictate specific foods that may not be eaten by girls and pregnant and/or lactating women. Many of these taboo foods are highly nutritious, and lack of them can result in iron deficiency, anemia, or even malnutrition and pregnancy-related deaths. The increased nutrients and calories required during pregnancy and lactation may be thwarted by taboos on protein and vitamin-rich foods such as eggs, because tradition predicts a negative physical or character effect in the girl, woman, or newborn. For example, vitamin-rich green peppers are not given to young girls in some traditional Ethiopian highland communities because of the belief that the peppers increase their sexual desire and early maturation.

These practices are all interwoven with religious beliefs and local superstitions. When a mother or child suffers illness or death, the cause is often explained as evil spirits. A lack of understanding of how the human body functions, even by community health workers or traditional birth attendants (TBAs), can trigger a supernatural explanation, with blame being attributed in the wrong direction. The misapplication of local magic and herbal remedies may also be a lethal combination. Difficulty in labor or delay in delivery may be interpreted by others as punishment for marital infidelity, and confession is demanded for continued, successful delivery. Local TBA approaches to obstructed labor may also be ineffective or harmful, causing uterine rupture.

---

[56]   See UNICEF, *State of the World's Children 2007*, 4.

LEGAL ISSUES

To what degree can the sanctions of the law and human rights offer protection from harmful cultural practices and promote equity for girl children? As an example, most post-independence national legal systems in Africa provide for gender equity. Recent constitutional laws, however, frequently enshrine African adaptations of European law simultaneously amidst older customary, religious, and civil laws and practices, creating a sometimes-confusing coexistence of legal contradictions. What different constitutional, religious, and customary laws in one country or province say about female ownership of land, for example, may not coincide. Where women's equity in law has increased because of recent legislative changes, contrary customary laws tend to override.

Within the realm of reproductive rights, African law past and present tends to focus on the childbearing role of women, who are often not empowered legally or socially to exercise control over their own fertility, as in the numbers or spacing of their children. Local customs of dowry or bride price often mandate that the husband controls all aspects of his wife's life, her contacts, his discipline of her, her success as a child-bearer. Under many customary laws, a woman may have no right to her husband's property when he dies. This attitude projected backwards fosters an inflated value for boys, and deflated value for girls, in terms of their contribution to their birth families. The frequent inability of women to own land, and to access credit, training, and government extension services, is directly reflected in the devaluation of women's household economic and social worth. In general, women, whether single, married, divorced, or widowed, have fewer legal rights to land, property, and inheritance. This creates particular hardship where there is a disproportionately high number of female-headed households, as in post-genocide Rwanda and areas devastated by AIDS.

THE FUTURE? A WAY FORWARD

As the "African Platform for Action: African Common Position for the Advancement of Women" (1994) puts it, "The girl child of today is the woman of tomorrow. In order that she may grow up with the health, confidence and education necessary for her to take her place with dignity and equal to man in society, special attention needs to be focused on her."

This needed special attention has gained a foundation through events of the past few years, and is beginning to bear some fruit in the realm of development assistance. As the development paradigm appears to have shifted over the past fifty years, from:

- goods and technology transfer, to
- service delivery, to
- community participation, to
- community ownership, to
- people's movements,

the paradigm for engagement with gender seems to have also shifted, from:

- ignorance of the gender impacts of development, to
- assumptions of development's equal benefits, to
- special projects focused on women, to
- mainstreaming gender within development, to
- gender-oriented capacity building and policy development.

The focus for gender is more frequently now on building the capacity of girls and women, boys and men within communities, through formal and informal education, economic training, and awareness of gender equity and the harmful effects of some traditional practices. Gender is being institutionalized within the laws, policies, and practices of state, civil, and market sectors.

It is now recognized that the underlying community power structures, which dictate how girls are socialized and keep them in positions of powerlessness, must be transformed for real change to take place. As declared in the "Platform for Action" from the 1995 Beijing Conference, "initiatives should be taken to prepare girls to participate actively, effectively and equally with boys at all levels of social, economic, political and cultural leadership."[57] But shifting power structures toward such equity requires a critical mass of people who work in concert within their own communities to reject harmful practices, promote worthy, beneficial, and alternative practices, and persuade others to join them. They must in particular enlist the FGM excisors, the parents, the religious, traditional, and elected leaders, and any others who have previously had an interest in keeping these harmful practices alive, to work together with sensitivity to traditional values, cultural change, and issues of power, status, and authority.

Among the recommendations by Kurz and Prather,[58] a number are worth repeating and adapting here:

1. Focus investment on girls as an investment in women—increasing girls' education has proven results in their increased future earnings, reduced future fertility, and reduced maternal mortality and child mortality. Investments in women have a larger multiplier effect for the family than investments in men, because women contribute a larger portion of their income to the family.[59]

2. Include gender balance in the provision and utilization of services.

3. Direct awareness and communication exercises toward not just attitude changes—focus on those that demonstrably result in behavioral changes.

---

57   United Nations, "The United Nations Fourth World Conference on Women."
58   Kathleen M. Kurz and Cynthia J. Prather, *Improving the Quality of Life of Girls* (New York: Association for Women in Development, 1995), 59–65.
59   See further in UNESCO, *World Education Report* (New York: UNESCO, 1995).

4. Advocate for the rights of women and girls, and include targeted policy changes.
5. Include boys and fathers as agents of change.
6. Analyze and present all data separately for girls and boys by age.
7. Build program sustainability through coalitions, networks, and partnerships with community-based organizations and local civil society organizations.
8. Evaluate and conduct operations research to identify and verify best practices, to strengthen interventions.

Regarding the recommendation above on education, it is worth pushing our thinking further in both appreciative and radical directions. In the appreciative direction, we must acknowledge that the educational systems in developing countries hold great potential for the girl child and her future. With the right quantitative (increased female enrollment and decreased dropouts) and qualitative improvements (relevant curriculum and skilled teachers focused on developing girls' critical thinking and adaptive skills), girls can develop into women with the right tools for understanding and analyzing the strengths and weaknesses of the social, political, and economic environments in which they live and struggle.

In the radical direction, if true change in the status quo is to take place, including the elimination and/or replacement of harmful traditional practices and the removal of oppressive structures that render girls and women powerless, then consciousness-raising and transformation become the mission of education systems, with the girls themselves as the real change agents in their own societies' and communities' structures. Unfortunately, the educational systems of most developing countries remain traditional in methodology, with students and teachers working toward rote learning and regurgitation of memorized information, not fostering independent, critical thinking. But a first step is to help girls inside and outside formal education systems to begin to know and question why they must give birth to so many children, so often work endless hours without respite, be beaten and sexually abused, and be denied access to property, training, and credit.

Finally, progress forward is not necessarily straight ahead to the target. The journey, and in fact even the target itself, may change. Girl child champions and human rights practitioners must learn the dance that works most appropriately and effectively, even if it means having to adapt their own models and methods. The story of the shifting struggle against FGM is a case in point. In the 1980s, the World Health Organization and many private agencies declared war on FGM, calling for its complete abolition globally in every form practiced. But over the past decade or two, as development health professionals and human rights activists have worked within communities practicing FGM, the understanding of FGM as a total violation of the dignity, human rights, and personal health of girls has been challenged.

Citing the case of an NGO in West Africa, Ignatieff speaks of the unfolding FGM story as a parable about the cultural learning of 'outsiders' that is necessary if human rights practice is to be legitimate as well as effective.[60] As the outsiders in the West African example, NGO development and human rights workers had to modify their understanding and their terminology, and then question the right of human rights activists to intervene. They discovered that though painful, the FGM rites were not necessarily life-threatening, and were enthusiastically supported by many villagers, who value its role within an important public transition period for girls who are becoming socially and culturally validated as women of worth. And within their own community contexts that widely support the tradition of FGM, where it is the essential pre-condition for marriage, individual girls simply cannot by themselves renounce the rite, without broad community development and buy-in to an alternative rite of passage.

For the broader range of traditional practices harmful to girls, this thrusts into the light the increasingly important question of how 'insiders' and 'outsiders' should deliberate and work together toward a common understanding of human rights and real changes

---

60   See Michael Ignatieff, *The Rights Revolution*.

of traditional practices.[61] In the case of FGM and other practices, it is common for the outsiders to bring to the dialogue and intervention a western preconception of individualism, while the insiders come from within the strong collective, deliberately communitarian orientation of many developing communities. Where it is the practice for the women of a whole village together to be informed, deliberate with their elders, and then choose and declare a strategy corporately, there is little room for individual decisions.

This leaves the girl child 'outsider' champion or health professional with a dilemma—if the community decides to keep a harmful or dangerous practice, what then? In the case of a community choosing to retain FGM, should she help to support the community to make the genital cutting safer, more hygienic, and less painful, or step back entirely from the practice and risk her overall relationship with the community?

The call to equity for the marginalized, in this case for girl children undergoing harmful traditional practices, must also be translated into the call to work with integrity, and effectiveness on the ground in the village. This is not the world of high ideals and global conference rhetoric. Harmful practices occur in situations of local power imbalance, weakness and unequal structures, and effective interventions for girl children must work incrementally over time, beginning with effective alignment and appreciation of local institutions and customs. By necessity, we are called to be facilitators of a process, not bulldozers toward a fixed destination, in a tactical dance to celebrate for girl children that which affirms their lives, equity, and wholeness, and to find creative alternatives for that which harms them. There is no tidy ending in mind for this story, but the whiff of progress is in the air.

---

61   See Michael Ignatieff, *Human Rights as Politics and Idolatry* (Princeton: Princeton University Press, 2001).

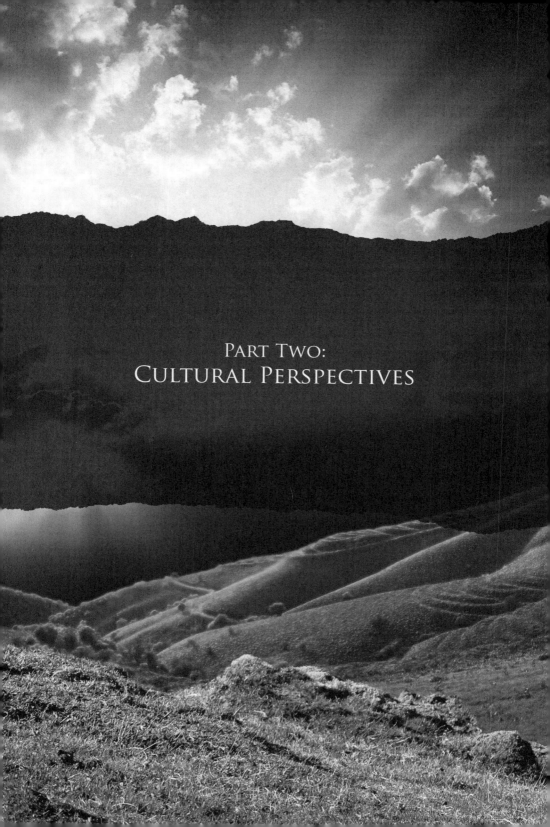

PART TWO:
CULTURAL PERSPECTIVES

The girl child and those who promote her cause need the intelligence and agility of the monkey, the courage and strength of the lion, the beauty and elegance of the giraffe, the adaptability of the hippo, and the focus and sureness—without the slowness—of the tortoise to enhance her chances of survival. Many of these characteristics come from Christ's teachings, from the power of the Holy Spirit, that allows us to walk with the girl child in her painful despair and toward solutions to these problems.

DR. OLIVIA N. MUCHENA,
DEPUTY MINISTER OF LANDS AND AGRICULTURE
FOR ZIMBABWE IN WORLD VISION, ED.,
THE GIRL CHILD: ENHANCING LIFE, SUSTAINING HOPE, 90–91

CHAPTER 4

A GIRL CHILD IS BORN: AN EXAMPLE FROM AN AFRICAN CONTEXT

Vongai Nzenza

Activity buzzed outside the quiet hut. Toria didn't care; she was in too much pain! Is this what labor is all about? she wondered. Was all the recognition one received after giving birth worth all this agony? Where was the husband who had contributed to her pain? Just carrying a life within one's body for nine months was overwhelming enough. Would he ever know how painful it was to give birth? Although Toria was experiencing an indescribably elated feeling, the pain was unbearable. The labor had now lasted almost fifty-two hours. Would this child ever come out and leave her alive?

Toria's mother had walked for three days, stopping only at night, to be present when her daughter faced a mother's most painful experience. Most young women in the villages died giving birth. There was no way MaiToria (Mother of Toria) was going to miss this occasion in case her daughter passed through the footsteps of her many cousins. Every year, countless stories spread of young brides facing death on their straw labor mats.

MaiToria continued to wipe the sweat from her daughter's forehead. She had stopped offering comforting words; Toria's mother-in-law strongly disapproved of the cries Toria had been making. She claimed Toria was a spoiled daughter, brought up to complain about everything. She insisted that Toria was a very lucky girl whose educated husband earned money, but never gave anything to his own mother, just because of Toria.

MaiToria seemed to assume responsibility for these claims about her daughter. A mother is always blamed for a daughter's unacceptable behavior. MaiToria lowered her head as the mother-in-law continued with her complaints. Toria could not endure any more. She screamed, infuriating the mother-in-law even further. The quiet of the hut had disappeared.

As if to make matters worse, the smoke from the center of the hut began causing tears in everyone's eyes. The birth attendant, the fourth woman in the house, screamed as well. "I am the most experienced traditional attendant in this area," she shouted. "As far as South Africa they know of me. MaiToria, your daughter is at fault. She has to name the man she had sex with besides her husband, because this behavior is the reason the labor is taking so long. Without that confession, she is going to die!"

Toria screamed back, "I have slept only with my husband and no one else, so there is no one to name." MaiToria, very embarrassed by this conversation, began to think her daughter might have had a sexual encounter with a man other than her son-in-law. She commenced persuading her daughter to name the man.

"Amai (Mother)," Toria begged. "Are you beginning to believe these people more than...?"

The mother-in-law cut Toria's complaint short as she broke in with, "I just cannot believe my son could fall in love, worse marry such a stupid girl. It is her mother's fault. We cannot completely blame Toria, can we?" She continued to talk negatively until Toria's mother started to talk to her daughter.

"My daughter, I understand how you are feeling right now. Pregnancy labor can make everyone stubborn. But put that aside and humble yourself. Just say with whom you slept, besides Ismael your husband."

Toria's anger, fueled by these affronts, screamed, "I slept with Peter, John, Mark, and...who else do you want me to name?" Her sarcasm had no time to penetrate the thinking of the three elderly women, for at that moment a baby girl popped into the world.

The baby cried like a normal newborn, but the women sat as if in total shock. Then the mother-in-law screamed, "You slut! To make matters worse, you give birth to another prostitute. My son would never have fathered a girl child as his firstborn. Get up from your labor mat and go to your village. I am not going to contribute to the upbringing of a prostitute by a prostitute!"

Mother-in-law went from screaming to moaning, speaking as if to herself, "What is my son going to say when he comes back? Poor Ismael. He works hard to look after this prostitute, and what does he get in return? Nothing but embarrassment. If only he had seen the pregnancy growing, he would have known that this was not his child. Working in the mines of South Africa does not help him to work out his home matters. My son! I feel sorry for my son. He works six months at a time with no chance to come home. And when he comes what does he get? Nothing but misery and embarrassment." She spat out the last words, expressing her grief and exasperation.

Instead of shouting with joy, MaiToria began to cry. Toria looked at her then requested to see her baby. The sight of her firstborn produced smiles of joy. The birth attendant displayed her wisdom and her professionalism by cutting the umbilical cord and smearing cow dung below the navel. Toria admitted how tired she felt, and the mother-in-law further demonstrated her disgust by spitting in the fire. Toria, not realizing the women truly believed she slept with other men before her marriage and that the baby belonged to someone else, said, "I think she looks like Ismael's sister!" Outraged, Mother-in-law slapped Toria on the cheek. "My daughter Dadi would never look like the daughter of a prostitute," she screamed.

With that remark, Toria realized what the old woman was thinking. She looked at her mother, who was staring down at her with shame. "Mother! What is the matter with you? You should be proud that I gave birth!" MaiToria looked at her daughter without answering. Then she begged the mother-in-law to be allowed to stay the night. Toria, looking puzzled, asked her mother why she should be begging for a one-night stay. "Go to sleep, my daughter, and I will see if I can get you some soup. You are tired," her mother replied. Toria smiled and fell into a deep sleep.

The mother-in-law, assuming that this baby was not her grandchild, refused to pay the birth attendant. So MaiToria had to compensate the birth attendant by giving up her cardigan and her sarong. Usually the payment is a goat and a chicken, but MaiToria was not prepared for this, and neither could she afford it. The only cash she had would be used to put Toria and the baby on the bus, and she would have to walk uphill for three days to get back home. She knew they could not stay there much longer, because if Ismael came home the embarrassment would be too much to swallow.

Although everyone treated MaiToria and her daughter with disgust, they still expected MaiToria to cook for them since she was the in-law from the woman's side. With her head lowered to her shoulders, a sign of submission and shamefulness, she asked for and received permission to use the mother-in-law's pots. Luckily, she had brought some dry meat, tomatoes, and peanut butter with her. As her grandmother used to say, you always carry presents for those you are visiting. MaiToria toiled, trying to cook a good meal. The rain outside made it even more difficult; all the firewood was wet. She cooked, keeping an eye on her grandchild. The last thing she wanted was to lose her granddaughter, no matter how she came into the world.

The baby began to cry, and MaiToria awakened Toria to feed the child. Opening her eyes, Toria smiled and with the help of her mother positioned the baby on her breast. The baby began to suckle. Toria had no energy to talk, but a sense of amazed wonder swept over her. For someone only seventeen years of age, she had been through a lot over the past two days.

"You're lucky," the birth attendant commented. "It takes some women up to two days before milk that satisfies the baby begins to flow. At least there are some positives about you," she added, with a small mocking laugh to please the mother-in-law.

Fortunately, all the men in the compound and other people were not allowed to see a baby girl and the mother for two weeks. (If the baby was a boy, the father could come into the hut to see his son.) No visitors made it easier for MaiToria. She didn't have to face a lot of people with questioning looks. After the meal, which everyone seemed to enjoy, the birth attendant and the mother-in-law went to sleep on the right side of the fireplace, in the middle of the hut. MaiToria slept on the other side with her daughter and granddaughter. In her heart, she felt happy that her daughter was alive.

Early in the morning, MaiToria helped her daughter wash and get situated on the bus at five o'clock in the morning. In spite of Toria's refusal to leave before Ismael returned from the mines, the mother-in-law was adamant that Toria must leave. Slowly, she got on the bus, and MaiToria commenced her three-day journey on foot.

Toria did not give much thought to what was happening. She was still in terrible pain from a difficult labor. Journeying along, she felt like falling asleep to never come back to life again. Looking at her beautiful baby gave her strength. In the long, curly black hair, big eyes, long fingers, and well-defined though very thick lips, Toria could see Ismael. Momentarily forgetting the reason for her journey, all she could think of was how pleased Ismael would be to hold the baby in his arms.

As Toria smiled to herself, the woman next to her commented, "I know! It is the joys of motherhood. No one can explain this feeling, although they say some never get it after giving birth. I have met a woman in those circumstances. It is a pity because I would really like every woman or mother to experience the joy of motherhood."

Toria looked up, amazed at this woman's observations. "How did you know?" she asked.

"I know," the woman replied. "You look tired, like you have just come out of labor. Anyway, where are you going by yourself in such a state? With all these potholes, your uterus will not survive. You must be in pain."

Without replying, Toria began to cry. The woman moved closer, and with one arm took the baby from Toria's arms. She cuddled Toria on her shoulder with the other arm. "Cry as much as you like," the woman consoled her, "and then if you want you can tell me the problem." Toria explained what had happened. Shaking her head, the woman replied, "I am sixty-five years old. I have been through a lot, my daughter. If you are only seventeen, you still have a lot to learn. Our male-dominated society is terrible. For this reason, you are on this bus right now."

Toria tried to explain that her husband was a nice man, but it was her mother-in-law who was the problem. The woman told Toria to be quiet and let her explain what was happening. "In a patriarchal society, women are happy to live under suppressive conditions controlled by men. Call it what you like, men have dominated this culture so that women carry out the laws put in place for them. The sad thing is that we women do not realize it. We go along with it, calling it 'culture.' Look at the policemen. They arrest peaceful protesters who demonstrate against corruption in governments and see themselves as carrying out the law. Who puts this law in place? The government, of course. And what happens when the government becomes corrupt? The police protect the politicians running the government. Just like us women: we do all the fighting, protecting whose culture?

"Culture is good, but not when it makes other humans suffer. What was okay long ago is no longer okay. Culture has to change to meet the ever-changing needs of our society. Schooling for everyone would be a start so that people will be able to question and make informed choices.

"I did not have much education. I gave birth to nine girls and no boys. I was divorced after nine children. I made a commitment to my girls that they would all have an education. I struggled. The last-born is in Form 4 now, and all have very good jobs. I never thought women could drive big cars, but my daughters have made me see a world I did not know existed. I look at my daughters now, and forget all the trouble I went through in educating them.

"Their father tried to demand money from them to look after the children of his second marriage. It was very interesting to see my ex-husband demanding the girls' salaries. 'They are women,' he reasoned, 'and might not be able to use the money wisely.' At one time during his arguments, my oldest daughter told her father to come to her work and help her make decisions. Her father answered that he wouldn't know what to do with computers. My daughter told him she assumed, since he was a man, he would know what to do. Her father laughed and apologized, saying he could see the sense.

"I do have respect for my ex-husband. He is willing to learn, and he is now sending his daughters from his second marriage to school. He reckons he was unlucky for marrying women who can give him only girls. My daughter who is a doctor told me that it is not the woman's biology that decides the sex of a child but the man's. I find this difficult to understand, but I suppose she knows a lot.

"Getting back to the point, whatever you do, my child, make sure you send all your children to school, whether they are boys or girls. Take your time, my child, and things will fall into place. Surely this husband of yours knows the real truth. The most important thing now is to look after this special girl child of yours." The woman had to shout her last sentence through the window of the bus as Toria got off at her parents' village.

Toria arrived in Chisumba Village in mid-afternoon. No one expected her since the trip was not planned, and her mother, walking, would not arrive for another two days. Toria managed to walk off the bus but could go no further. The pain was unbearable. Since her parents' home was a few kilometers from the bus stop, helpful villagers, organized by the local storekeeper, wheeled Toria home in a wheelbarrow. Although no one asked why she was traveling in this state, people could sense a big problem. BabaToria (father of Toria) did not ask either. He decided to wait for his wife's arrival.

BabaToria put the blame on his wife for having brought up a prostitute. He had nothing to do with it, he said. Girls belonged to mothers, and boys belonged to fathers. This allegation destroyed MaiToria for, sadly, she herself considered it her fault. She decided not to discuss the issue with her daughter until she was fully well. To hold the discussions, Toria's aunt from the father's side had to be present, since it is cultural to have a female to represent the father.

On the day of the questioning, MaiToria was extra quiet as she could not predict the end result. Toria's aunt would decide what would happen to Toria. Living with the family forever would be a disgrace. Most likely, Toria would have to leave the village, leave the baby, and find work in the city. If no job could be found, she would resort to prostitution and run the risk of contracting HIV and AIDS.

> *If no job could be found, she would resort to prostitution and run the risk of contracting HIV and AIDS.*

As the discussions commenced, Toria was given no chance to speak. Her mother did most of the "guilty" talking, and the aunt was very angry. Four other women were also present at this questioning. After each one had spoken, they gave Toria a chance to talk. "I cannot understand," she began, "why you do not just ask me if the baby is Ismael's or not." The aunt spoke before Toria could say more.

"Toria, now that we all know you are a disgrace to the family, you will have to leave your baby and find a job to fend for your daughter. We think it is wise for you to leave this family in two weeks, at the latest. No one can feed the child of a prostitute. Your mother will have to look after this evil thing that you brought into the world. It is now two weeks since you gave birth, and your child doesn't even have a name because of your doings. I will not have my brother look at you every day and wonder how many men have slept with his daughter."

Toria could take no more. "Aunt, give me a chance to talk," she cried. "I have never slept with any men besides Ismael. Everyone is assuming I am guilty before I am even tried. Ask Ismael. He will tell you I was a virgin when we met. I went to live with his family afterwards. Who could I have slept with when I was living with his mother who always wanted to know what I was doing? Even sitting down to rest was illegal in her eyes. She was like a foreman to me. Every day, I had to work all day long since Ismael left for the mines. This baby is truly and honestly Ismael's baby and I have nothing else to add to what I have said, except to say I am not going to leave my baby at this young age and before I have talked to Ismael himself."

MaiToria was shocked. She reminded Toria that she, herself, had confessed in front of her mother-in-law. Toria explained that the unbearable labor pain caused her to make the sarcastic remarks. Finally the decision was made: wait another six months until Ismael comes to claim divorce.

Nine months later, Ismael arrived with his uncles to claim back his wife. Thinking all her problems were over and the issues had been clarified, Toria went back with Ismael to his village. On arriving, she found her mother-in-law very inhospitable. She still believed that the baby was not Ismael's and that if Ismael was so stupid as to accept his wife then he should get a second wife in compensation. She said she would not rest until Ismael married a second wife. The uncles also kept nagging him to get a second wife even if he still wanted Toria. Ismael contended that he had no need for a second wife since he was already involved with a lot of girls in South Africa and was never home to see the two wives anyway. The uncles argued that wives are to be used for the fields and to bring more boys into the world. Toria had given birth to a girl, and marrying another wife would give more chances of having a boy.

After a few days, and to his mother's satisfaction, Ismael brought home a sixteen-year-old girl as his second wife. "Just a child," mused Toria. "At least I was seventeen when I got married."

Toria found the experience painful, but she looked on it as culturally acceptable. Her father had married two more wives since MaiToria had given birth to four girls before the five boys came along. Her father's second wife had given birth to five girls and divorced BabaToria due to ill treatment as a result of her not giving birth to boys. Reminded of the lecture she had received on the bus going to her village, Toria still did not see how one could change one's culture.

Finally, her daughter was named. Tapiwa. During the naming ceremony, Toria could trace the footsteps her daughter would take through life. Already the in-laws had plans for the grandchild. They considered her a God-given working girl due to the circumstances in which she had been born. Too much gossip had gone on during her birth, which meant Tapiwa had been born to serve the family.

A year passed, and Toria gave birth to a bouncing baby boy, and so did the second wife. The in-laws were very happy. In six years, Toria had four children, one girl and three boys. The second wife had three children, two boys and one girl. When Tapiwa was five years old, it was decided that she should move in with Ismael's parents so that she could be trained to look after a household of boys as well as to be groomed by the grandmother to be a good wife. Toria cried very much knowing what this move would entail for her daughter. She argued that her daughter was only five years old. What was Tapiwa to learn that Toria herself could not teach? Her arguments went unheard.

Strangely, VaTakai (grandmother) became very attached to Tapiwa. Tapiwa resembled this grandmother very much, even in mannerisms. Very strong-willed she was. A pity that her grandmother's strength and willpower were used for wrong purposes. At one time, the midwife who brought Tapiwa into the world said jokingly to Tapiwa's VaTakai, "Are you not embarrassed that you threw Toria out and yet Tapiwa has grown up to be just like you?" VaTakai was embarrassed, but argued that she had been fighting for her son's rights since her son was not present. The midwife laughed and exclaimed, "The reason women will never be free is because of us women ourselves. We treat each other badly to please the men!"

Defensively, VaTakai replied, "Men are stupid, and we have to behave this way so we can uphold the country!" The midwife walked away saying she did not understand what that meant and would not listen to any further excuses on behalf of men.

Tapiwa's first month with her grandmother was full of drills. "Sit properly, Tapiwa, with your dress covering your knees as a good wife should sit. Tapiwa, you only have nine more years before you are married off. You should sit like a good wife." VaTakai scolded her every day. Tapiwa had to wake up at 5 a.m. to fetch water, light the fire, and boil the water for her grandfather to wash. She also swept the house while everyone else was in the field. These chores were considered to be the easiest she could do since she was still too young to work in the fields.

Toria lived not far from VaTakai's house. She could see her daughter working and the boys kneeling down to be served. At only six years of age, Tapiwa was dressed like an adult, and she had to extend her respect to even the young boys simply because they were boys. Any behavior unbecoming to a good wife was met with reprimands and accusations of being a bad wife. A girl should never look or behave in such manner, she was told.

At nine years of age, Tapiwa spoke with dignity, causing one to think she was much older. She was also quite intelligent. Although VaTakai was against Tapiwa going to school, somehow Toria managed to convince the grandmother that Tapiwa must go to school. Attending school meant double work for Tapiwa. Now she had to wake up at four in the morning, fetch water, do the usual chores, and then walk six kilometers to school. To be on time meant walking part of the way in the dark. Being late to school meant two lashes with a leather whip on the backside. Also, girls had to arrive fifteen minutes early to polish the floor with crushed green leaves, fetched from the bush on the way to school. At the end of class, boys could leave the school early, and girls remained to sweep the classroom, ready for polishing the next morning.

Going home from school meant running all the way. If one walked, the household chores would not be done on time. Some days, firewood had to be collected from far away since most of the trees had been cut near the households. In addition, if girls did not run and boys caught up with them, it meant abuse. The boys could choose to beat up girls at will, or throw them to the ground and pretend to be having a sexual encounter. Tapiwa hated this harassment. It made her feel as if the encounter was really happening. Other boys would always cheer when one of them managed to throw a girl down.

In grade four, during the last term of the year, Tapiwa could not handle the amount of work required at school and at home. She told VaTakai. Very pleased, VaTakai commented that she never understood the need for schooling anyway. She herself had survived with no schooling, and she now owned two cows. Her friend who had gone to school and could read and write owned only one goat, so why bother going to school if it does not really bring livestock!

Tapiwa took this argument to her mother, which brought Toria almost to tears. She explained to Tapiwa that while it was difficult to manage school as well as work at home, the benefits in the end were immeasurable. Tapiwa asked her mother why she had not gone to school if it was so important. Toria sat with her daughter and for hours that day tried to explain the disadvantages of being born a woman and what it meant in life. She recalled the conversation she had with the woman on the bus the day after Tapiwa was born. She explained how she had been taken out of school so that her brother Mufudzi could get schooling because he was a boy.

The argument was that Mufudzi would look after the family, but Toria would be married off, thereby not benefiting the family. Toria's father had been so firm that no one opposed. Mufudzi went to the University of Zimbabwe and then to England. Contrary to the belief that Mufudzi would look after the family financially, in England he got married and moved to Nigeria—the last they had heard of him. Toria became very emotional and began to cry, thinking of how much Mufudzi could have helped her parents, mostly her mother, in alleviating their poverty.

Tapiwa still did not see the benefit of a girl going to school. So, Toria pointed to an example of one girl in her class who had managed to go through college. She was now a teacher in Tapiwa's school and did not need to go to the fields at five in the morning. "Look, Tapiwa," her mother said. "This woman's children go to school without struggling for food or going to the fields before school. Above all, she also looks after her parents, and the parents even wear shoes to church. She has proved wrong all the beliefs that girls marry off and do not look after their parents."

Tapiwa could not believe it that Mrs. Jeche, who dressed so well and whose fingers looked so fragile, had gone to school with her mother. Mrs. Jeche's children ate bread for breakfast and wore shoes with white socks. Her children had four meals a day while Tapiwa had only two meals a day. Incredible, Tapiwa fantasized, that her mother could have been just like Mrs. Jeche, and Toria herself could be the daughter wearing black shoes with white socks!

She compared her mother's work-worn fingers with Mrs. Jeche's fingers. To see herself as one of Mrs. Jeche's children was completely unimaginable, yet the thought gave Tapiwa a feeling of fullness that she could not explain. Although she was only ten years old, she felt herself gathering great strength to push herself through school. She looked at her mother and smiled.

Besides finding it physically difficult to go to school, Tapiwa worried about school fees. She knew how difficult it was for her mother. To provide the school fees as well as the required building fund charges, Toria had hired herself out to work in other people's fields, as well as her own, and made arrangements with the school to work with the builders making bricks for the building. The headmaster had been very supportive.

Grandmother VaTakai argued that this was madness. She contended that if education for a girl child was so important, the girl's father would have agreed to pay it like he did currently for Tapiwa's brothers. Ismael was in full agreement with his mother that schooling for girls was a waste of time and would not even entertain discussions that referred to him paying fees for girl children. If Toria was interested in sending her girl children to school, she was free to raise the funds for the expense.

Seeing the struggles her mother went through to keep her and the other three girls in school, Tapiwa became more determined to do well. She was now sixteen. Two of her brothers had decided to drop out of school and join their mother in farming. Toria did not push them because she could see that her husband had already allocated land to them, unlike the girls. As soon as the boys turned eighteen, they would go with their father to South Africa and work in the mines. In spite of their mother's warnings, the boys could not wait to go. They anticipated receiving the same respect their father got during the few times he came home. After all, they were men and could decide what they would do with their lives rather than listen to their mother—a woman.

Tapiwa could have finished lower secondary education except for the lack of money. When she was to go into Form 3, her mother could not raise the required money. Toria was now pregnant with her ninth child and the pregnancy was not an easy one, so half the time she spent lying down. Toria blamed herself for getting pregnant again. She forgot that she had no say in the number of children she could have. Her husband had to decide that. Ismael came home only once a year for six weeks.

During that time, he always managed to get both of his wives pregnant. He paid school fees for the boys, but everything he ate had to be produced by the wives. All he gave in return was a dress for each wife and a few second-hand clothes for the boys. As far as he was concerned, the girls could always find ways of surviving until they got married, then he could get his *lobola* (bride price). Of course wealth belonged to him, not his wives. Remember, he was the father, and they were only mothers—nothing more.

Toria gave birth to a stillborn baby, and she was sick for a long time. Tapiwa had to quit school and move back home from her grandmother's to nurse her mother. Tapiwa became the mother, the breadwinner, and the cook for all the children. Her job also included making sure her brothers' clothes were washed and ironed. The boys demanded it and saw it as their right.

VaTakai was a bit disappointed with Tapiwa for not finding a boyfriend and marrying. Tapiwa had sworn that she would not marry until she had an education that would get her a job. Toria continued to push her daughters firmly, and Tapiwa, while she stayed at home, worked to earn the fees for the other girls to continue schooling.

When Toria was back on her feet, Tapiwa went back to school, but when it became too difficult for her mother to raise the required fees, Tapiwa decided to talk to one of the teachers at her school to see if she could find some help. The male teacher was not helpful except to discourage Tapiwa. He told her that she was a woman and girls of her age should be married and washing their husband's feet rather than sitting behind a desk with a full breast as she was. His solution was for Tapiwa to become his wife.

Feeling totally disillusioned, Tapiwa's last resort, though her mother discouraged such a move, was Mrs. Jeche. Toria did not realize that she had brought up her girls to be so strong. Tapiwa went straight to Mrs. Jeche, who was still teaching in the primary school, and told her the problem. Mrs. Jeche proved to be very helpful. She gave Tapiwa a list of names to whom she could write explaining her situation. Tapiwa did not see this as an immediate solution. In no way would she get a reply by the following term when the fees would be due. She started crying, and Mrs. Jeche, touched by this reaction, asked Tapiwa what she thought would be a solution. Tapiwa's eyes lit up brightly, and she said, "I will work for you, and if I can't work enough to pay off my fees, I promise I will pay it back somehow." Mrs. Jeche could not give her a reply at that moment.

Tapiwa, surprised by her own quick thoughts, now worried that her mother would refuse to allow her to work for Mrs. Jeche. She decided not to worry: she would deal with her mother when the time came.

Tapiwa arrived home from school at sunset. Tapiwa found her mother grinding nuts to make peanut butter. Her mother had become very frail since her last illness. Things had never been the same although she pretended to be all right. Tapiwa could not help but cry as she watched her mother from the back of the house. Her mother did not realize that her daughter was watching her. Tapiwa stayed behind the house for a little while thinking very deeply. She promised herself that she would see to it that her mother lived to enjoy the fruits of her labor through her daughter Tapiwa. Not only that, she also would make sure that many women around her village would not live the way most women did right now. Tapiwa was so deep in her thoughts she did not see her brother coming up behind her.

"What are you doing, woman! Is the water ready for my bath yet? You know I need my warm water at sunset, but you seem to be forgetting a lot these days!"

Tapiwa looked at her brother with anger she could not explain. She thought she should get the respect she deserved from this brother who was two years younger than she. Just being a woman did not warrant this treatment. If anything was to change, she decided, it should start now. If her promise to the women of her village that one day they and their daughters would be treated with respect, the change would have to be put into effect now!

"Go get the water yourself," she said firmly to her brother. "If you were man enough, you would respect everyone and think about human feelings. Being a woman does not warrant the treatment you are giving me. From now on, you get your own bath water."

Neither her brother nor her mother could believe their ears. Toria thought, "It's not actually bad that the boys get their own water." Somehow she felt responsible to say something but decided against it. Her mother's lack of comment surprised Tapiwa, and at first she was very pleased by the silence. But then she said to herself, "No, silence is not enough if things are to change."

"Amai (mother)," she said determinedly, "You cannot just keep quiet. If you support my speech, then please say so. If you are against it, still the more you should say something! It is the silence that perpetuates the suffering you have gone through during your lifetime.

Say something!"

"Tapiwa, I understand your anger," her mother replied. "Are school fees the issue? Things will settle down, and a solution will be found. Don't put your anger on everyone."

Tapiwa's brother was in full support of this, but Tapiwa would not be silenced! "No, Amai! It is not right. It is not just the fees. It is everything—this house, this village, this country, and this world. Being a woman is not a sin, but we are treated like we have committed some sin. I am not going to take it lying down."

The brother walked away, claiming that Tapiwa was possessed by this so-called education. He blamed his mother for pushing education into the girls for no real reason. God would judge Tapiwa for not accepting her position as it was in society. Toria was not pleased with Tapiwa or her son, but she somehow felt Tapiwa was right. She, however, did not have the energy to enter the debate. She felt a satisfied feeling that her job had been done, but she asked herself, how have I done the job, and what job was it?

Tapiwa continued in her struggle for education and freedom. Watching her daughter's progress, Toria kept remembering the night this girl child was born.

Girls are the world's most squandered gift. They are precious human beings with enormous potential, but across the world, they are generally the last to have their basic needs met and the first to have their basic rights denied.

WORLD VISION, *EVERY GIRL COUNTS*, 6

Gender equality will not only empower women to overcome poverty, but also their children, families, communities and countries. When seen in this light, gender equality is not only morally right—it is pivotal to human progress and sustainable development.

UNICEF, *STATE OF THE WORLD'S CHILDREN 2007*, X

CHAPTER 5

MY STORY, THEIR STORIES: GIRLS IN WESTERN CONTEXTS

Desiree Segura-April

Barbie, pink, frills, diets, blonde, thin, dolls, playing house, talking, talking on the phone, boy-crazy, pretty, Cinderella, knight-in-shining-armor saves damsel-in-distress, pretend not to be smarter than the boys, ballerinas, makeup, popularity contests, cheerleaders, in-style clothes, sexy, girl-next-door, innocent. Those are some of the words and phrases that come to mind when I think about my experience of growing up a girl in the United States of America.

Granted, it's impossible to know if I would have used those words and phrases to describe my experience at that time. In fact, it is highly likely that because of my education and my extensive reading in the field of women's studies and girl child issues, these images are highlighted differently than they would be for the average girl growing up in America. Yet, I am constantly struck by the way in which my experience rings true to the trends and issues that emerge from the literature describing the challenges of girlhood in the western context. I like to think that I was able to grow up unscathed by these socializing factors, but the more I read and reflect, the more I realize I am a product of the very same influences that I hope to be able to help girls overcome.

My purpose is to explore these factors from a very personal perspective by simply sharing my story with you. It is my hope that my story will serve as a case study to identify some issues to consider for understanding the lives of girls in western contexts today.

DIVERSITY WITHIN ˝WESTERN˝ CONTEXTS

Before I share my story, I must note that the category "girls in western contexts" is somewhat misleading because there is a tremendous amount of diversity encompassed therein. There are a wide variety of countries, socio-economic classes, and cultural backgrounds represented. All of these areas contribute to a girl's experience of life in deeply profound ways. Thus, it is impossible to generalize completely what life is like for a girl in a western context. My particular context was within the middle class, educated, white, and small-town society of the United States. My story will hence be very different from that of a girl of color who grew up in a poor neighborhood in an urban setting.

"Many research studies treat girls as a homogeneous category, rather than probing issues of race, social class, culture, and sexuality, and the interplay of these with gender."[62] Accordingly, the generalizations that I will suggest in this chapter are simply for the purpose of understanding trends and generalities. It must always be kept in mind that they do not reflect the reality of *all* girls in *all* contexts.

After I share my story and the issues that it raises, I will summarize some of the issues that girls may face, as identified by a variety of researchers and authors. Even that won't do justice to the wide array of experiences of so many girls. Therefore, I would ask the reader to attempt to maintain a creative tension between the generalizations of life as a girl in a western context and the specific experiences of each and every girl. We must view every girl as unique, special, and deserving of understanding, while at the same time, we must attempt

---

62   Lynn Phillips, *The Girls Report: What We Know & Need to Know About Growing Up Female* (New York: The National Council for Research on Women, 1998), 3.

to understand trends among girls and issues that affect them if we are to minister with them.

MY STORY: A CASE STUDY

My story begins with a simple, naïve prayer. My mother was a new Christian when she became pregnant with me. My parents were both teachers, but when they decided to attempt to become pregnant again, she resigned from her position. She was implicitly encouraged by the school administration to resign if she were going to become pregnant. Due to other circumstances, her health insurance would not cover the delivery costs unless I was born after May thirty-first. The due date given by the doctors was the twenty-fifth of May. This is where the prayer entered. My mother was still "testing the waters" with her newfound faith; she was not totally convinced that this God she had committed her life to could really make a difference in everyday affairs. And so she prayed, "God, if you really exist, then you'll make sure this baby isn't born until after May thirty-first." I was born on the first of June! My parents gave me the name "Desiree," which means "desired one."

A girl baby being "desired" by parents is not completely unusual in a western context. Unlike some non-western contexts, there is no evidence to show that there are more abortions of girls than boys based on a desire for boy babies over and above girl babies. There are, however, some studies that indicate a preference for boys, even in western countries.[63] So the fact that I was named "the desired one" makes my case somewhat unique. I truly believe that God chose to bless my parents by hearing their prayer and allowing me to be born after my due date. Moreover, I believe God blessed them by giving them a *girl* who would eventually grow up to be a woman who would seek justice for *other girls*. That is why I share this part of my story with you today.

---

63 Neera Kuckreja Sohoni, *The Burden of Girlhood: A Global Inquiry into the Status of Girls* (Oakland, CA: Third Party Publishing Co., 1995), 18–20.

As a "desired child," I grew up knowing I was deeply loved and cherished. I never doubted the love of my parents, and ultimately this led to a natural acceptance of the love of God. I became a Christian at a very young age and don't even remember not knowing Jesus as my friend and Savior. Obviously, the depth of my understanding and my relationship with Jesus grew over time, but I was raised knowing that I was a child of God, created in His image and worthy of love and dignity.

THE BATTLE OF THE BULGE

This understanding of infinite worth was often in conflict with the messages I received from the world around me. Even as a very young girl, I remember thinking I was fat because I had curves while most girls were still "straight as a bean pole." In reality, my weight as a girl was always within normal healthy ranges on the medical charts. My mother was always dieting and always slightly overweight, so I grew up believing that weight control would be a constant, never-ending battle that I would ultimately lose.

My "Barbie" dolls were Donnie and Marie Osmond and Cher. I always thought the Cher doll was huge and so unlike what a girl should look like (sorry, Cher). Marie, on the other hand, was petite but voluptuous where appropriate. That's what I wanted to look like. To this day, I struggle to fight those old tapes that play in my head and tell me that my body is not acceptable or beautiful because it is not small and petite. (And I am still within normal healthy weight ranges on medical charts.) I know intellectually that what is most important is to be healthy and to take care of "God's temple." Nevertheless, emotionally I still have to fight against those girlhood messages, which degrade me as a human being because of my physical body type.

This is something that is rarely discussed in churches or theological institutions. When it is discussed or written about from a Christian perspective, it is generally to propose a "Christian" approach to weight management. Yet, issues of self-esteem and body image are on the top of the list of obstacles faced by girls in western societies. Eating disorders, sexual exploitation, and teenage pregnancy are some of the consequences of these obstacles. The Church for the most part has neglected to address these issues with girls (and boys). This is an area that must be explored much more if we are to truly understand growing up female in a western context and how the Church can help girls have healthy self-images.

> *Issues of self-esteem and body image are on the top of the list of obstacles faced by girls in western societies.*

COMBAT WITH THE "DUMB BLONDE" STEREOTYPE

Not only did I struggle with my body image, but I also battled with society's portrayal of the "dumb blonde" girl always winning the gorgeous guy. While I *was* blonde growing up, I certainly *was not* dumb. In fact, I was always self-conscious about my somewhat above normal intelligence. From the time I was in first grade, I was placed in advanced classes in many subjects, and in third grade I was placed in a "gifted program" at school. I just wanted to be "normal," so I never told anyone my scores on things. I often knew the answers to questions in class but wouldn't raise my hand unless no one else did or I was directly called upon to answer. I lacked confidence in myself and wished that I could be "pretty" instead of "smart." Inwardly I felt proud of my achievements, but I always had a sense that if I shared them with others, no one would like me, especially not the boys.

Even in college, I remember pretending not to know certain things with guys so that they would think they were smarter than I. Thankfully, I finally realized that those games were boring and that I did not want to date men who were threatened by my intelligence anyway.[64] When I entered the Ph.D. program, I was the first female Ph.D. student at the school.[65] We had a weekly discussion seminar with all of the doctoral students and professors (there was also only one female professor out of seven), and I spoke only once or twice in three years because I felt intimidated. I think that was my own problem, not theirs, but it stems from the way I was socialized as a young girl.

I was the second person in the history of the program to receive the highest marks possible on the qualifying exams. When this occurred, I was surprised by the reactions of my male student colleagues. While they were congratulatory, there was a definite sense of competition and embarrassment that a woman had "set the standard so high" and essentially "outdone" them.[66] I must admit that even at this level, I almost felt embarrassed by my achievement, and I know that those feelings date back to how I felt growing up as a girl.

FIGHTING DEPRESSION

I also struggled with depression as an adolescent girl. I remember for several months during my first year in high school experiencing a sense that I had become void of all feeling. I didn't necessarily feel sad, but I also couldn't feel happiness or joy. I recall describing afterwards that it was like there was a wet, heavy towel laying over my heart that made it impossible to feel anything. Feeling extremely sad would have been better than no feelings at all. Most of the people around me were unaware of my depression because I had learned to mask my feelings and act as though everything was fine.

I finally found relief from that experience of prolonged depression when I went to a church retreat. I understood anew that God loved me for who I was, not for what I achieved or how "popular" I was. I now

---

64   I'm thankful that in 1994 God saw fit to give me the gift of a creative, wonderful, intelligent (and handsome) man from Costa Rica to be my husband. He has been my most faithful "fan," supporter, and encourager in the pursuit of my Ph.D. and constantly challenges me to do things that use the gifts God has given me.

65   The school had offered a Doctor of Missiology program for about ten years when I started, but the Ph.D. in Intercultural Studies program was only in its second year. While I was the first woman in the Ph.D. section, there were already a few women in the D.Miss. program, although they also made up only a very small percentage of the students in the program.

66   Several actually "jokingly" used these words with me.

know that many girls suffer from depression, but at the time I felt I was the only one. Those patterns from my girlhood continue to affect me.

Occasionally I still experience bouts with depression, although they are much shorter in duration now (a day or two at a time). This is another area that the Church has generally neglected but must be explored if we are to minister to the needs of girls and women.

CHALLENGING THE CHURCH'S STANCE ON WOMEN'S ROLES

Finally, my story would not be complete without a discussion of my experience of the Church in relation to the roles of women in church, society, and the home. I was raised in a church that made a decision to have only men as elders. This decision was made when I was about twelve years old. Before this time, women served as deaconesses in the church, leading ministries of hospitality with children and other women, teaching adult classes, and in participating in music ministries. So, as a young girl, I observed many women participating in the church, but mostly in traditionally "female" roles.

In my adolescent years, these roles became even more restrictive as the church re-organized its leadership structure and reduced the sanctioned leadership positions from including deacons, deaconesses, and trustees to only elders. Women were not allowed to become elders. They continued to serve in the roles indicated above, but were no longer decision-makers in any of these ministries. Seldom did a woman even teach an adult Sunday School class anymore, although this did happen occasionally. A woman would not be hired as the pastor either because the new structure required the pastor to become an elder.

As for women's roles in society and the home, there was a subtle undercurrent of teaching that a mother's role was to be at home to care for her husband and children. If she worked outside the home, that work was only to supplement the family income and should not interfere with her primary roles of mother and wife. Likewise, the wife was taught to be subservient to her husband; the vocabulary used was to be "submissive," but the understanding was subservience and even inferiority. While this wasn't actually preached or taught, it was implicit within the structures, underlying teachings, and roles within the majority of the families in the church.

Within my family, both of my parents participated in church activities and served in different ministry roles. However, I later learned that my mother believed at the time that my father should be the "spiritual leader" in the home, and, therefore, she refrained from leading us in any formal faith development activities because she felt she would be usurping his role. Unfortunately, my father was a brand-new Christian when I was born and did not really know how to be a "spiritual leader." Consequently, our faith development at home was limited to prayers at meals and before bed, occasional spontaneous discussions about the Bible, and a commitment to values and ethics that were basically Christian in nature. I think this is another illustration of how gender expectations limited my development because I think I would have benefited from learning more spiritual disciplines as a child, and I still struggle to incorporate them into my daily life as an adult.

As a child, I was not aware of the way in which these role expectations influenced me. It was not until I went to a Christian college and began sensing a call to full-time ministry that I experienced an inner conflict. I started to question both the explicit and implicit teachings of my church. This was a very emotional and difficult quest because the church had been my "extended family" all my life and provided a major source of support and community for me. As I studied the Bible and commentaries, I discovered a different interpretation. I began to believe that overall, the Bible teaches about mutual submission between spouses and that all people receive gifts of the Spirit, regardless of gender. I also learned that these gifts are to be used for the mutual building up of the body of Christ and in service within society. Thus, I believe that gender should not be considered when designating leadership and/or ministry roles in the church, nor should it dictate a person's vocation. I struggled to reconcile these understandings with my experience of my "home church." While I still felt very connected to the people of the church, I no longer felt I could participate as a member of that church because our fundamental beliefs were too different. Furthermore, I would not be allowed to exercise the gifts that I felt God was calling me to use in my future vocation.

I share this part of my story only to illustrate how the teachings of the Church (or other faith communities) can greatly affect the opportunities available to girls and even the ways in which they believe God can use them. Thankfully, I was able to move beyond the constrictive nature of the church in which I was raised because of further education. Nevertheless, I fear that many, many girls are growing up in churches today that continue to teach limited roles for women. This limits girls from reaching their full potential as children of God.

BLESSINGS, JOYS, & OPPORTUNITIES

On the other hand, I did have many other opportunities as a girl to grow, develop, and move toward what God created me to be. I had complete access to education throughout my girlhood, and my teachers constantly strove to challenge me and to help me develop my intellectual abilities. In high school I won an award for the highest achievement in math and science, areas in which studies indicate girls in western contexts tend to do poorly.[67] I played on a variety of sports teams with other girls, and if I had desired, I could have played on teams with boys in most sports also. (Though this was not common and would have been viewed as "strange" by most of the people I knew, including other girls.) I participated in music, including band and choirs, and served as a drum major for several years. The training I received in all of these areas helped me develop confidence and poise and brought pleasure and enjoyment to my life.

---

[67] I must admit that I did struggle in both math and science, especially in calculus and physics during high school, and this was likely due to my earlier socialization. However, I had an incredible calculus and physics teacher who met with me almost every day during lunch and explained the concepts to me over and over again, never tiring of using a different way to explain it until I understood. Therefore, it was only through sheer hard work on my part (and his) that I was able to eventually succeed in these areas! Nevertheless, the studies would indicate that I broke the norm by "excelling" in math and science (and so did that teacher by helping me).

At home, I was encouraged to express my opinions, and my thoughts and feelings were heard by my parents, other family

members, and friends. My parents always told me I could do anything I wanted when I "grew up." In fact, they encouraged me to explore non-traditional fields for women and probably would have been disappointed had I not chosen to pursue further education and a vocation outside the home. I observed both of my parents taking part in the household tasks, although they tended to split them along somewhat traditional lines. As well, they both had careers outside the home, although as I mentioned above, my mother took time off from hers when I was born until I entered first grade. As I said before, I always felt loved, and God's love also permeated our home.

Overall, then, my childhood was a mixture of positive and negative experiences. While there were some limitations as a result of gender issues, there were also many positive influences that helped me to grow and develop into a competent, "successful" person and a mature child of God.

What about girls today?

That is my story, but it is only one case study among many. I am no longer a girl, and some things have certainly changed since I grew up. I hope that some of these changes have been for the better, while I also fear that others have changed for the worse. I must admit that when I catch glimpses of women in the media today, I am shocked by their clothing (or lack thereof), the overwhelmingly sexual nature of most portrayals, and the body images that are even more dominated by thinness and perpetual youth than when I was a girl. On the other hand, in most sectors of U.S. society, women are given the opportunity to pursue vocations at all levels now, even some that were rarely pursued when I was a child. Additionally, most can consider a variety of options for roles within the home and church (although this still varies widely among denominations and faith traditions). So, while my story is only one person's story, as a case study it represents some of the trends and issues faced by many girls. Let's explore some of those trends and issues as researchers and authors represent them today.

TRENDS & ISSUES FOR GIRLS IN WESTERN CONTEXTS

Once again, it begs mentioning that we must keep in mind the complexities of the lives of girls and realize that any generalization cannot fully represent *all* girls in *all* western settings. "Much of the existing developmental research still extracts girls from these contexts and speaks of girls or youth in general, without probing the important intersections of race, social class, sexual identity, and so forth in girls' construction of their textured and multi-layered identities."[68] Therefore, in the following discussion, let us always remember that these issues will be worked out within a variety of contexts, and the experience of girls within those contexts will also vary greatly.

The main categories for understanding the issues that many girls face in western contexts include gender equity and gender discrimination, identity and self-esteem, education, health, and violence. Many of the issues overlap within these categories, but we'll look at each category separately and focus on the major issues within each one. In reality, of course, the issues are intertwined.

GENDER EQUITY & GENDER DISCRIMINATION

The area of gender equity and gender discrimination is broad. It encompasses a wide range of issues with varying degrees of subtlety and severity. "The belief that girls are worth less than boys is woven through a complex web of history, practices, and attitudes [found within] culture... tradition... politics... religion... sexuality... laws... economics... [and] images/media."[69] It is within this complex web that the root causes for gender inequities are found, and one must seek to understand all of these areas in a girl's life.

---

68   Phillips, *The Girls Report*, 14.
69   David Kupp, "Growing Up a Girl: A Tough Life," *Voices*, no. 1 (1994): 3.

Many studies have been done to show how parents in western contexts treat boy and girl babies differently.[70] These differences are not necessarily discriminatory, but they do contribute to the way in which a girl is socialized. "It has also been established that the sex-role training of girls in and outside the home fosters dependency in western societies. The socialization of boys is oriented toward aggressiveness, achievement, and self-reliance, and that of girls toward docility, nurturance, and responsibility."[71]

Girls from around the world, including many from Canada and other western countries, participated in a conference called "Girls! Stories Worth Telling" where they shared ideas and participated in workshops. Some of the words or phrases they identified with the concept of gender equity in a western context included "girls change their names when they marry and have to change their identity; equal opportunity for girls; equal pay and equal access to jobs."[72]

Discrimination against girls has been studied mostly in school settings, although it is often not viewed as discrimination. "Unlike apartheid and racism, gender prejudice is not acknowledged as a formally articulated behavioral precept or doctrine. But it clearly exists and has an impact on the female life-cycle."[73] In most western contexts, the discrimination is very subtle, and in recent years some studies have argued that girls are succeeding more than boys are in some instances.[74] Still, others indicate that teachers do tend to treat girls and boys differently. While this may not always be considered discrimination, it does contribute to a girl's experience of life and ultimately what she learns about herself and her opportunities.

---

70   Barbara Mackoff in *Growing a Girl: Seven Strategies for Raising a Strong, Spirited Daughter* states that "a number of 'Baby X' studies—where the *same* infant was labeled either a boy or a girl—suggest that from the moment of their arrival, adult caretakers provide dramatically different social and emotional experiences for infant sons and daughters" (New York: Dell Publishing, 1996), 26; see also the extended notes and bibliography in this book for many examples of these studies.

71   Sohoni, *The Burden of Girlhood*, 16.

72   World Vision Canada, *Girls! Stories Worth Telling: Report and Conference Manual* (Toronto: World Vision Canada, 1998), 10–11.

73   Sohoni, *The Burden of Girlhood*, 7

74   Christina Hoff Sommers, "The War Against Boys," *The Atlantic Monthly* (May 2000).

IDENTITY & SELF-ESTEEM

The experience of gender inequity and/or discrimination contributes to a girl's sense of identity and self-esteem, which is the next category we will explore. This area has been discussed in depth by a number of secular researchers and writers, along with some Christian ones. Many of these books include strategies to help parents in a western context raise daughters to have a positive sense of identity and self-esteem.[75] There is a general consensus among most authors that almost all girls suffer from low self-esteem at some level and struggle to establish their own identity. On the other hand, some argue that "girls' identities are far more complex than overall high or low self-esteem scores can indicate."[76] Once again, we must recognize that a girl's context (social, cultural, religious, and so on) will greatly affect her sense of self.

Some of the factors that contribute to a girl developing a healthy sense of self include spending time with mentors from her community, learning to believe in her own self-worth and ability to succeed, participating in activities where she is encouraged and supported, having a place to discuss issues related to sexism, having supportive families who allow her to express feelings, analyzing the images produced by media, and focusing on her character and how she contributes to society, rather than physical appearance.[77]

This is also the arena in which the Church could have a great impact by helping girls to develop an understanding of being created in God's image. The teachings of the Church have the opportunity to greatly influence a girl's identity and understanding of her role and purpose in life. Unfortunately, the Christian Church has often

---

[75]　See, for example: William Beausay and Kathryn Beausay, *Girls! Helping Your Little Girl Become an Extraordinary Woman* (Grand Rapids, MI: Fleming H. Revell, 1996); *Mackoff, Growing a Girl*; Lisa Graham McMinn, *Growing Strong Daughters* (Grand Rapids, MI: Baker Books, 2000); Mary Pipher, *Reviving Ophelia: Saving the Selves of Adolescent Girls* (New York: Ballantine Books, 1994); Virginia Beane Rutter, *Celebrating Girls: Nurturing and Empowering Our Daughters* (Berkeley, CA: Conari Press, 1996).

[76]　Phillips, *The Girls Report*, 9.

[77]　Phillips, *The Girls Report*, 15; World Vision Canada, *Girls! Stories Worth Telling*, C-i.

taught girls to devalue themselves. The roles that women and men fulfill in the Church, combined with the way in which Church leaders and volunteers participate in a girl's life, have the potential to either positively or negatively affect her development of a self-concept that is intimately connected to her faith in God. A relationship with Jesus Christ, along with healthy relationships with other adults and peers in church, are powerful contributing factors to a girl's positive self-worth and understanding of her identity as a precious child of God.

EDUCATION

A girl's identity is also formed through her experiences of formal education, which is the next category for our consideration. "Other than families, schools provide perhaps the most critical context in which girls can develop a sense of intellectual competence or failure, personal worth or marginalization, and optimism or despair about their futures."[78] In western contexts, there have been a multitude of studies done over the past thirty years in an attempt to evaluate how educational experiences contribute to and perpetuate gender stereotypes and how they can help to overcome them. In most western settings, it is not whether or not girls have access to education, but rather, whether boys and girls are treated differently and whether the quality of the education is equitable.

Within western schools, one of the issues girls face includes gender-role stereotyping. This begins even in preschool and is perpetuated by books, curriculum, teachers, peers, and other role models who reinforce certain roles for boys and men and others for girls and women. Women's accomplishments and voices are often not represented in school curricula (along with those of men of color and people from non-western perspectives). Non-inclusive language is often still prevalent in many textbooks and in discussions held by teachers with students. Math, science, and technology continue to be areas where girls and women are underrepresented. Boys are socialized to thrive on competition and individualism, whereas girls are socialized to seek

78   Phillips, *The Girls Report*, 55.

cooperation and relationships with others. In recent years, education has begun to focus more on cooperative learning, but competition continues to influence most classrooms, especially at higher grade levels.[79]

A perhaps more subtle influence is seen in the interaction between teachers and students and students with one another. Several extensive studies have shown that sexism is still prevalent in the way that teachers treat boys and girls in their classrooms. Although some progress has been made through educational reforms and grant programs for raising awareness among teachers, most of the research indicates that there are still many subtle ways by which girls are treated differently than boys. For example, boys are more likely to be called upon than girls, and consequently many girls eventually choose not to volunteer their answers.[80] This leads to what is described as a "loss of voice" for girls, especially in middle school.[81] In addition, boys often receive more feedback about their work from teachers than girls do.

This subtle sexism may even influence some girls to quit school. Girls may also drop out or be expelled from school because of excessive absenteeism due to having to support their families or help with younger siblings at home or pregnancy. As well, in some contexts girls form role expectations for themselves by which they value being married and having children more highly than preparing for a vocation outside the home.

HEALTH

Education is very important for helping girls overcome obstacles they face in the next category, which focuses on issues related to health for girls. Again, there are a wide variety of challenges that

---

[79] The entire section on education is based on findings in the following sources: American Association of University Women, *How Schools Shortchange Girls: The AAUW Report* (New York: Marlowe & Company, 1995); American Association of University Women, *Gender Gaps: Where Schools Still Fail Our Children* (New York: Marlowe & Company, 1999); Peggy Orenstein, *SchoolGirls: Young Women, Self-Esteem, and the Confidence Gap* (New York: Doubleday, 1994); Myra Sadker and David Sadker, *Failing at Fairness: How Our Schools Cheat Girls* (New York: Touchstone, Simon & Schuster, 1994).

[80] Sadker and Sadker, *Failing at Fairness*.

[81] Lyn Mikel Brown and Carol Gilligan, *Meeting at the Crossroads: Women's Psychology and Girls' Development* (Cambridge, MA: Harvard University Press, 1992).

girls may face in this arena, depending upon their circumstances

and socio-economic backgrounds. It is very important that girls be viewed wholistically[82] and that their spiritual, emotional, mental, and physical well-being be considered. "At the 1994 *Healthy Girls/Healthy Women Research Roundtable* sponsored by the Ms. Foundation, researchers and practitioners grappled with the question, 'What is health?' Participants noted that little is known about girls' healthy development, since traditional research focuses on illness, pathology, and disease."[83] As a result, most of what is known is framed from a "negative" perspective, such as how girls are *unhealthy*, rather than what contributes to good health.

With this framework in mind, some of the western issues that are most commonly discussed in the literature include eating disorders, sexually transmitted diseases including HIV and AIDS, teenage pregnancy, depression, and other emotional disorders, and the use of drugs (including alcohol, tobacco, and others). Let's look briefly at each of these issues in more detail.

Western culture is virtually obsessed with body image, and the stereotypes perpetuated by the media provide impossible models for young girls. A recent World Health Organization study in Europe states that:

> *The extent of dissatisfaction with body size (feeling too fat) varies across countries but is consistently higher among girls than boys, this gender gap widening with age. On average around a quarter of 11-year-old girls, increasing to over 40% of 15-year-old girls, consider themselves to be too fat.*[84]

---

82 I am choosing to use the spelling of holistic/wholistic that begins with a w in order to emphasize the term whole, which focuses on completeness. The Merriam-Webster dictionary lists the spelling of wholistic with a w as a variant spelling of the word holistic.

83 Phillips, *The Girls Report*, 17.

84 WHO Europe, "Young People's Health in Context: Selected Key Findings from the Health Behaviour in School Aged Children Study," Fact Sheet Euro 04/04, 3, http://www.euro.who.int/document/mediacentre/fs0404e.pdf.

Often, this obsession with body image and weight leads to girls suffering from a variety of eating disorders such as anorexia nervosa and bulimia. Sources vary widely in their estimates of actual frequency of eating disorders among girls. Notwithstanding, both indicate that weight and body image are key issues for girls in western societies. At the very least, this can cause emotional and physical stress, and at its worst, death may result.

Unfortunately, even Christians have contributed to girls and women becoming obsessive over dieting and weight control. One author humorously points out that in Christian books on this topic, "the message, whether blatant or subtle, is that fat-is-sin-and-the-righteous-are-thin-amen."[85] All joking aside, we must question whether this message is truly biblical or simply a reflection of societal pressures.

With this in mind, exercise and participation in sporting events are two issues in the category of health that can have both positive and negative influences. Healthy participation in exercise and sports has been shown to be very important during a girl's development, not only in regard to physical well-being, but also emotional and mental (and I would argue even spiritual). In the U.S., this has been greatly encouraged by Title IX, which in 1972 required schools that receive federal aid to provide athletic opportunities for all students, regardless of gender.[86] On the other hand, exercise or sports can become negative when they are participated in excessively or become an obsession fed by an unhealthy desire for thinness, which was already discussed above.

This excessive focus on body image also contributes to an overemphasis on sexuality among girls, which often leads to early sexual activity, girls contracting sexually transmitted diseases, and high rates of teenage pregnancy. Along with emotional trauma related to early sexual activity, girls often suffer greater physical consequences than boys do. According to the Joint United Nations Programme on HIV/

85   Janet Tanaka, "Will Size 22 Fit Through the Pearly Gates?" *Daughters of Sarah* (September/October 1989): 16.
86   Phillips, *The Girls Report*, 18.

AIDS, three fourths of young people who are living with HIV around the world are young women.[87] For girls, there is a much greater risk of complications in pregnancy than for adult women, including higher maternal and neonatal mortality rates, premature births, and low birthweight.[88] Additionally, adolescent girls often feel that abortion is their only viable option, and complications from this procedure (often done in secret) constitute a major health risk for teenage girls.

Often, one health-related problem leads to others; "eating disorders have been found to be correlated with clinical depression, anxiety disorders, low self-esteem, and substance abuse in adolescent girls."[89] Depression and other emotional and/or mental disorders are prevalent among girls in western contexts. While actual rates vary among different ethnic groups, girls are generally twice as likely as boys to experience depression, and a higher percentage of girls than boys have seriously considered suicide.[90] It is also becoming increasingly more common for girls to participate in self-mutilation, such as burning or cutting themselves.

Perhaps as a response to emotional problems and/or to social pressures, girls are also at risk for abusing alcohol, tobacco, and other drugs. It is harder to determine the difference between boys and girls in these categories because most of the research does not separate gender-specific factors. Without diminishing the consequences of substance abuse itself, perhaps the greater risk is the way in which it contributes to other areas of health concern for girls. For example, girls who have been drinking are more likely to engage in unprotected sexual activity, often leading to unwanted pregnancy and sexually transmitted diseases. Furthermore, alcohol and drug consumption contributes to a higher possibility of violence committed against girls, including but not limited to rape and assault.

---

87 Joint United Nations Programme on HIV/AIDS, "Women and Girls," UNAIDS, http://www.unaids.org/en/PolicyAndPractice/KeyPopulations/WomenGirls/.

88 Kathleen M. Kurz and Cynthia J. Prather, *Improving the Quality of Life of Girls* (New York: United Nations Children's Fund, 1995), 21.

89 Phillips, *The Girls Report*, 21.

90 Phillips, *The Girls Report*, 24, 25.

VIOLENCE

Violence is a category closely related to that of health because often a girl's health is jeopardized as a result of violent acts committed against her. While both boys and girls are the victims of violence, "Younger women and adolescent girls are especially vulnerable to gender-based violence. Nearly 50 percent of all sexual assaults worldwide are against girls 15 years or younger."[91] The types of violence vary from sexual abuse to battering to harassment to psychological abuse to date rape to sexual exploitation, and so on. These can happen on an individual level, where a particular girl is insulted, violated, or oppressed; on a broader societal level, where violent customs are imposed upon all girls in a society; or at an extreme level where a girl is murdered or the experience of violence causes her to kill herself.[92] Most often, the perpetrators are people the girls know, are family members, and are predominantly males, although some mothers also abuse their children.

Girls are more likely to be the victims of violence perhaps because of the differences in the socialization of boys and girls in many western contexts. Boys are generally encouraged to be aggressive, and studies show that from a very young age they have greater behavioral problems, including fighting, bullying, using force, and more. Girls, on the other hand, are socialized to be meek and gentle, to resolve conflicts through mediation rather than force, and to be concerned with relationships with others.[93] When these gender roles and behaviors are taken to an extreme, violence against girls (and later women) results. Girls become victims, and often fall into the trap of permanent victim-status, which simply invites more violence.

The Church has often been a part of this socialization process, and this has not always been "good news" for girls. In fact, many denominational doctrines still include teachings that encourage the

---

[91]. United Nations Population Fund, "Adolescents Fact Sheet," UNFPA, http://www.unfpa.org/swp/2005/presskit/factsheets/facts_adolescents.htm#ftn7.

[92]. Sohoni, *The Burden of Girlhood*, 131.

[93]. Sohoni, *The Burden of Girlhood*, 132.

gender roles and stereotypes that lead to violence, especially within marriage and families. If girls themselves aren't abused, they observe their mothers being emotionally (if not physically) battered in many so-called Christian homes in the name of "submission." In other cases, it is simply a matter of the sinfulness of human nature, rather than a doctrinal issue. Either way, the Church has generally failed to address these issues on a tangible level.

WILL YOU LISTEN TO THEIR STORIES?

Addressing these issues, however, is the topic of another chapter. In conclusion, I would like to emphasize that the issues raised herein are only a small beginning toward understanding the lives of girls in western contexts. The complex nature of our societies makes understanding girls and the issues they face an ongoing challenge. It is also important to recognize that there are many positive things happening in the lives of girls; they have many areas of strength. We have focused here primarily on their challenges because they have often been overlooked or trivialized in many western contexts.

My hope is that this chapter (and the book as a whole) will encourage you to be intentional to take some time to listen to the stories of the girls in your life, your church, and your community.[94] I believe that in so doing, we will hear both joys and struggles. In listening to their experiences, we may hear about some of the things described at the very beginning of this chapter—Barbie, diets, blonde, thin, dolls, playing house, talking, pretty, knight-in-shining-armor saves damsel-in-distress, pretend not to be smarter than the boys, in-style clothes, sexy, and so on. Their lists of words and phrases describing their experience of growing up a girl will likely be very different from mine.

---

[94] Along with talking to girls you personally know, one way you might begin doing this is by reading some girls' stories found in the following sources: Pamela Haag and American Association of University Women Educational Foundation, *Voices of a Generation: Teenage Girls Report About Their Lives Today* (New York: Marlowe & Company, 2000) and Sara Shandler, *Ophelia Speaks: Adolescent Girls Write About Their Search for Self* (New York: HarperPerennial, 1999). Although some of the material may be offensive, it may also be instructive to visit the following websites designed especially for girls: www.evemag.com; www.girlzone.com; www.gurl.com; www.newmoon.org; www.teengrrl.com; www.teenvoices.com; www.terrifichick.com.

My dream is that more girls' lists will eventually include: valued for who I am, excelling in math and science (and all other subjects), strong, independent, intelligent, content with my body, creative clothing that expresses my unique personality, free to serve God and others, safe from abuse, confident, healthy relationships with adults and boys... and much, much, more.

Thank you for listening to my story. I pray you will take the time to listen to many, many more girls' stories—both of those girls you know and love and those girls who desperately need to be known and loved.

Children are a heritage from the LORD,
offspring a reward from him.

PSALM 127:3

Gender equality will not only empower women to overcome
poverty, but also their children, families, communities and
countries. When seen in this light, gender equality is not
only morally right—it is pivotal to human progress and
sustainable development.

UNICEF, *STATE OF THE WORLD'S CHILDREN 2007*, x

CHAPTER 6

A PERPETUAL ROBBING: LOSSES FOR THE GIRL CHILD IN THE ROMANIAN CONTEXT

Sue Bates

The thief comes only to steal and kill and destroy; I have come that they might have life, and have it to the full.

John 10:10

Thieves are interested only in themselves; Christ's interest is in the welfare of his children. Throughout her life, the girl child experiences many significant robbings by the "thief": her childhood, her innocence, her God-given and society-declared childhood rights, a sense of identity—knowing her true self, one who has been created in the image of her heavenly Father, and having an individually designed inheritance wrapped up in God's promises to give her "a hope and a future" (Jeremiah 29:11).

Being robbed of such treasures as justice, hope, and love is indeed a crushing load for girl children to bear. Robbings result in losses and deficits in a child's life; they are central to a child's traumatic experiences and woundings. Losses also affect every aspect of a child's life developmentally. One must understand these losses to be able to intervene on behalf of the child, focusing interventions on restoring her God-given treasures. Identifying vital losses suffered through the robbing of the girl child will guide and equip you to respond holistically to her needs.

DEFINING THE ROBBING

Webster's dictionary offers several definitions of "rob": to take something away by force; to take personal property by violence or threat; to remove valuables without rights; to deprive something due, expected, or desired; and to withhold unjustly or injuriously. These all are apt descriptions of the robbing experienced by the girl child! An understanding of the impact suffering from such robbing is crucial to understanding not just the physical but also the spiritual and emotional needs of the girl child.

In talking to girl children in India, Joseph Ammo states that the most startling and saddening revelation to emerge from conversations is that all the girls, virtually without exception, had often wished they had not been born female.[95]

Most of them could not think of any advantage attached to being female except that as girls they were able to help, love, and look after their parents. On the other hand, they could easily point out several disadvantages associated with their gender. One of the most aggravating aspect of being female was the curtailment of their freedom and mobility, especially from the pre-adolescent stage onwards. They felt that even their homes were like a prison with their movements constantly monitored. These types of situations contribute to the robbing of girls' self-image, self-esteem, and self-confidence: all vital ingredients to healthy, normal childhood growth and development.

ROMANIA'S CHILDREN

Living and working with neglected girl children in Romania, one is continuously reminded of the painful robbing of normal, everyday

---

[95]   Joseph Ammo, "The World According to Adolescents," South Asia Forum 2001, http://www.hsph.harvard.edu/.

treasures from them: family, the center of their world; warm and loving nurture; daily provision for food, shelter, and medical care; discipline; opportunities for education—all things a child needs for healthy growth and development, for safety and protection.

The situations these girls confront paint vivid scenarios depicting the injustices heaped on the girl child. And indeed, girl children do feel these injustices very keenly.

BACKGROUND TO CHILDREN'S SITUATION

On December 25, 1989, while enjoying our traditional Christmas dinner, we were mesmerized by startling images on the television. Amidst a sea of faces brightly lit by candles, the people were chanting and singing songs of victory. Nicolae Ceaucescu, the dreaded dictator of Romania, had been overthrown and sent to meet his Maker.

The Romanian people dreamt of a rapid recovery and a return to freedom and civilization. They were sick of the oppression, the lack of food and basic necessities, the deprivation of basic rights due every human being. But they were soon to discover just how much damage had been done under those dark years, damage that even today has not been reversed and perhaps never can be undone. Just after the Revolution, the dreaded news was revealed to the whole world when ABC's *20/20* aired a documentary of the horrid conditions in many Romanian orphanages. Conditions in the orphanages made Charles Dickens' *Oliver Twist* seem almost humane. The pained faces of neglected and abused children shook the world.

These children have now grown up and are passing on the legacy of care they inherited to their children. How can the young girls know how to lovingly nurture and parent a child when, as babies and small children, they were left in their iron cribs to rock themselves for self-stimulation and warmth? Often they were without caring caregivers or, if they were caring, they were untrained and understaffed. Such caregivers did not have time or energy for the compassionate touches or individual attention and care that each young child needed. And as teenagers, they were left behind by their society, experiencing neglect in all areas of their lives: physically, spiritually, socially, and in every way possible.

Education was a major area of neglect; they were not given an opportunity to attend school. So, when orphans reached the age of eighteen, they were forced to leave their institutionalized home totally unprepared for life. In Romania, there is no "safety net" to care for them or to help them adjust. They are dumped out on the streets to live in dangerous parks, deserted apartment blocks, underground canals where the street kids live, or even with pimps and perverts.

One day, Cristi, a young orphan living on the streets, called us and reported a large group of young girls who had been kicked out of the orphanages and were now living in the park. We immediately went to see how we could help. The girls were living like animals: sleeping on the ground, some with blankets, but also with the sand fleas and just plain dirt. We took them blankets, clothes, and hot meals every day while trying to find a place for them to stay, but people either claimed to have no room or made it clear that the girls were not wanted.

The girls were forced to spend their days begging, stealing, fighting off pimps, or bathing in the polluted Dimbovita River that runs through Bucharest. All the while, they also were trying to keep what sanity they had left after being raised in the orphanage. One night it was raining and flooding heavily; we were late taking them their meal. When we arrived at about half-past nine at night, the kids came running out to our car and said, "Come quickly, some men are here to take off Gabi and Lalela." We hurried to the back of the subway stop, and there were three men who had posed as plainclothes policemen. They were from the mafia and were going to kidnap these two girls to be used as prostitutes. We asked to see their identity badges, they had none.

When the men were driven off and the girls rescued, they were trembling with fear. Gabi said, "If I would have been forced to live like that I would have killed myself." Because of the flooding, we were late, yet right in God's timing for their rescue. The girls, too frightened to go back to the streets, have now made our house their home.

As we listened, we gradually learned the girls' stories. When Gabi was a small child, she was put in the orphanage because her mother claimed she was mentally retarded and did not want her. Lalela's family was extremely poor, and thirteen children were just too many to feed. So Lalela was left in the same orphanage with Gabi.

We feared for the girls when we saw how unprepared for life they were. And yet, thousands of young people continued to be thrown out on the streets to fend for themselves. We prayed with them, studied the Bible with them, talked to them, tried to set an example to them, and also attempted to be firm and yet fair. Nothing we did seemed to have an effect on them.

We previously had taken in the children of street children—second-generation street kids. The mothers who lived on the street did not want to leave their babies and small children to be raised in the streets and underground canals. So, the older girls helped us care for the babies.

Only these little children and babies could accomplish what we found impossible. Before our very eyes, we witnessed the love and bonding between the older girls and these little babies. The small children changed the girls' attitudes; now, their main concerns were for these little ones. Every day, they dressed the babies up so nicely and brought them to me to admire. If they only knew how this filled my heart with joy!

Today, Fatima dressed Carol in a pretty pink dress and adorable pink hat and brought her to me; both had wonderful smiles. And when they see me picking up a child assigned to their care, they swell with pride. Secretly they hope their child will be my favorite! These girls, having lost trust with ill-meaning and exploitive adults, have difficulty accepting our love. Similarly, they have difficulty accepting God as One who loves them. Yet they trust these helpless, defenseless babies to give and receive love. In reality, God is melting their hearts by pouring out his love through these infants. These little babies are teaching the girls how to love and live again, being able to not only give but also receive love.

LOSSES

As adults, we recognize that everything about us has a foundation based on our past: our parents, our education, our church, our society, and our friends. The kind of person we are—our personality, fears, insecurities, and tendencies—all have their roots in our past. What is in the pasts of these girls? You will definitely find multiple losses that have caused deep emotional wounds.

These girls have been robbed of a well-balanced personality, a sensitive conscience, an understanding of their God-given dignity, and a chance to develop a godly character. Their health and their happiness as expressed in a carefree childhood also are significant losses, resulting in a lost opportunity for a normal life as a child and as an adult. Without education, they do not have knowledge of their personal history, or knowledge of the Bible and other great literature. Indeed, they lack the basic tools of reading and writing that enable them to mature and grow intellectually.

Illiterate, poor, deficient in social skills, lacking self-esteem and the ability to establish meaningful relationships or to respect other people and their property, these girls often lose their place in society. Of utmost importance, they also lose their place in the church family. Often, they also lack the spiritual and moral development to enable them to think on a spiritual level, especially concerning right and wrong.

When robbed of their family, girls suffer the lack of not only the safety, protection, and provision a family provides, but they also experience the loss of normal everyday occasions that little girls take for granted: being taken to the zoo, going on picnics, attending special events, receiving night-time cuddles and a mother's goodnight kiss, or feeling a father's strong hand of love embracing them. The loss of family also means a loss of identity and belonging to a part of a caring, loving family.

The loss of family, affection, and a sense of acceptance and belonging results in tremendous emotional losses for the girl child that will be carried over into adulthood:

- good memories of childhood and life;
- innocence;
- wonder and awe of a God who is neither physical nor material;
- the ability to reason;
- the chance to laugh and cry with understanding;
- the ability to trust people;
- proper discipline and correction;
- and a sense of being needed and of belonging.

These girls have also suffered immense spiritual losses. The injustices they have endured stifle the moral development needed to discern right from wrong. They have had no spiritual role models to guide them. In addition, society has looked down on them as trash, no good for anything, worthless. How can they help but believe that God, too, must view them this way? And, how can these views inspire hope within them of ever having a role and sense of importance in this life, let alone becoming part of God's family? All too often, God's childhood gifts of creativity, wonder, and curiosity are gone.

IS THERE HOPE?

Will they ever understand the unconditional love and compassion of God? Will they know his presence in the midst of their suffering? Will they be able to believe, "The Lord is a refuge for the oppressed... He does not ignore the cry of the afflicted?" (Psalm 9:9–12). How comforting it would be if they knew that over and over in Scripture, God declares that he sees and hears the suffering of the oppressed.[96]

They, above all, have been robbed of their ability to see God as a loving Father or to know Jesus as the One who wants to be a close friend, sticking closer than a brother. And to know that Jesus loved them so much, that he gave his life for their salvation and deliverance.

---

[96] See Exodus 22:22–24; Psalm 9:12, 17–18; 10:17–18; 12:5; Isaiah 41:17; Amos 4:1.

Eventually, the girls are robbed of life-sustaining hope. Paul Cedar describes what it is like to be without hope:

> *Life without hope is like a beautiful flower cut off from the stem. Like a precious child who has nothing to eat. We cannot live very well or very long without hope. Without it, we shrivel and die.*[97]

So what is left? Are they like zombies or robots? Not at all. They may be challenged or limited, but our God is a God of restoration. In spite of all that Satan and humankind with their wicked ideologies could do against these girls, they could never be robbed of the image of God in them. His image may be blurred and distorted, but it is there. "For you created my inmost being, you knit me together in my mother's womb. I praise you because I am fearfully and wonderfully made" (Psalm 139:13–14). And our God who redeems will restore that image to his likeness. But remember, we ourselves must have confidence in a hope for the girl child; the children must sense that expectancy of hope within us. Again, our assurance is derived from our belief that each girl has been created in the image of God and, therefore, is of utmost worth and value to him.

Our interventions must seek to restore in some way the losses suffered. As we seek justice for girl children, making opportunities for them to develop their God-given gifts and talents, and developing support programs that can provide justice for all children, we can help to restore their hope. Tomorrow can be different. As the Psalmist reminds us,

> *No one whose hope is in [God] will ever be put to shame.*
>
> *Psalm 25:3*

---

97   Paul Cedar, "Where Is Hope?" *Pursuit* 1, no. 4 (1993): 1.

PART THREE:
HURDLES CONFRONTING THE
GIRL CHILD

If girls are not viewed by families and societies as having a critical role in social development and are not provided needed opportunities to learn and grow, they may become mothers with children who are likely to die in infancy. Those children who do survive are likely to be less healthy, less educated and less confident, and the cycle will continue. An investment in girls can be considered an investment in national development.

KATHLEEN M. KURZ AND CYNTHIA J. PRATHER,
IMPROVING THE QUALITY OF LIFE OF GIRLS, 1

CHAPTER 7

HARMFUL TRADITIONAL PRACTICES

Phyllis Kilbourn

She is born into indifference and reared on neglect. The girl child is caught in a web of cultural practices and prejudices that divest her of her individuality and mold her into a submissive, self-sacrificing daughter and wife. Her labor ensures the survival and well-being of her family but robs her not only of her childhood but also of her right to be free of hunger, ignorance, disease, and poverty.[98]

While children around the world continue to face various forms of adversity in the twenty-first century, girl children in particular are subjected to multiple forms of oppression, exploitation, and discrimination due to their gender. Forms of discrimination against girl children are numerous and vary depending on the traditions, history, and culture of a particular society.

Countries worldwide are rich in their cultural practices that cover all aspects of life. Those practices include marriage procedures, childbearing, naming ceremonies, childrearing/socialization, puberty rites, funeral rites, and religious ceremonies, to name a few. Lives are molded by cultural practices embedded in the very fabric of everyday life. In spite of some common threads, each of the ethnic groups within a culture has unique and distinct practices that are geared toward

---

98   United Nations, "Convention on the Rights of the Child," Geneva: Office of the High Commissioner for Human Rights, 1989. Article 19 and Article 24.

protecting each member of that society as a child and as an adult. The rules governing each ethnic group's practices are not always written, but are present in the day-to-day governing of that ethnic group.

An analysis of girl child issues within these groups, however, quickly reveals that long-practiced customs, taboos, and superstitions that degrade women and girls are also entrenched in many communities and societies. In an earlier chapter, we learned that such practices also lie at the root of the discrimination against the girl child. Sometimes, even society's sacred writings are interpreted as being opposed to female–male equality and some religious sayings and beliefs contradict respect for women and girls. This is particularly true in rural areas where opportunities for women are limited by custom, the demands of child rearing, and the difficult work of subsistence farming.

Many cultural beliefs are rooted in violent, harmful, and trauma-producing practices that adversely affect the health and welfare of women and girls. These harmful traditional practices persist in spite of their extraordinarily harmful nature, the huge social and economic cost of their effects, and the violation of international human rights laws they entail. Often they are not questioned. They preserve tradition, and their practice may even be seen as morally superior conduct. Communities and national governments perpetuate harmful practices through laws that discriminate, or through lack of enforcement of laws meant to protect girls.

Underlying harmful cultural practices is the socialization of both girls and boys that encourages girls to assume low status, which, in turn, discourages their confidence and participation. When boys are socialized into rigid and sometimes violent rules, their own growth is limited, and their sisters' low status is also perpetrated. This socialization provides the rationale and norms—both implicit and explicit—for harmful traditional practices against girls.

No matter how destructive or traumatizing these practices might be, they are rooted in cultural concepts that connect them to legitimate needs such as bride prices being linked to making provision for parents' current needs while son preference is linked to the legitimate need for someone to care for parents in their old age.

The following describes four of the strongholds of culture that threaten the lives and development of the girl child: infanticide, female genital mutilation, early marriage, and honor killings. These demonstrate the tremendous emotional and physical toll such practices extract from the girl child.

INFANTICIDE

Seventy-nine million females are missing in South Asia alone.

Some girls are rejected even before birth. In 2000, a United Nations report estimated that 79 million females are missing in South Asia alone and attributed this number to sex-selective abortion and infanticide, as well as food favoritism.[99] Infanticide is the intentional killing of baby girls due to the preference for male babies and the low status accorded women in many countries, notably China and India. This aborting of female fetuses is a rapidly growing trend, especially following a sex determination test. Women often experience extreme pressure from their families to kill female children, especially from the second female birth onwards. Cultural acceptance of female infanticide perpetuates the low status of girls.

Most of the examples of sex selection given in the following pages will come from India, where the introduction of ultrasound equipment has made sex selection an easy, widespread practice. As technology increases, these practices are more likely to occur in all places where cultural norms value male children over female children. Daniel Goodkind verifies this extensive spreading of the practice: "Societies that practice sex selection in favor of males (sometimes called *son preference* or *female deselection*) are quite common, especially in China,

---

[99] A. Gettis, et al., *Introduction to Geography*, 9th ed. (New York: McGraw-Hill, 2004), 200; WV accepted the general designation: UN report, 2000; see United Nations Population Fund, "Ending Violence Against Women and Girls," in *The State of the World's Population 2000*, ed. UNFPA (New York: UNFPA, 2000), http://www.unfpa.org/swp/2000/english/ch03.html.

Korea, Taiwan, Singapore, Malaysia, India, Pakistan, New Guinea, and many other developing countries in Asia and North Africa."[100] For the purposes of this chapter, we will look at India as a case study of what occurs in many parts of the world.

The Indian Medical Association, a nationwide network of doctors, states,

The increasing use of ultrasound methods to identify the sex of an unborn child with a view to aborting the female fetus has spread from a few elite centres to an ever-increasing number of sex identification shops all over the country.[101]

The transvaginal ultrasound can reveal the sex of a baby within thirteen weeks of conception. The Pre-Natal Diagnostic Techniques Acts, passed in 1994, bans termination of a pregnancy after twenty weeks, and thus, the ultrasound allows women to 'beat' the ban.

The selective abortion of the female fetus results in deliberate killings of female infants by the crudest and the most violent methods imaginable. Such practices do not stem from poverty as much as from a preferential attitude toward boys and a rejecting attitude toward girls.

Tests to determine the sex of a fetus were banned in India in 1994, after clinics with ultrasound machines started mushrooming across the country in the early 1990s. Extensive reports confirmed that the machines in most clinics were not being used to determine the health of a fetus but to check its sex. Thousands of women were opting for having abortions after learning they were carrying girls. A survey conducted in Mumbai in 1984 showed that of the 8,000 fetuses aborted after sex determination tests, 7,999 were female. Yet sex-determination tests remain widely available in both cities and in rural areas, where the tests are conducted openly. A January report in the Indian Medical Association's "Family

---

100 Daniel Goodkind, "Should Prenatal Sex Selection be Restricted? Ethical Questions and Their Implications for Research and Policy," *Population Studies* 53, no. 1 (1999): 49–61, http://links.jstor.org/sici?sici=0032-4728(199903)53%3A1%3C49%3ASPSSBR%3E2.0.CO%3B2-D.

101 Bishakha De Sarkar, "Killing Daughters to Avoid Watering Your Neighbour's Plant," *The Telegraph*, Lucknow, India, n.d.

Medicine India" journal said it estimated about 5 million female-selected abortions are carried out in India every year.[102]

Most people blame the increase of this practice on the misuse of advanced medical technology such as ultrasound and sonography to detect the sex of unborn babies. Uttar Pradesh, where female feticide is on the rise, has seen the growth of ultrasound clinics operating in the state mushroom to 4,000. Mobile vans with mini ultrasound machines make ultrasounds available in the most remote villages. This has resulted in a dwindling number of females—879 as against the national 927 girls per thousand males.

While infanticide is a centuries-old practice in India, the difference now is that instead of being killed later, the children are systematically deprived in all aspects of life, including the right to be born.

Women are forced to abort their fetuses due to extreme family pressure. The argument for female feticide centers on the premise that it is better to abort a female fetus than to let a girl child grow up unwanted and unloved—unloved because to get a daughter married, a dowry has to be arranged, and men demand huge sums of money and gifts from the bride's family during marriage. In the cases where brides are unable to meet the demand, they are tortured and sometimes killed after they are married. Sons, on the other hand, bring dowries.

Sons also provide for their aged parents and light the funeral pyre, but married daughters go away. Some societies, such as India and China, have patriarchal societies that have traditionally preferred sons to daughters, and the preference continues to be especially strong in rural and semi-urban areas.

Recently, a group of India's top religious leaders came together in New Delhi to make a passionate plea to end the growing trend of feticide, calling it "cold blooded murder." Swami Jayaendra Saraswatiji Maharaj, one of Hinduism's most revered monks, stated, "Female feticide is a crime against humanity. People forget that to carry on with life, a girl child is a must."[103]

---

[102] De Sarkar, "Killing Daughters."
[103] Roy Anirban, "Indian Religious Seers Call to End Female Foeticide," Reuters News, June 24, 2001, New Delhi.

FEMALE GENITAL MUTILATION

Before we start thinking about our communities, our fears for our cultures, and our fear of the disintegration of our traditions, we have to think about one single girl. A child who is held—scared, petrified, and screaming through a very traumatizing experience—having a very sensitive part of her body cut.[104]

From infancy to adulthood, the procedure of female genital mutilation (FGM) is still being performed. Within some traditional cultures, it is a significant rite of passage for young girls. Whatever age a person experiences FGM, it can cause health problems and even death due to complications from the procedure.

FGM has inflicted pain, illness, and death on young girls for more than two thousand years. Today, nearly 130 million women and girls globally have endured this experience.[105] The pain from FGM lasts, intensifies, and recurs: at the cutting, at sexual contact, and at childbirth. Many women die from immediate or long-term complications of FGM such as hemorrhaging, infection, septic shock, and complications in childbearing. Many of those who survive suffer emotional trauma as drastic as the physical pain.[106]

While medical personnel, human rights activists, and international organizations have been trying to discourage FGM because it is harmful and a violation of human rights, traditionalists argue that FGM "retains the community and symbolically endorses the growth of young girls into womanhood."[107]

Defining FGM

Female genital mutilation is a generic term for various forms of surgery performed on the external female genitalia. It is usually performed as either a religious ritual or as a way to gain acceptance

---

104 See Juliet Evusa, "A Change of Attitude: A Thematic and Critical Analysis of Female Genital Mutilation Debates Across the Media from 1986 to 2001" (presented at "The Children of the World: Risk and Hope" conference, Ohio University, Ohio, April 5–7, 2001).

105 UNICEF, *State of the World's Children 2007: The Double Dividend of Gender Equality* (New York: UNICEF, 2006), 4.

106 Kelly Morris, "Feature: Issues on Female Genital Mutilation/Cutting—Progress and Parallels," *The Lancet: Medicine and Creativity* 368 (December 1, 2006): S64-S67, http://www.proquest.com/ (accessed January 8, 2008).

107 Evusa, "A Change of Attitude."

within the society. Despite diseases, medical problems, and deaths resulting from crude and unsanitary surgical instruments, the tradition continues, seriously affecting many women's lives. FGM also increases the risk of HIV infection since unsterilized instruments are shared among participants.

The details of circumcision vary between cultures, but the basics are the same. There are three types of FGM practiced on girls sometime between infancy and womanhood. The most moderate, called *sunna*, is the cutting off of the clitoris hood. *Excision* is the removal of the clitoris and all or part of the labia. The most extreme form, *infibulation*, involves the removal of all external genital parts and the stitching of the vulva with thread or thorns, leaving a tiny hole for urine and menstrual blood. On the wedding night, the opening must be widened.

In cultures where FGM is an accepted norm, female genital mutilation is usually performed by traditional practitioners, including midwives and older women who have limited or no medical training or educational background in medicine.[108] The operations are performed under local or no anesthesia, causing the child intense pain. Too, with the child struggling, there often is inaccurate cutting and damage to other organs. The health consequences of FGM last far beyond the operation. A later chapter describes the often-horrendous medical problems stemming from this practice.

The age at which FGM is carried out varies from infants a few days old to, occasionally, into adulthood. The younger the child, the more accurate the cutting. In communities where FGM has a high social value, girls and women who are not mutilated may be ostracized from their communities.

Prevalence

Female genital mutilation or "circumcision" is common to women in at least twenty-five African countries and several parts of the Middle East. Less known is that FGM was common in the United States and the United Kingdom until the 1950s, prescribed as a cure for such

---

[108] For more on the health ramifications of FGM, please see the ninth chapter of this volume.

"female deviancies" as lesbianism, masturbation, nymphomania, and even epilepsy.[109] In 1996, after decades of lobbying, the U.S. Congress passed legislation making it a crime to perform FGM on a minor.

According to the Population Reference Bureau, more than 3 million girls undergo FGM annually.[110] An estimated 130 million girls have been subjected to this procedure, and FGM is practiced in at least twenty-eight African countries, and by various people groups in parts of Asia and the Middle East.[111] Though FGM has been banned and denounced by many national governments and international organizations, the practice is still common in many parts of the world. According to the Center for Reproductive Rights, the most severe form of FGM, infibulation, accounts for "approximately 80% to 90% of all circumcisions in Djibouti, Somalia and Sudan," and up to 92 percent of women in the most affected regions experience FGM in some form.[112] In addition, FGM is still practiced by many immigrant families in North America and Europe.[113]

History & Culture Behind FGM Practice

Assumptions supporting FGM date back many centuries. Women dare not defy this practice even if they disagree with it, because social acceptance is critical to their survival in the community. In most traditional societies, circumcision is considered a religious practice, even though neither the Qur'an nor the Bible requires it. For some, it is a tradition. For others, their society and their status as women forces them to obey. Many mothers and grandmothers perpetuate this practice.

All of a female's identity, all of her future, is just to get married and to get her daughters married. FGM is thought by many to make

---

109 Jill Dudones, "Unkindest Cut," *Ms. Magazine*, March 29, 2007.
110 D'Vera Cohn, "The Campaign Against Female Genital Cutting: New Hope, New Challenges," Population Reference Bureau, http://www.prb.org/Articles/2007/CampaignAgainstFemaleGenitalCutting.aspx.
111 United Nations Population Fund, "Frequently Asked Questions on Female Genital Mutilation/Cutting," UNFPA, http://www.unfpa.org/gender/practices2.htm#12.
112 Center for Reproductive Rights, "Female Genital Mutilation (FGM): Legal Prohibitions Worldwide," February 2005, http://www.crlp.org/pub_fac_fgmicpd.html.
113 See N. Eke and K.E.O. Nkanginieme, "Female Genital Mutilation and Obstetric Outcome," *The Lancet* 367, no. 9525 (June 3, 2006): 1799–1800, http://www.proquest.com/ (accessed January 8, 2008).

a girl more sexually attractive to her husband. But the main purpose of circumcision is to control the women's sexuality and to protect traditional social customs. Circumcision ensures that the girl will not have sex before she is married as it is too painful. Also, it is important to please the man, who insists on having a virgin. In many cases, if he marries and realizes that this girl is not circumcised, he will divorce her the next day.

Cultural Beliefs & Myths

To gain an understanding of the background of the problem, and the importance of the practice in a given culture, it is helpful to examine the cultural beliefs and myths given for the practice of FGM. The quotations below are statements made by men and women of various ages in Burkina Faso, Mali, and Guinea.[114]

a) Psychosexual Reasons

> *"The female sex is the root of all evil. It causes the collapse of mores and traditions, is full of lust and completely uninhibited."*
>
> *"Sexually transmitted diseases and AIDS are spread by uncircumcised girls because they are insatiable and always unfaithful."*
>
> *"You must reduce women's sensitiveness at all costs, to stop her being unfaithful."*

---

114 World Vision Canada, "The Girl Child—Background," in *Children at Risk Training Packet* (Canada: World Vision, n.d.).

Psychosexually, the objectives or assumed impacts of genital mutilation can be summed up as the following:

- reduction in the sexual enjoyment of women;
- control of female sexuality;
- preservation of virginity before marriage and faithfulness afterwards; and
- increase in men's desire.

b) Sociological Reasons

> *"What a young woman learns during circumcision will stand her in good stead throughout life."*
>
> *"Circumcision is part of our tradition. We have inherited it from our ancestors. We are obliged to continue it."*
>
> *"Circumcision purifies a girl and makes her proud. If a girl is not circumcised, the other girls will shun her."*

Sociologically, circumcision is seen as a status quo that cannot be changed. It was always like this and will always be like this. It is a precondition for participating in society and a precondition for eligibility to marry.

c) Religious Reasons

> *"Circumcision goes hand in hand with Islam, and must be performed before a girl can take part in prayers."*

While genital mutilation is practiced by some members of most religions, no religion has FGM as a requirement.

d) Aesthetic/Hygienic Reasons

> *"An uncircumcised girl is impure."*
>
> *"Islam demands circumcision for reasons of hygiene."*

e) Economic Reasons

> *"Circumcision is a source of income for the traditional practitioner and for health service staff."*

Since this cultural tradition runs deep, the traditional practitioner is showered with many lavish gifts. Also, a higher dowry can be demanded for a circumcised woman.

f) Myths

> *"If the clitoris touches the head of a baby during childbirth, the baby will die."*
>
> *"The clitoris makes a man impotent."*
>
> *"An uncircumcised girl behaves like a boy."*

Legal Status

All forms of female genital mutilation are widely condemned by international health experts as damaging to both physical and psychological health. Further, they also view FGM as a violation of human rights, an infringement of the rights of the child and of the right to health and physical integrity.[115] Still, FGM is widely practiced in regions worldwide, among many religious and ethnic groups.

Cultural Alternatives

Efforts to curtail this painful, debilitating, and often life-threatening practice have focused on education and legislative initiatives. Already, ten countries in Africa have enacted laws to criminalize FGM. Perhaps offering alternative rites of passage that satisfy the cultural meaning of the practice without inflicting bodily harm would encourage more governments to outlaw this practice. As women are becoming educated on the dangers of the FGM procedures, they are opposing the practice. In Kenya, for example, many families have substituted an alternative rite of passage where girls spend a week in seclusion, learn life skills from women in the community, and take part in a 'coming of age' ceremony.[116] Another alternative practice involves only a slight symbolic incision of a girl's genitals rather than the complete procedure. Recently, the Coordinating Committee on Traditional Practices Affecting Women's and Children's Health (CPTAFE) held a large public ceremony celebrating the "laying down of the excision knife" in which some traditional practitioners of FGM pledged to discontinue the practice.[117]

Nevertheless, most of those who perform FGM oppose its eradication since it is so lucrative for them. In the Masai culture in Kenya, for example, many girls are forced to be married as young as ten

---

115 United Nations, "Convention on the Rights of the Child," Geneva: Office of the High Commissioner for Human Rights, 1989. Article 24.

116 Plan UK, *Because I am a Girl: The State of the World's Girls 2007* (London: Plan International, 2007), 43, http://www.plan-uk.org/pdfs/plan_uk-girls_report2007.pdf.

117 WiLDAF/FeDDAF—West Africa, "Female Genital Mutilation, a Daily Fight to Eradicate [sic.] this practice in Guinea for the Rights of Women and Girls," Women, Law and Development in Africa, . http://www.wildaf-ao.org/eng/article.php3?id_article=77

years. They are usually circumcised before they are accepted as wives by elderly men chosen by their families. In addition to the psychological and physical risks that they experience due to these practices, the girls are often also left without any basic education.

In another example of cultural alternatives, a group of Masai girls created change in their community by speaking up and seeking assistance. In general, Masai men have many wives, and culturally, it is expected that every time a visitor comes to the family, one of the wives will automatically spend the night with the visitor. This local way of showing hospitality has now led to 120,000 out of 300,000 Masais in the area becoming infected with HIV.

Not wanting such a fate, twenty-five Masai girls escaped from their communities to the compound of the Narkok Full Gospel church, an indigenous national church with 200,000 members in churches throughout the country. They pled with the church to protect them against being forced into being circumcised followed by early marriage. They also wanted an opportunity to be educated.

Without any external support, the church began accommodating these girls. However, the church soon realized that feeding, clothing, and paying school fees was not enough. The girls were in need of permanent work to earn an income. They now are engaged in sewing classes.

With the local church understanding that the root problem was in the community, they realized that their relationship with the girls' communities and their own communities needed to be re-established. How to change these deep cultural practices was definitely a challenge. Fortunately, some of the Masai people have already understood the destructive nature of the cultural habits and are looking for change. Also ,the Kenyan government has officially banned female circumcision and early marriage. The local officials are working with the church in supporting these girls. The officials also have requested that the church start working with the girls in their communities.

The stated objectives of the project are to:

- take care of the escaped girls and arrange basic education with local church resources;
- implement preventive community development work based on community health education-values, empowering the Masai communities themselves to overcome the destructive aspects of their cultural behavior;
- start some income-generating activities to cover the administrative costs of the program and the costs of the vocational programs for the girls.

Sitting down to chat with the Narkok girls recently, I was amazed at the hope they now have of achieving lifestyle dreams and goals. They are grateful for the educational programs that have opened previously closed doors, enabling them to pursue their long-sought career goals. Some of the girls desired to enter the medical profession as a doctor or a nurse; others wanted to become a teacher or a lawyer. All held the hope that one day they could return to their villages to use their skills and education, making it easier for a new generation of girl children.[118]

EARLY MARRIAGE

Child marriages can be found across the globe, but they are pervasive in parts of Africa and South Asia. In some cases, marriage agreements take place for girls as young as two or three years of age, and sometimes before birth.[119] Though some girls marry and leave home soon after the agreement, most go to the husband's home when

---

118 UNICEF, "Sara...Daughter of a Lioness," Episode 3, Tape 367 VHS (UNICEF, 1998). UNICEF has produced a series of comic teaching books that focus on these issues. The third in the series, *Daughter of a Lioness*, focuses on the adventures of Sara, an adolescent girl who is gradually emerging as the heroine and a role model for girls' as well as boys' empowerment in Africa. The story addresses the issues of harmful traditional practices, focusing on FGM. Sara is targeted to be circumcised, but manages to get out of the situation by using her assertiveness and critical thinking life skills. At the end, she also mobilizes the community against FGM. The book is full of action and suspense. The story can be widely used to create awareness and initiate behavior change against FGM and other harmful practices, and to educate on children's rights.

119 UNICEF, "Early Marriage: Child Spouses," *Innocenti Digest*, no. 7 (March 2001): 2.

they are ten to thirteen years old. The United Nations Population Fund notes that, "despite the sanctions on child marriage...more than 100 million girls are expected to marry in the next decade."[120]

Many young women across the globe are married before their eighteenth birthdays: 42 percent in Africa, 29 percent in Latin America and the Caribbean, and 48 percent in Southern Asia. Early marriage is most common in countries with high rates of poverty and conflict and low levels of schooling, healthcare, and opportunities for employment.[121]

Girls are subjected to early marriage for many complex reasons. Usually, they have no choice but to accept the marriage arrangements. They are very young and have been socialized not to protest decisions made by their parents, other older relatives, or their community. Saying "no" might mean painfully turning their backs on their entire community and identity. Even if they do have the courage to leave, most girls lack education or other resources needed for economic survival outside their families.

Weinishet, sixteen, speaks in a shy, hesitant voice, a mark of the trauma she experienced as a young child. "I was married at the age of seven," she says.

"My husband was much older than me. He waited until I was nine years old to have intercourse. It was very difficult. He passed away when I was twelve years old. I was pregnant at the time, but lost the baby after a difficult labour, which went on for days. I do not want to re-marry. I do not want any man to come near me."[122]

Following the trauma of being removed from her family and being forced into an early marriage, Weinishet had to experience intercourse at the very onset of puberty. She also suffered the death of her first pregnancy before she was psychologically, mentally, or physically mature.

---

120   United Nations Population Fund, "Child Marriage Fact Sheet," UNFPA 2005, http://www.unfpa.org/swp/2005/presskit/factsheets/facts_child_marriage.htm (accessed January 8, 2008).

121   United Nations Population Fund, "Child Marriage Fact Sheet."

122   UNICEF, "Life After Early Marriage," UNICEF Innocenti Research Centre, 2, http://www.unicef-irc.org/presscentre/presskit/innocentidigest/storiesid7.pdf.

The period of adolescence is one in which a child is slowly transformed into a mature adult. This process involves biological, intellectual, and psychological change. Yet for the girl child, the growth into maturity is acknowledged almost exclusively in terms of physiology. The onset of puberty signals that a girl, now capable of reproduction, ceases to be a child and is thus transformed into a woman.

The child is forced to leap from childhood into adulthood, skipping a vital phase of development. Early marriage not only violates the rights of the child, but also clearly compromises her health and development.

Dowry

The rationale behind early marriages is usually economic. The bride price, or dowry, is a welcomed source of income for the bridegroom's family. Dowry is defined as "the property a man receives from his wife or her family at the time of their marriage."[123] Dowry was originally a wedding gift to a daughter from her family—money, jewelry, clothing, or household items. The gifts were a kind of insurance, giving the wife some personal wealth in case of mistreatment by her new family or a failed marriage.

Like any system, dowry has its abuses. Today, it has become common for the groom's family to demand a large amount of money or goods as well as the bride. Giving of a dowry has degenerated into a financial bargaining point between two families, and the girl has become the commodity to be bought and sold. The dowry is not only given at the time of marriage but, in many cases, the dowry is a demand that continues even after marriage. Far too often, this lucrative practice encourages men to marry girls for whom they have little or no love.

As a rule, the more educated and affluent the bridegroom, the higher the requested bride price. Therefore, the amount for dowries soars, especially if it means the family will benefit socially. Because of dowry, the girl child ultimately is viewed as a burden to the family.[124]

---

123 Ram Ahuja, *The Indian Social System* (New Delhi: Ravat Publications, 1997), 94.
124 "Bartered, Battered, Burned," *The Telegraph*, March 31, 2001, http://www.telegraph.co.uk/arts/main.jhtml;jsessionid=C4A KL02E1THRDQFIQMGSFF4AVCBQWIV0?xml=/arts/2001/03/31/bofir31.xml (accessed December 21, 2007).

Even though dowry has been outlawed in some countries, the practice continues; the occurrences of dowry harassment and deaths also have increased. A UNICEF report stated that in India, over a dozen women die every day as a result of disputes about dowry, mostly in kitchen fires designed to look like accidents.[125] Often, custom is stronger than law. And between 2001 and 2005, India's National Crime Records Bureau reported 33,694 cases of "dowry death," cases where brides were murdered because their dowries did not satisfy their new families.[126]

Effects of Early Marriage

Forcing children, especially girls, into early marriages can be physically and emotionally harmful. It violates their rights to personal freedom and a childhood in which they can be free to grow and develop holistically. Further, early child marriages put girl children at risk for having their educations interrupted, feeling the psychological impact of being taken away from their homes and families, and experiencing more sexual violence and unprotected sex.[127] Nevertheless, there have been few attempts to view child marriage as a human rights violation.

According to the United Nations Population Fund, the older women are when they marry for the first time, the more education they complete, and "conversely, getting and keeping girls in school may be one of the best ways to foster later, chosen marriage."[128]

Many child brides suffer emotional trauma from the shock of leaving their homes and being forced into an intimate relationship with a man they do not know. Because the girls have not yet matured, pregnancy and childbirth can hurt their uterus or other parts of their body, the effects leading to long-term injury or death. These girls also endure domestic violence, including rape.[129]

---

125 "Bartered, Battered, Burned."
126 National Crime Record Bureau, "Chapter 5—Crime Against Women," Crime in India—2005, http://ncrb.nic.in/crime2005/cii-2005/CHAP5.pdf, 242.
127 United Nations Population Fund, "Gender Inequality and Reproductive Health," UNFPA, http://www.unfpa.org/swp/2003/english/ch2/index.htm. For recent activity by UNICEF in this area, see http://www.unicef.org/protection/index_earlymarriage.html.
128 United Nations Population Fund, "Gender Inequality and Reproductive Health."
129 "Bartered, Battered, Burned."

Factors Leading to Early Marriage

Girls are subjected to early marriage for many complex reasons. Without a doubt, poverty is a major factor forcing girls into early marriages. Poverty-stricken parents are often persuaded to give their daughters in marriage to men who are willing to pay a good bride price. However, the girls often soon learn they have simply been lured into prostitution.

In many countries, it is common for girls to be married young because the family can pay a less expensive dowry. Poor families see the practice as a way to improve the family's economic status, to strengthen ties between marrying families, to ensure that girls are virgins when they marry, and to avoid the possibility of having a daughter be unmarriageable later in life. Also, the traditional desire to protect girls from out-of-wedlock pregnancies is a prime factor that pushes girls into early marriage.

Though early marriages may mean a less expensive dowry, which appeals to poverty-stricken parents, they have more serious implications for the girl. Early marriage is the launching of yet more harmful practices, including loss of educational opportunities, poor health from strenuous work and lack of nutritious food, early pregnancies, and a life of poverty.[130]

Not only do these girls face lives of incredible hardship, but they also face stigma and marginalization that confront women who leave their husbands. Girls who have left report their families as being mad at them for bringing shame upon them. Often, girls are cut off completely by their families and communities.

Government Attempts for Change

Some governments are serious about changing the practice of early marriage. In India, for example, they have passed "The Child Marriage Restraint Act," making marriage of a girl under eighteen years of age illegal and punishable. The mean age of marriage now is about 19.3

---

[130] UNICEF, "Child Marriage," Child Protection from Violence, Exploitation and Abuse, http://www.unicef.org/protection/index_earlymarriage.html.

years compared to around thirteen years at the beginning of the century. Some states, as an incentive to following this law, have introduced schemes for the girl child to be given a lump sum of money if she marries after eighteen years of age. The government has also launched multi-media campaigns to create public opinion against child marriages and to mobilize social forces to prevent early marriages from occurring.[131]

Yet cultures resist change. In places like Rajasthan, child marriages remain so popular that virtually every city, town, and village takes on a holiday atmosphere ahead of the day set by astrologers for the annual Akha Teej Festival—the moment judged most auspicious for marriages. And once again, girls as young as four will prepare for their wedding night.[132]

HONOR KILLINGS

Murder of women in the name of "honor" of the family is an age-old practice across many parts of India, Pakistan, the Arab world, and other locations. Women may be hunted and shot, strangled, or stabbed to death by family members—fathers, husbands, brothers, or uncles—for adultery, sexual misconduct, or any other non-sanctioned behavior, regardless of the reason. One of the aspects of "honor killings" that distinguishes them from the murder of female family members in other countries is that the criminal justice systems of the countries in which honor killings occur often tolerate them. Honor killings seem so paradoxical a term when one considers a custom that rewards families for killing their own daughters, or husbands their wives—those they claim to love.

---

[131] Sarala Gopalan and Vijay Bhaskar, "Response of the Government to the Girl Child" (paper written for the South Asia Forum, 2001), 12–13, http://www.hsph.harvard.edu/grhf/SAsia/forums/girlchild/response.

[132] See John F. Burns, "Child Marriages, Though Illegal, Persist in India," *The New York Times*, May 11, 1998, http://www.ishipress.com/indiamar.htm (accessed December 21, 2007).

The following recounts an honor killing:

In 1998 Sarhan Abdullah murdered his sister because she had been raped—by her brother-in-law, as it turned out. "I shot her with four bullets in the head," he told the Ottawa Citizen *three years later. "I was treated as a hero in prison." When Sarhan was released after six months, his family gave him a ceremonial sword and he rode home triumphantly on a horse. "My horse was white because I had cleansed my family's honor."*[133]

Sarhan was sentenced to one year in jail but was set free after six months when the judge announced that Sarhan acted out of great anger, and justified the short sentence. According to one report, women in certain parts of the world "run the risk of violence if they talk to an unrelated man, marry someone without family approval, have premarital sex, or become pregnant outside of marriage."[134]

In cultures where honor killers are hailed as heroes, the cultural understandings of morality can originate with the fact that men in their culture feel that everything a woman in their family does reflects on their manhood. Men are expected to control their female relatives. Virginity before marriage and fidelity afterward are 'must' requirements. If a woman strays, it is widely thought that only by killing her can the man restore his dignity.

In addition, a woman's purity reflects on a family's reputation. A family is shamed if there is even a rumor that a daughter is not a virgin, or if she refuses an arranged marriage, has an extramarital affair, or is disobedient. Rana Husseini graphically illustrates this: "In many families, they believe that once she tarnishes the image, it's just

---

133 Laura Jamison, "Killing for 'Honor': Legalized Murder," Amnesty International USA, http://www.amnestyusa.org/amnestynow/legalizedmurder.html.

134 Human Rights Watch, "Jordan: Victims Jailed in 'Honor' Crime Cases," *Human Rights News*, http://hrw.org/english/docs/2004/04/16/jordan8465.htm.

like breaking glass. It can't be fixed. So the only way to fix it is to kill her."[135]

RESPONSE

In many countries, attempts to enforce compliance with international and human rights norms or to stop harmful traditional practices merely provokes cultural indignation and stiff resistance. To change deeply rooted cultural practices requires fundamental changes in societal attitudes. These changes must occur within the context of health, human rights, and women's empowerment. It is encouraging to note that many countries are pushing the issues to the forefront in political as well as medical circles. Claiming that some international initiatives disregard established patterns of cultural life, some countries are even taking their own initiatives to outlaw harmful traditional practices. Some governments are going so far as to introduce legislation to criminalize banned harmful practices and planning safe, culturally sensitive alternatives that fulfill ritual cultural requirements. Others, however, feel that banning harmful cultural practices such as FGM will simply drive them underground and thus endanger the lives of many more girls.

Culturally respected initiatives, aimed at elevating the issue in the community's own agenda and eliciting a community response, will be necessary to affect long-term changes that impact attitudes and values. Our best efforts must be aimed at instilling within families and societies the value and worth of the girl child. Mother Teresa stated, "I have come to realize more and more that the greatest disease and the greatest suffering is to be unwanted, unloved, uncared for, to be shunned by everybody, to be just nobody."[136] We must strive to eradicate this deeper "disease" afflicting the girl child.

May we be encouraged to use our voices and our best efforts to 'eradicate the diseases afflicting the girl child,' and to empower her to lay claim to her great inheritance of hope from a God of justice and

---

[135] Rana Husseini, interview by Diane Sawyer, *20/20*, ABC, 1998.
[136] Mother Teresa, *My Life for the Poor* (New York: HarperCollins, 2005).

compassion. In claiming her inheritance, she will know how "wanted, loved, and cared for" she truly is—both by those around her and by her heavenly Father.

You, LORD, hear the desire of the afflicted;
you encourage them, and you listen to their cry,
defending the fatherless and the oppressed,
so that mere earthly mortals
will never again strike terror.

PSALM 10:17–18

CHAPTER 8

EXPLOITATION AND VIOLENCE

Phyllis Kilbourn

When we think of childhood, our usual first thoughts are of happy, laughing children enjoying a time of age-appropriate activities leading to healthy growth and development. Play, school, friendships, home responsibilities, and community relationships all intertwine to give children a safe passage to adulthood.

But as we learned earlier, for millions of children around the world, especially the girl child, childhood is just the opposite. Instead of childhood being about home and family, school and play, it revolves around a vicious cycle of exploitation, violence, and loss. In all countries, the girl child is shortchanged by the culture in educational institutions, politics, policy, health care, the law, and the media. She is also particularly vulnerable to exploitation and abuse.

Since 1989, the United Nations Convention on the Rights of the Child has provided a point of reference for measuring progress in children's rights. One summary of the declaration states:

> *The girl child has the birthright to be loved and nurtured, to learn, to play, and to discover her community and world, and her rights and responsibilities within. And above all, she has the right to grow into her unique and full human potential, free from coercion, exploitation and abuse.*[137]

Instead of these rights being honored, the girl child's life today is filled with rejection and violence that leaves her deeply scarred emotionally, physically, mentally, socially, and spiritually. Often, physical punishment, emotional humiliation, and sexual abuse become her daily lot. As Graeme Irvine comments,

> *To the world's shame, and irrespective of culture, the utilization of children for selfish purposes continues to our day. Child exploitation has never been a simple matter of the rich versus the poor, although surely it is one dimension of the problem. The root issue is disregard for those who are weaker than one's self and it is a pervasive mentality that can manifest itself at any level of society.*[138]

Exploitation is further fueled by the fact that those on the leading edge of poverty have few choices or alternatives available to them. Especially when it comes to girl children, it is almost certain they will not have a choice.

A child enters the world with unquestioning trust, totally defenseless and completely dependent on adults for protection and care. Children who have been abandoned or rejected often become powerless, voiceless, and vulnerable. Girls born in cultures where they

---

137   World Vision Canada, *Girls! Stories Worth Telling: Report and Conference Manual* (Toronto: World Vision Canada, 1998), 9. See United Nations, "Convention on the Rights of the Child," Geneva: Office of the High Commissioner for Human Rights, 1989. Preamble; Articles 2, 9, 19, 28, 29, 32, 34, and 39.

138   Graeme Irvine, "Taking the Child Seriously," *Together* 42 (1994): 3.

are devalued are especially at risk. If we truly are serious about the plight of the girl child, we have to challenge the cultural and value systems that make them subject to exploitation and violence.

GENDER-BASED VIOLENCE

In all societies, to a greater or lesser degree, women and girls are subjected to physical, sexual and psychological abuse that cuts across lines of income, class and culture. Violence against women both violates and impairs or nullifies the enjoyment of their human rights and freedoms.[139]

Violence against girls (and women) is extremely broad and deeply instilled in most cultures of the world. Studies of very young boys and girls show only that although boys may have a lower tolerance for frustration and a tendency toward rough-and-tumble play, these tendencies are dwarfed by the importance of male socialization and peer pressure into gender roles.[140]

The prevalence of domestic violence in a given society, therefore, is the result of inferred acceptance by that society. The way men view themselves as men, and the way they view women, will determine whether they use violence or coercion against women and girls.

As demonstrated in earlier chapters, violence is tightly intertwined with cultural practices that devalue the girl child. However, there are injustices that the girl child is subjected to that are not related to traditions, customs, or beliefs, but to political and economic forces that the girl child is caught up in simply because of poverty and her sex.

Being female and poor exposes girls to situations in which they are more helpless and therefore can be more easily exploited, abused,

---

139   The United Nations Fourth World Conference on Women, "Beijing Declaration and Platform for Action," United Nations, http://www.un.org/womenwatch/daw/beijing/platform/violence.htm. Paragraph 112.

140   United Nations Population Fund, "Involving Men in Promoting Gender Equality and Women's Reproductive Health," United Nations, http://www.unfpa.org/gender/men.htm.

and sexually violated. The violence to the girl child is less visible and is considered less significant than violence shown to boys. For the girl child, violence closes the door to any legal aid or voice that would address her needs and concerns.

Linda Hawkins reminds us that gender-based violence is also minimized by the inability to talk about the violence, which is often sexual and traditionally is not discussed.[141] Moreover, the domestic violence that occurs in families may be defined as "private" business, occurring in "private space." The categorization of gender-based violence as "private" serves to condone inactivity, minimize the importance, and perpetuate the violence.

DOMESTIC VIOLENCE

Domestic violence is inflicted upon children sexually, physically, and emotionally. Such violence robs children of the safety and protection of home and family along with the parental love and nurture needed for healthy development. Poverty and an ensuing sense of hopelessness are major factors behind domestic violence. Frustration at not having adequate resources is vented through anger and actions against children.

Sexual Violence

The western world is seeing an unprecedented rise of incidences related to domestic sexual violence among adolescents. The root causes for this are varied. Adolescence is a time of potential crisis for both females and males. The need to fit in and respond to peer pressure and social expectations can be particularly difficult for teenagers. Boys in many societies are acculturated to exercise power over others, and one of the ways this shows itself is through sexual violence. As adolescents internalize the cultural norms that reinforce sex-role stereotyping, they also increase their vulnerability to experiencing violence and abuse, as victims and/or perpetrators.[142]

---

[141] Linda Hawkins, "Because They Are Girls," in *A Safe World for Children*, ed. Melanie Gow (Monrovia, CA: World Vision International, 2001), 38.

[142] Plan UK, *Because I am a Girl: The State of the World's Girls 2007* (London: Plan International, 2007), 23, http://www.plan-uk.org/pdfs/plan_uk-girls_report2007.pdf.

Most violence against children and adolescents—as with adults—is committed by family members or friends. A study on the incidence of sexual assault in Massachusetts (USA) reported that out of 7,254 incidents reported to publicly funded rape crisis centers over a three-year period, only 18 percent of the women stated that their attacker was a stranger.[143] Among child victims under age thirteen, 62 percent were assaulted by a parent or relative; strangers accounted for only 3 percent of the reported incidents. According to UNICEF data, 73.6 percent of Chilean girls and boys are the object of some physical or psychological violence from their parents.[144]

Physical Violence

In St. Petersburg, Russia, Rainbows of Hope staff workers soon learned a major reason why so many children choose to live in sewer pipes rather than homes. With poverty at a destructive high, many being forced into eating every other day, parents have lost hope. When coming home at the end of the workday, rather than nurturing the children, they hit the vodka, seeking a release from the hopelessness that engulfs them. Often, the children are unmercifully beaten, causing them to escape from the harsh realities of home life to a safer environment.

Emotional or Psychological Abuse

Violence does not have to be physical; emotional abuse can be as destructive to a person's well-being as physical abuse. Emotional abuse is considered a pattern of behavior that can seriously interfere with a child's cognitive, emotional, psychological, or social development. Emotional or psychological abuse can be verbal or nonverbal. *Verbal abuse* includes yelling, name-calling, blaming, and shaming. Isolation, intimidation, and controlling behavior fall under *nonverbal emotional abuse*. Additionally, abusers who use emotional or psychological abuse often throw in threats of physical violence. The aim of emotional abuse is to chip away at one's

---

143 Debra J. Robin, "Educating Against Gender-Based Violence," *WEEA Digest*, Women's Equity Publications, 4.
144 Renata Delgado-Schenk, "Children's Rights in Chile: Alternative Report on the Implementation of the Convention on the Rights of the Child by Chile," World Organization Against Torture (Geneva: United Nations, 2007), 11, http://www.undp.org/rblac/gender/itsourright.htm.

feelings of self-worth and independence; the abused comes to see himself or herself as unworthy of love and affection.

Other types of abuse are usually more identifiable because marks or other physical evidence is left. Emotional abuse, with little or no visible proof, can be very hard to diagnose or even to define. Emotional abuse, however, leaves hidden scars that manifest themselves in numerous ways, including patterns of attitudes and behavior. Insecurity, poor self-esteem, destructive behavior, angry acts (such as fire setting or cruelty to animals), withdrawal, poor development of basic skills, alcohol or drug abuse, suicide, and difficulty forming relationships can all be possible results of emotional abuse.

A commonly held belief is that physical abuse is far worse than emotional abuse. However, children who are constantly shamed, humiliated, terrorized, or rejected suffer at least as much, if not more than if they had been physically assaulted. The scars of emotional abuse are very real, and they run deep. Often, these scars are carried over into adulthood.

Impact of Domestic Violence

Domestic violence impacts children's lives in many ways. A study in Nicaragua showed that 63 percent of the children of violence-affected families repeat school years and abandon school at an average age of nine years, in contrast to the national average of twelve years.[145]

Violence also limits a girl's options to protect herself. In much of the world, girls are subordinate, voiceless, and imperiled, even in the best of times. They have no power to put a stop to the violence.

The rise in and consequences of domestic violence raise an imperative for educators to consider the incidence of violence against adolescents as a serious issue, and for agencies working with the girl child to be knowledgeable and equipped to provide help and to refer to appropriate services.

---

[145] Aparna Mehrotra and Rini Banerjee, "Life Without Violence: It's Our Right," UNDP, http://www.undp.org/rblac/gender/itsourright.htm.

VIOLENCE OUTSIDE THE HOME

Beyond the home, children enter into different landscapes of violence directed against them through such activities as war, sexual exploitation, street life, and child labor. These, however, are not clear-cut categories, nor are they the only ways poverty and societies perpetrate violence and abuse against the girl child. A girl living on the streets, for example, will probably be engaged in child labor, likely prostitution, be exposed to HIV and AIDS through forced sexual abuse, and suffer vicious attacks by gang warlords. The following depicts situations where children find themselves the objects of violent abuse.

War

Armed conflict and war brutalize children in many ways, separating them from their parents and exposing them to acts of violence. The experiences and subsequent impact of war on girls leave them with severe psychological problems. In war, girls are forced to actively engage in armed conflict, go through exploitive situations stemming from loss of family and subsequent displacement from home and often the community, suffer physically from lack of nutrition and health care, and be targeted for violence and abuse, especially sexual abuse and rape. The vulnerability of girls causes them to suffer disproportionately.

Globally, approximately 300,000 girls and boys under eighteen years are currently involved in war and armed conflict.[146] Girls are conscripted for a variety of roles: as fighters or combatants, to be "wives" of the adult soldiers, or to serve in support roles such as carrying loads or cooking. Such a role is in stark contrast to their traditional role, in many cultures, of working alongside their mothers in the home—cutting firewood, carrying water, cooking and cleaning, helping with younger siblings, or looking after goats and sheep in the fields. War is not a role they have prepared for; it is instead a role that inflicts severe losses and trauma.

---

[146] International Programme on the Elimination of Child Labour, "Armed Conflict (Child Soldiers)," International Labour Organization, http://www.ilo.org/ipec/areas/Armedconflict/lang--en/index.htm.

For example, let us consider a group of former child soldiers in Uganda who made drawings of terror. The girls drew caricatures of the soldier "husbands" to whom they had been given. One drawing was all black except for a big red eye. When explaining her drawing, the girl said, "This is the face of death."[147]

Another story tells of girls in Sri Lanka who are brainwashed and trained to be suicide bombers. Given a cyanide tablet to hang around their neck to swallow in the likely event they are caught, death is always the ultimate destiny.

War also forces girl children to become refugees. Women and girls comprise the majority of the world's refugee and internally displaced populations. Often, the traditional values that uphold the care and protection as practiced in the refugees' home communities are neglected as they struggle to simply survive. Having fled to refugee camps in search of safety and assistance, they often find more insecurity and depravation. Diseases run rampant through the camps, food is diverted from those who need it most, and sexual abuse is almost a given.

Street Children

The United Nations estimates that there are 140,000 to 200,000 children, both boys and girls, living on danger-filled city streets. Just as there are thousands of children living on the streets, so there are thousands of reasons why they have been forced to call the streets their home: abuse in their homes, poverty, abandonment, boredom, becoming orphaned, being unaccepted in their village, or fearing reprisal for serving as a child combatant—each child has his or her own story.

These children, without parental or adult supervision, support or guidance, are very vulnerable. They must survive by any available means, which often means ending up in prostitution or being sexually exploited. Pimps and the mafia see the children as markets of exploitation for

---

147   World Vision Canada, *Girls! Stories Worth Telling*, 20.

financial gain. Along with using them in prostitution, they help fulfill the great demand for child pornographic materials and videos.

While interviewing Dowling, a Mongolian police officer, and Sarantunga, a three-year veteran street girl, Kristine Weber learned a lot about what life means to females on the street. Dowling admits that society does not look at the situation of the street children. He states, "So many girls are abused by so many people—the police, teachers and men in the street."[148] Due to the added pressure of life on the streets as a female, many of the street girls have serious emotional problems.

Sarantunga relates many fears of being a girl on the street, including the fear of pregnancy. Surviving on the streets for three years, she knows the ropes of survival. "I usually approach men near the cinema," says Sarantunga. "I get five or six thousand tugrik (US$12 or US$14) from them and then on the way to where they want to have sex, I run away." More than once Sarantunga has been caught and beaten, receiving black eyes or a bloody nose.

She has a vague understanding of pregnancy but no clear idea of sexually transmitted diseases:

> *I don't understand how a baby could get inside of me because babies are so big and I'm so small," she said looking puzzled. "Last month I got my period for the first time and I didn't know what it was and I got really scared and started crying. Now I know I can get pregnant but I still don't see how this is possible.*[149]

Casa Alianza, a home for street children in Guatemala, paints another chilling scenario of life for a Guatemalan street girl, Alejandra. Her story also highlights the multiple abuses girls are often forced to endure when making the streets their home.

---

[148] Kristine Weber, "Out in the Cold: The Street Children of Mongolia," People's News Agency, http://www.prout.org/pna/mongolian-street-children.html.

[149] Weber, "Out in the Cold."

> *Yesterday morning Alejandra gave up on the cruel world in which she had to live. Abandoned by her family, violated by her stepfather, beaten by the cops, raped by adults, cold, hungry, and tired. The slight fifteen-year-old fell asleep on the top of a small shop in Zone 4 of Guatemala City on Thursday night. Sleep was her only respite from the suffering.*
>
> *And early the next morning two "men"—a generous term for the bastards—came and, seeing the homeless girl asleep, lifted two huge slabs of concrete and hurled them down at her about fifteen feet below. They knew they would hurt her. They knew they could kill her. And that is probably why they did it.*
>
> *Alejandra could no longer take the pain and suffering after her skull was crushed. The few medical personnel available at the San Juan de Dios public hospital—where doctors are on strike and where the administrators are rife with corruption so there is insufficient medicine—were unable to cope and so Alejandra passed on to something better. God knows, nothing could be worse than this hellhole for Guatemala's street children.*[150]

Learning that 20 percent of Indonesia's street children were girls and that most street children's projects targeted boys, the Asian Development Bank launched a poverty reduction scheme in Yogyakarta to help female street children. The project helps female street children with counseling services and health and medical care in collaboration with non-governmental organizations (NGOs). Kus Hardjanti, task manager for the project, stated, "We will provide prenatal and postnatal care for pregnant girls and young mothers. We will also treat girls with sexually transmitted infections, train social workers to deal with

---

[150] Bruce Harris, "Casa Alianza," http://www.casa-alianza.org/es/news.php (accessed August 18, 2002).

female children, and organize public information campaigns against child prostitution."[151]

In the follow-up report, the Asian Development Bank relates that more than 950 young women were assisted, supported, and trained, and that "the number of girl street children in the target group was reduced significantly from 724 to 300 over a period of 3 years."[152] Further plans are under way to replicate the Yogyakarta scheme in other urban centers. The scheme will establish counseling centers for street girls who are at risk of, or have experienced, sexual abuse; evaluate different approaches to prevention and rehabilitation; and develop culturally acceptable, cost-effective, and sustainable programs to help the government, NGOs, and social workers address the needs of female street children.

CHILD LABOR

Child workers are found in a wide range of economic activities, largely due to family poverty. The largest number work on family-based farms, in sweatshops, as domestic helpers, or in the areas of prostitution, street vending, and manufacturing. Often, the activities in which child workers are engaged inflict great harm on the children and accordingly are labeled as exploitative. Exploitative labor is detrimental to the child's health, welfare, and development. Such exploitative labor is also characterized by the employment of very young children, as young as five years. In most work situations, girl children are at especially great risk of sexual exploitation.[153]

When talking about child labor, one must be aware that there is a difference between children having to work in the home or public venues to assist poverty-stricken parents and those being oppressed in exploitative labor markets. However, discrimination can favor the

---

151 Omana Nair, "Hope for Street Girls," *ADB Review* 33, no. 1 (2001), http://www.adb.org/Documents/Periodicals/ADB_Review/2001/vol33_1/street_girls.asp?p=gender.

152 Asian Development Bank, "Indonesia: Supporting Girl Street Children," *Seagen Waves* 1, no. 1 (August 2007), http://www.adb.org/Documents/Periodicals/SEA-GEN/vol01-01/ino-girl-street-children.asp.

153 See, for example, ILO-IPEC Geneva, *Hazardous Child Domestic Work: A Briefing Sheet* (Geneva: International Labour Office, 2007), 13.

boy child even in the home, thereby disadvantaging the girl child. In rural areas, for example, girls more often spend many hours gathering firewood and water, working in the fields, preparing food, and caring for younger siblings.

The girl child also works longer hours than her brother. This leaves her with little time or energy for play, friends, or school. And as to employment outside the home, her employer trains and pays her less, and she becomes a second-class citizen within her social, economic, and legal system. Children not only are engaged in occupations that are hazardous to their health, but also are involved in working long hours with little provision for food or comfort. They receive little if any pay.[154] In some countries, for example, girls work long hours bent over looms, a position that will crush their not-yet fully formed chest walls, damaging their lung capacities or permanently injuring them in other ways. The infamous match and explosive factories are noted for giving children the most dangerous tasks, again putting young lives at risk.

With long hours, insufficient food, exhaustion, no time—or energy—for play or school, and exploitive labor options, the girl child is robbed of a meaningful childhood along with normal childhood development; even her health is compromised. Domestic labor, vending, and sexual exploitation, work venues for millions of young girls, are prime examples of exploitation and violence in girls' labor market.

Domestic Labor

One of the most hidden forms of exploitation is domestic service, where tens of millions of young girls, ages six and up, work long hours in the homes of relatives or strangers as housemaids or servants. Often, they are employed by wealthy and middle-class families. These girls are among the most exploited children in the world. Working from before dawn until late into the night, these girls are hidden behind

---

154   International Labour Organization, "Provisional Record, Ninety-Sixth Session, Geneva, 2007" (report of the fifth sitting of the International Labour Conference, June 8, 2007), 10/7, http://www.adb.org/Documents/Periodicals/ADB_Review/2001/vol33_1/street_girls.asp?p=gender.

closed doors and have no protection from the cruelty and lust of their employers. They are often poorly fed, have meager accommodation facilities, and do not experience the benefits of laws that could serve to protect them from physical, sexual, and emotional abuse.

Many find themselves socially isolated from family and friends. Those who find jobs as housemaids usually find they are not free from sexual exploitation and harassment. In many cases, their masters inflict physical and emotional abuse and mistreatment on the girls, including sexual molestation and physical torture. Learning to do housework properly is an integral part of a girl's education, but many employers are quick to exploit girls by passing too many chores on to them. This often is the same fate girls experience in the classroom, where they are likewise assigned cleaning chores. The worst-case scenarios, however, are those from children who are sold or bonded to serve as maids. These girls are exploited by overwork and denial of childhood rights along with sexual and physical abuse.

Children's rights groups in Cote D'Ivoire, for example, are concerned about the rising employment of young girls aged between four and eight years as maids. The Ivorian girls are usually taken away from their rural homes by an illicit network run by Abidjan-based women whose role is to supply maids for a fee. The transactions usually take place at Boundoukou, a distance from Abidjan where false relatives literally sell the girls to women agents from Abidjan. Girls from large, poor families are usually targeted.[155]

After making magnificent promises to the families, the young girls are dispatched to private homes as house helpers for a monthly stipend, depending on their ages and the employee's purchasing power. However, the wages are paid to the so-called guardian, who does not give a cent to the girls. The social services also revealed that the young girl-maids live under appalling conditions. Most of the girls are not only bullied by the children of their employers, but are sometimes raped by the head of the household.

---

[155] Africa News Service Files, "Child Labour: A Blight in Cote D'Ivoire," January 16, 2001.

It is reported that the girls generally sleep in the kitchen or in the living room and are prohibited from using the indoor toilets. Sometimes, they are not allowed to rest or to be given medication or cared for when they are sick.[156]

Vendors

Many girls, including street children, wander the streets to sell petty goods at all hours of the day or night. They risk traffic hazards, irate customers, being cheated out of a fair price for their goods, and physical and sexual abuse.

On a recent visit to Sierra Leone, the author heard several stories of young girls selling peanuts from door to door to help with the family income. Often, these girls were snatched and dragged into the house and raped by one or more men. The mothers, aware of this situation, simply shrugged their shoulders and explained, "Someone has to sell the peanuts." As a result, there is a growing number of child mothers in the capital: girls who are rejected because of their undeserved fate.

Global Trafficking of Children

Perhaps the most destructive form of child labor for the girl child occurs through sexual exploitation. More than 1 million children, mostly girls, are physically, sexually, and psychologically exploited in the global sex trade every year. Girls are lured away from their homes with promises of better lives by enterprising businesspeople. Then the girls are sold into prostitution. Sometimes, parents unwittingly sell their daughters into servitude, not knowing they will end up as prostitutes. Some parents know their daughters will end up as prostitutes but for reasons of poverty sell them anyway.

Children entering the sex industry are put at risk of contracting HIV and AIDS and other sexually transmitted diseases. In 2007, more than 33 million people were infected with HIV.[157] In many cultures,

---

156   Africa News Service Files, "Child Labour."
157   UNAIDS, "Fact Sheet: Revised HIV Estimates," Joint United Nations Programme on HIV/AIDS, http://data.unaids.org/pub/EPISlides/2007/071118_epi_revisions_factsheet_en.pdf.

men believe that having sex with a virgin will cure STDs, including AIDS. And to obtain this healing, younger and younger girls are sought out. This erroneous belief puts millions of very young girls at risk of abuse, disease, and physical injury.

> *When you have met an old lady of thirteen years who has already lived a life of such abuse that she is now selling her body for 20 cents and waiting for the right opportunity to commit suicide and you multiply that young girl's experience by a hundred, a thousand, tens of thousands and possibly even hundreds of thousands, then you realize that what we are talking about really is a crime against humanity.*[158]

Richard Halloran relates a compelling story of modern-day slavery that was given at a conference on trafficking in women and children. A thirteen-year-old Mexican girl was tricked into prostitution in the United States, told that she could make more money working in Texas than she could by waiting tables. Two men arranged her immigration papers and transportation, promising to find her another job if she didn't like the first one or bring her back to Mexico if she became homesick.

She and several other girls walked four days and nights through the desert and across the Rio Grande into Texas and were then driven to a trailer in a deserted area of Florida. Her story of life there enables us to grasp the horrific situations our girls are forced into.

---

[158] Ron O'Grady, *The Child and the Tourist: The Story Behind the Escalation of Child Prostitution in Asia* (Bangkok: ECPAT, 1992).

> *"Only then was the little thirteen-year-old girl told that she had been sold to a brothel and would have to work off her debt by sexually servicing men," Allen said. "She was a virgin, and she didn't know what they were talking about, but she knew it was bad, so she refused. She was then brutally gang-raped to induct her into the business."*

For the next six months, she was forced to service ten to fifteen men every day. "Twice she was impregnated, twice forced to have an abortion, and twice she was back in the brothel the next day," Allen told the hushed audience in the convention center. The traffickers circulated her through trailer brothels and private parties, where she was passed around. She was pistol-whipped and raped if she resisted.

The girl was rescued when two girls ran to neighbors, who called police. "She had multiple sexually transmitted diseases, scar tissue from the forced abortions, and was addicted to drugs and alcohol," Allen said. "She had posttraumatic stress syndrome, including severe depression and suicidal thoughts. She was physically, mentally, emotionally, and spiritually broken. This is a modern-day form of slavery," Allen asserted.[159]

Worldwide, about 1.2 million girls and boys a year are trafficked for sexual exploitation and forced labor,[160] generating an estimated US$5 to $7 billion for traffickers. Kevin Bales, a researcher and author, agrees: "There are more slaves today than at any other time in human history," with 27 million people in one form of slavery another.[161]

Radha Paul states that situations of sexual exploitation are much more difficult to deal with compared to what girls experience because

---

159   Richard Halloran, "The Rising East: Millions Victimized by Modern-Day Slavery," *The Honolulu Advertiser*, November 19, 2002.

160   UNICEF, "Children in Unconditional Worst Forms of Child Labour and Exploitation," *State of the World's Children 2006*, http://www.unicef.org/sowc06/pdfs/figure3_7.pdf.

161   Kevin Bales, *Understanding Global Slavery: A Reader* (Berkeley, CA: University of California Press, 2005), 151; Kevin Bales, "Slavery Today," Free the Slaves, http://www.freetheslaves.net/NETCOMMUNITY/Page.aspx?pid=301&srcid=208.

of tradition and belief.[162] However, these situations are increasing and need our intervention on behalf of the girl child just as much as long-term transformational development.

Holistic Ministry

Trafficking and other forms of sexual abuse of children are a vital concern for Christian missions. Such abuse insults a central tenet of the Christian faith: that all people are created in the image of God. God never intended for girls' bodies to become only "economic assets." Bruce Bradshaw points out,

> *While the immorality of child exploitation is a major issue, child exploitation is not simply a moral problem. Condemning the immorality of the issue does not solve it. Instead it masks the nature of the problem by simplifying it. The immorality of child exploitation is a symptom of greater economic and social problems. Child exploitation results when the survival strategies in rural communities fail to support the social and economic welfare of a community.*[163]

A key ingredient in stopping all forms of exploitive labor practices is to provide resources for alternative incomes for children and their families. Girls in Sierra Leone who have been sexually exploited in the workplace are now given the opportunity to engage in soapmaking, tailoring, and a number of small business ventures that Rainbows of Hope, a mission-based organization, has launched. In time, the girls set up their own small businesses and become respected businesspeople in the community.

Without income-generating skills, girls have a bleak future, unable to develop their potential, which would enable them to rise above poverty. Instead, they will be confined to the most degrading and exploitative

---

162 Radha Paul, "What About the Girl Child?" *Together* (January–March 2000): 14.
163 Bruce Bradshaw, "Preventing Child Exploitation through Community Survival Strategies," *Together* (April–June 1990): 1.

work, in conditions so hazardous that they likely will not live long lives. Girls doubtless will pass the same fate on to their own children, perpetuating a cycle of poverty and misery that afflicts so many girl children today.

Advocating for changes in exploitative labor practices that are gender-biased, or that disrespect the rights of the girl employee, is also vital to assure that both girls and boys have safe working environments that are conducive to mental, physical, and emotional health.

RESPONSE TO VIOLENCE & EXPLOITATION

Archbishop Njongonkulu Ndungane recently urged all males in the vicinity of Cape Town to join the Men's March to protest violence and abuse against women and girls. The marchers' plans included handing the following declaration to President Thabo Mbeki at the gates to Parliament in Cape Town:

If the men in this country fail to take a stand against the abuse and violence perpetrated against women and girls, there is little hope of stopping the tide that threatens the stability of the nation.

Daily we learn of little girls being abused and killed. We have statistics on how many women are raped every minute of every day. The economic and social exploitation of women and female children is an insidious aspect of our culture and we know that abuse has many shapes and forms. This sin against the female of our species is ultimately a sin against all creation.[164]

---

[164] Njongonkulu Ndungane, media statement, Pan African News Agency (Cape Town, South Africa), November 2, 2000.

As the various forms of violence and exploitation against the girl child are coming to the attention of societies worldwide, educators are realizing that preventing girls from becoming victims of violence is vital, and early intervention is essential. Education that addresses these issues, including societies' attempts to solve problems through aggression, must be a prime intervention. When aggression as a means of solving problems is modeled by adults and leaders, children learn that violence is an appropriate response to problems.

Exploitation and violence rob girls of the freedom to develop to their full potential. Violence also occurs in cycles; someone who was abused as a child is likely to abuse her children, perpetrating a cycle of violence. School-based approaches are valuable as they reach large numbers of children at ages when education can be particularly effective. This is desperately needed. However, the problem must also be tackled in all social settings: home, church, community, and educational institutions. Only then will the cycle can be broken.

Health is a state of complete physical, mental and social well-being and not merely the absence of disease . . . Healthy development of the child is of basic importance; the ability to live harmoniously in a changing total environment is essential to such development.

CONSTITUTION OF THE WORLD HEALTH ORGANIZATION

CHAPTER 9

HEALTH AND NUTRITION ISSUES

Nancy LaDue

The essential health and developmental needs of children are expressed in the constitution of the World Health Organization as follows:

> *Health is a state of complete physical, mental and social well-being and not merely the absence of disease... Healthy development of the child is of basic importance; the ability to live harmoniously in a changing total environment is essential to such development [and that] governments have a responsibility for the health of their peoples which can be fulfilled only by the provision of adequate health and social measures.*[165]

---

[165] Constitution of the World Health Organization as adopted by the International Health Conference, New York, June 19–22, 1946; signed on July 22, 1946 by the representatives of 61 States (Official Records of the World Health Organization, no. 2, p. 100) and entered into force on April 7, 1948.

In Antigua, Guatemala, where I work, the effects of poverty are constantly played out before one's eyes. Walking past the market, you soon come upon many Native American women and girls struggling to sell their goods. One wonders if these girls will ever have an education or if meaningful opportunities will open up for them to achieve their full potential. Do they ever get time to run and play? Have they ever seen the inside of a classroom? Do they know anything other than work? What does this mean for their health? Will their essential health and developmental needs be met?

The Guatemalan women—like women worldwide—are confronted with many health concerns related to their working and living conditions, along with the challenges of poverty and gender discrimination. Women's health concerns largely stem from early marriage, male preference, lack of education, unfair and unsafe workloads, poor health care and nutrition, sexual and physical abuse, violence, exploitation, and poverty. There never is just a single issue affecting a woman's health; the root causes of health issues are multifaceted. Existing research shows that today's girls and young women are confronted by a range of obstacles and barriers along the path toward healthy development. Our challenge is to discover the extent to which growing up female impacts the healthy development of girls and young women from birth to adulthood. When we understand this, we can plan holistic health care programs to improve the welfare of the girl child.

HEALTH: EVERY CHILD'S RIGHT

When the constitution of the World Health Organization was drafted more than fifty years ago, the writers emphasized health as a fundamental human right. They condemned all forms of distinction or discrimination in health: race, religion, political belief, or economic or social condition. However, they forgot one vital distinction— discrimination on the basis of gender. Awareness about gender discrimination in health is relatively recent; it not only reflects a preference for sons but also an underestimation of the worth of the girl child. As far as medical treatment is concerned, a child is a child. The social reality in many parts of the world is different—a boy is a boy, and a girl is a girl.

As we have seen throughout this volume, the effects of gender discrimination take many forms. Let us now re-examine these effects from the perspective of the health consequences of being born a girl: girl children receive less access to adequate nutrition, face more health risks due to harmful traditional practices, live and work in dangerous situations, are severely affected by poverty, have less access to proper health care, and experience many health consequences due to gender-based violence. Gender discrimination is fraught with health issues for the girl child from birth and throughout her life.

MALNUTRITION

One of the biggest health concerns witnessed in girls is malnutrition. Therefore, health and nutrition are major components of interventions for improvement in their growth and development. When lives are geared toward survival, or adequate food is withheld from children, nutrition is an alien concept to them. When they are hungry, they will simply eat whatever is available, whether rotting fruit and vegetables, other bits of food they forage from garbage bins, or stale leftovers found on their brothers' plates.

In contrast, many young women from wealthier nations are malnourished because of serious eating disorders resulting from society's expectations of girls that are based on body size and image. The idealized "thin is more glamorous and sexy" concept flourishes. Anorexia nervosa sufferers, documented as young as age ten, refuse to eat enough food despite extreme hunger. Bulimia nervosa involves binges of eating followed by self-punishment. The rise in eating disorders in wealthy nations has had a devastating effect on girls' health and in some cases has also resulted in death.

Causes

For the girl child, malnutrition starts at birth. Babies born to malnourished mothers experience low birthweight which results in a greater likelihood of death in infancy or childhood, stunting, mental retardation, and chronic health problems. Girls are further deprived nutritionally as mothers in boy-preference communities tend to breastfeed boys for a longer time than girls. Sometimes, girls are weaned earlier so parents can try for another (male) child. A shorter breastfeeding time results in baby girls missing out on breast milk's protection against disease and malnutrition. After weaning, girls continue to have less nourishing food than boys. In families where food is scarce, mothers often feed their sons and husbands first, leaving only the leftovers for themselves and their daughters. Some societies have strongly enforced food taboos. In Bangladesh, for example, girls are forbidden to eat beef, eggs, or fish while menstruating. Yet these protein-rich foods are valuable for growth and to help replace blood loss.[166]

Research has consistently shown that education for the girl child has a strong impact on infant and child survival along with healthy growth and development.[167] Lack of education has a two-fold consequence for the health of the girl child: her mother doesn't know how to plan for adequate nutrition in the diet, and lack of sufficient knowledge prevents her from obtaining a good job that provides an adequate salary to enable her to purchase nutritious food.

Many mothers love their children, but they simply do not have the knowledge or means to provide a healthy diet for them.

The Family Planning Association of Pakistan has established "The Girl Child Project" to help girls learn more about and help prevent discrimination. In one meeting, sixteen-year-old Shabnam Naheed shared these comments:

---

166 "Young Women," World Vision Australia (1992).
167 See, for example, J.G. Cleland and J. K. Van Ginneken, "Maternal Education and Child Survival in Developing Countries: The Search for Pathways of Influence," *Social Science and Medicine* 27, no. 12 (1988): 1357–68; UNICEF, *State of the World's Children 2007: The Double Dividend of Gender Equality* (New York: UNICEF, 2006), 2.

In my own family, my mother used to give meat to my brothers first and then to us girls. I learned during the workshop that this was not right. So I went home and told my mother that even the Prophet Muhammad has said to treat girls equally. Now we all eat well.[168]

Medical Problems

UNICEF has referred to malnutrition as the silent emergency; it has stirred little public alarm in spite of the fact that more than half of all child deaths worldwide are due to poor nutrition. One of the most serious forms of malnutrition, severe acute malnutrition, affects 20 million children across the globe,[169] and the deaths of more than 5 million children each year are related to malnutrition. In Southeast Asian nations alone, 3.1 million child deaths were related to malnutrition, and this situation is worsening in several countries throughout the world.[170]

The tragic results of early childhood malnourishment include stunted growth and brain damage. Mental retardation is a common birth defect seen when mothers have been iodine deficient. Malnourished children suffer from weakened immune systems resulting in frequent infections, lifetime disabilities, and even early death. It has been shown that severely underweight children are two to eight times more likely than healthy children to die in the next year. Of the children in low- and middle-income countries, 182 million (30 percent) have stunted growth or are underweight due to lack of proper nutrition.[171]

---

[168] Family Planning Association of Pakistan, "India: Seminar on Adolescent Girl's Health," *Women's International Network News* 28 (Autumn 1992): 25.

[169] World Health Organization, "Community-Based Management of Severe Acute Malnutrition," World Health Organization, http://www.who.int/child-adolescent-health/New_Publications/CHILD_HEALTH/Severe_Acute_ Malnutrition_en.pdf.

[170] Child Health and Development, "Child Survival in the South-East Asia Region," World Health Organization, http://www. searo.who.int/EN/Section13/Section37/Section135.htm.

[171] F. James Levinson and Lucy Bassett, "Malnutrition Is Still a Major Contributor to Child Deaths," Population Reference Bureau, 1, http://www.prb.org/pdf07/Nutrition2007.pdf.

Malnutrition and its related challenges of illness, stunted growth, and even death do not affect all children equally. Due to early weaning, preferential feeding practices, and other discriminatory practices, girl children are more likely to experience these harmful medical effects than boys.[172]

An Intervention Model

Jeff Anderson, Director of ACTION Philippines and the Street Impact team, talked recently about the "Fish and Bread Feeding Program" in Tondo. Fish and Bread is a six-month nutritional feeding program. Mothers are taught about the nutritional needs of children and how to meet them. The training includes learning new income-generating skills. The mothers are also provided with start-up capital to launch a simple cottage industry where they prepare simple foods to be sold at a local school and in the market. The six-month program ends with a meaningful graduation ceremony. Several children are alive today because of the medical and nutritional assistance they received in this program. And the mothers have not only learned how to better care for their children, but also are regularly involved in a church women's ministry that functions also as a support group. Grateful for what they have learned, they are quick to recommend other needy moms to sign up for the course. And those hearing the reports of these mothers are quick to sign up. Such a program would be an ideal time to talk about the nutritional needs of the girl child, encouraging parents to provide proper nutrition for all children.

HARMFUL TRADITIONAL PRACTICES

Traditional practices within families and communities often are detrimental to the health and well-being of children and women. Some of these widespread practices pose serious risks for girls.

---

172 In fact, around 450 million women in developing countries are stunted as a result of malnutrition. For more on this topic, see Plan UK, *Because I am a Girl: The State of the World's Girls 2007* (London: Plan International, 2007), 17, 30, http://www.plan-uk.org/pdfs/plan_uk_girls_report2007.pdf.

Female Infanticide

As discussed in chapter 7, the ancient practice of female infanticide has not been completely abolished. The timing for this to occur has been brought forward with the utilization of new technologies for the selective abortion of the female fetus. Ultrasound, amniocentesis, and chorionic villus sampling have been used for this purpose. This violation of the right of the girl child is particularly disturbing as it involves the medical profession and has been made possible by medical advances.

Multiple abortions take a toll on mothers physically and emotionally. The practice of female infanticide has also opened a gender gap, causing serious social upheavals.

Female Genital Mutilation (FGM)

According to UNICEF, more than 3 million girls undergo female genital mutilation (FGM) every year.[173] Of note is the insistence of many in the medical profession that this not be called circumcision but, rather, as the name implies, mutilation. For our purposes here, the terms will be used interchangeably. This traditional practice results in multiple physical, mental, and social health risks. The practice also is a flagrant human rights violation, performed on a child who cannot give informed consent. Health problems are extensive for girls who undergo this procedure, and the health consequences of FGM last far beyond the operation. At the time of the circumcision, there is an extremely high risk of infection and hemorrhage as well as pain and shock.

This procedure, described in another chapter, is often performed by a local unskilled person using unsterile razors, knives, or metal objects and without anesthesia. Traditionally, older women or midwives who have no educational background or formal training in medicine perform the circumcision. Botched operations can cause fatal hemorrhaging. Women often experience pelvic and urinary

---

173 D'Vera Cohn, "The Campaign Against Female Genital Cutting: New Hope, New Challenges," Population Reference Bureau, http://www.prb.org/Articles/2007/CampaignAgainstFemaleGenitalCutting.aspx.

infections, tetanus, epidural cysts, and retention of urine and menstrual blood. Over the years, FGM also causes girls intense pain, severe rips and tears, and major difficulties during sexual intercourse, pregnancy, and childbirth.

Early Marriage

Sixteen-year-old Nacema says,

Girls are seen as belonging to their future in-laws' families and any investment in their future is futile. They go to their husbands' homes at a young age, usually anywhere from thirteen to seventeen, the rest of their lives are spent looking after in-laws, and bearing and bringing up children to prolong and strengthen their husband's family line.[174]

Early marriage violates the human rights of girls and boys. This practice also impacts their physical and psychological well-being and hinders opportunities for education and personal development. Girls are particularly affected because it often leads to early pregnancy, subservience to their husbands and in-laws, a huge domestic work load, abuse and domestic violence, and restricted mobility. In addition, girls are often married off to older men.

In many societies, pregnancy is not considered a condition that requires special treatment, so the young mothers receive no prenatal or post-natal care. Just before and during adolescence, there is a "growth spurt" when the body can make up for some of what it missed earlier. Young girls experiencing motherhood, along with the accompanying malnourishment, are often robbed of this important growth spurt.

---

[174] Family Planning Association of Pakistan, "India: Seminar on Adolescent Girl's Health," *Women's International Network News* 28 (Autumn 1992): 25.

Early marriage, before the girl is mentally and physically prepared, results in increased deaths of young mothers as well as newborn babies. Furthermore, the time between pregnancies is often very close, not allowing girls the necessary time for recovery and healing. It is vital that these young mothers receive prenatal and maternal health care. Many maternal deaths, maternal and childhood diseases, and disabilities could be prevented if women had access to four services:

1. prenatal health care;
2. trained health personnel at birth;
3. emergency obstetric care if needed; and
4. modern contraception.

In the developed world, where these main components of safe motherhood are, for the most part, already in place, the average lifetime risk of maternal death in childbirth or from pregnancy-related complications is 1 in 4,000; in Sub-Saharan Africa, for example, the average is 1 in 16, and "99 percent of all maternal deaths occur in developing countries."[175]

LIVING & WORKING ENVIRONMENTS

The girl child who lives at home is often overworked. She might be given responsibility for all the household chores, including washing clothes, cleaning inside and outside the house, collecting water and firewood, cooking the meals, and providing continuous childcare. She may also be required to help supplement the family income with part-time work away from the home. She is left with no time for recreation or proper rest.

Other children, such as child laborers and abandoned children, work and live in unsanitary conditions in slums, on top of garbage heaps or city dumps, or even in sewer pipes. Surrounding their homes are open, overflowing drains, flies, and toxic fumes from traffic and

---

[175] UNICEF, *State of the World's Children 2007*, 5.

rotting garbage. Their makeshift homes do not supply adequate heat, sanitary facilities, safe drinking sources, or protection from the elements, insects, wild dogs, or thugs. Children who sift through rubbish all day return home without adequate water for a proper wash. And usually they do not have sufficient food to meet their nutritional requirements. Not surprisingly, malnourishment and illnesses such as fevers, coughs, malaria, scabies, and diarrhea commonly result from such living environments.

In poor health already, child laborers are confronted with on-the-job hazards: cuts on rusty metal or pieces of glass, body aches from age-inappropriate work assignments, heat- or cold-related problems, and the ever-present potential for sexual molestation. Some accidents, such as working in explosive factories or bending over looms day after day, result in permanent injuries and physical and mental handicaps: blindness, amputations, loss of hearing, or other physical or mental impairments.

POVERTY

Poverty plays a major role in the deadly health issues of the girl child. She has a tremendous risk of dying prematurely from contracting tuberculosis (TB), malaria, measles, tetanus, or whooping cough. Often, there is no health care available.

Mwaka is nine years old and lives in Kwale, at the southeast tip of Kenya. Like most of the children around her, Mwaka does not go to school. Her home is about ten kilometers from the nearest hospital, although there is a small, poorly equipped clinic and local dispensary closer by. Kwale goes through droughts every two to four years. The only water available is unclean, being shared with the village animals. Dry periods force people to walk up to twenty kilometers to find water. Kenya's infant mortality rate is 79 per 1,000 live births (UK, 5 per 1,000). Only 61 percent of the population has access to safe drinking water, and the life expectancy is forty-eight years.[176]

---

[176] UNICEF, *State of the World's Children 2007*, 103–105, 111.

What is the future for Mwaka and the millions of children like her in Africa? To survive into healthy adulthood, she will need to avoid, among other dangers, acute respiratory infections, diarrhea, diseases, measles, and malaria. Her chances will be governed largely by her exposure to poverty. By the time she reaches the age to become a parent herself, she will have to negotiate the twin threats of HIV and multi-drug resistant TB.

ILLNESSES & LACK OF MEDICAL CARE

According to UNICEF, malnutrition and illness are closely related. For example, illnesses such as malaria, anemia, and tuberculosis are common among the malnourished, along with an increased incidence of being underweight.[177] In children, malnutrition is synonymous with growth failure. Women are living longer than men, but they do not live healthier lives. Most of the deaths of women in the developing world result from communicable diseases as well as diseases related to childbirth. Since women live longer than men and women tend to marry older men, this increases the woman's chance of poverty and ill health in her older years, as she will most likely be a widow. This trend sets up the future for the girl child with little chance of change in her world.

Parents, especially in poor communities, are more likely to take their sons for treatment as soon as they become sick, but their daughters only if the illness becomes very serious. Sometimes, this is because there are taboos about girls being examined by male doctors. Or parents may be concerned for their daughters' safety if they have to travel a long distance for treatment. But there are also economic and social reasons. Perhaps a boy's physical strength might be vital to a poor family's income while marriage customs such as dowry may cause a daughter to be seen as an economic burden.[178]

---

[177] Levinson and Bassett, "Malnutrition Is Still a Major Contributor," 1.
[178] For more on this topic, see the seventh chapter of this volume.

Tuberculosis

According to the World Health Organization, one-third of the world's population is infected with TB, and a new infection occurs every second. Furthermore, tuberculosis killed 1.6 million people in 2005, and with the spread of HIV, even more deaths are likely because "HIV and TB form a lethal combination, each speeding the other's progress."[179] Killing more women than either breast cancer or pregnancy and childbirth-related conditions, TB most often affects women of reproductive age.[180] Due to discrimination and the neglect of health care for women, they are less likely to receive the necessary treatment for TB. The World Health Organization understands that the control of tuberculosis is a gender issue that must be addressed.

HIV & AIDs

The impact of HIV and AIDS on children is overwhelming. The Joint United Nations Programme on HIV/AIDS (UNAIDS) reports that "children under 15 account for one in six AIDS-related deaths worldwide and one in seven new HIV infections."[181] Most of these cases occur through mother-to-child transmission, which means that the mothers have also been infected with HIV. In fact, "some 15 million children under 18 have lost one or both parents to AIDS," and many of these must learn to take care of themselves and their siblings when their parents have passed away. Sub-Saharan Africa remains the hardest-hit region.[182]

Half of all people infected with HIV are between fifteen and twenty-four years of age, and children who live on the streets, refugees, and children who are at risk of sexual abuse due to civil conflict, status, or poverty arethe most likely to become infected.[183] Sadly, millions

179 World Health Organization, "Tuberculosis," WHO March 2007, http://www.who.int/mediacentre/factsheets/fs104/en/index.html.
180 Department of Gender, Women and Health, "Gender in Tuberculosis Research," WHO 2004, 5, http://www.who.int/gender/documents/en/tuberculosislow.pdf.
181 Joint United Nations Programme on HIV/AIDS, "Children and Orphans," UNAIDS, http://www.unaids.org/en/PolicyAndPractice/KeyPopulations/ChildAndOrphans/.
182 Joint United Nations Programme on HIV/AIDS, "Children and Orphans."
183 Joint United Nations Programme on HIV/AIDS, "Young People," UNAIDS, http://www.unaids.org/en/PolicyAndPractice/KeyPopulations/YoungPeople/.

of girls across the globe experience these risks daily. Adolescent girls are at extreme risk due to sexual abuse and exploitation, lack of knowledge about how to protect themselves, and vulnerabilities due to their immature vaginal tracts that are at greater risk of tearing during intercourse. Seventy-five percent of young people who are living with HIV around the world are young women.[184]

As Peter Piot, executive director of UNAIDS, pointed out recently, "We are starting to see the real impact of this epidemic in the worst affected countries. We're starting to see a sort of reverse development— an undevelopment—because of the tremendous human and social capital loss to this epidemic."[185] AIDS is spreading like wildfire into other populous areas, including India, Russia, and China.

Furthermore, there is a direct link between a mother's and her children's health. Not only can HIV be passed from mother to child during pregnancy, childbirth, and breastfeeding, but the threats to child survival from death or disability of a parent with HIV and AIDS are numerous. Orphaned girl children are especially at risk of receiving inadequate health care; often they end up living on danger-filled city streets.

Some of the most tragic emerging trends in the AIDS situation are the harmful myths centered around cures for AIDS. South Africa, which already has one of the world's highest incidences of AIDS, has been in shock over a surge in the rape of children and even babies. Referring to the court case in which six men were being tried for the rape of a nine-month-old girl, Kelly Hatfield, director of a group called People Opposed to Women Abuse (POWA), stated:

---

184   Joint United Nations Programme on HIV/AIDS, "Women and Girls," UNAIDS, http://www.unaids.org/en/PolicyAndPractice/KeyPopulations/WomenGirls/.

185   Peter Piot, "Uniting the World against AIDS" (speech, Woodrow Wilson Center for Scholars, Washington, DC, September 20, 2007).

> *It's one case of many. A lot of it is to do with the myth that a man will be cured of AIDS by having sex with a virgin, and how much more virginal can you get than a baby?*[186]

Studies show that gender-based violence puts women and girls at higher risk for HIV infection. Often, cases of child rape and assault are committed by male relatives of the victims.[187]

GENDER-BASED VIOLENCE

Gender-based violence, now widely recognized as a major public health issue and a violation of human rights, includes domestic violence, rape, honor killings, female genital mutilation, and trafficking in children and women. Domestic violence, rape, and sexual exploitation are acts of violence against girls found in most cultures. Sexual exploitation is used as a weapon of war, for sex tourism, pornography, and a host of other profit-making schemes. In many countries, abuse of women flourishes, or at least is tolerated, because women have no legal rights.

Domestic Violence

Of all the threats of violence against women and girls, domestic violence perhaps is the most prevalent. Such violence has no geographic or economic boundaries; it strikes those in developed as well as developing countries, the rich as well as the poor. Such violence takes many forms but includes incest, rape, sexual, physical, emotional, and economic abuse. Domestic violence has an international counterpart, too. Each year an estimated 1.2 million women and girls are trafficked around the world for forced labor, domestic servitude, or sexual exploitation.[188]

---

186 Sue Thomas, "AIDS Myth Fuels S. Africa's Child-Rape Scourge," Reuters News Service, Johannesburg, November 5, 2002.
187 See UNAIDS, "HIV/AIDS and Gender-Based Violence," UNAIDS 2003, 1, http://data.unaids.org/Topics/Gender/genderbasedviolence_en.pdf.
188 UNICEF, "Children in Unconditional Worst Forms of Child Labour and Exploitation," *State of the World's Children 2006*, http://www.unicef.org/sowc06/pdfs/figure3_7.pdf.

Injuries to women who are abused range from cuts, bruises, and broken bones to permanent disability and death. Some common mental health problems resulting when women are abused include depression, post-traumatic stress disorder, suicide, and alcohol and drug use. Pregnancy loss from abortion, miscarriage, or stillbirth is more prevalent among abused women, and children also suffer many physical and mental illnesses as a result of living with conflict between parents. In homes where women are abused, children usually are also abused.

Sexual Exploitation

One cannot imagine the physical and emotional traumas of a seven-year-old child who, having being snatched from her home and locked in a filthy brothel, is told she must service ten men per night. Girls engaged in the commercial sex trade (including sex tourism and pornography) are at risk of contracting HIV and other sexually transmitted infections, are at high risk of suffering from gynecological problems, and are highly vulnerable to acts of violence, including physical assault and rape. They may also have difficulty with menstruation, frequent urinary tract infections, vaginal scarring and tears, and, in the future, difficulties in pregnancy and giving birth.

Armed Conflict

Children are the most vulnerable victims of war. War has claimed the lives of 2 million children in the past decade alone.[189] For the children who survive, they will endure poor nutrition, unhealthy conditions, and disrupted health care, as well as injury and trauma. Children must endure harsh living conditions as they are driven from their homes, facing long marches to places of safety. Struggling to survive in over-crowded refugee camps with unsanitary conditions, children face many health problems: malnutrition, diarrhea and dehydration, dysentery, cholera, acute respiratory infections, measles, typhoid, and malaria.

---

[189] Office of the Special Representative of the Secretary-General for Children and Armed Conflict, "Children Affected by Conflict," United Nations, http://www.un.org/special-rep/children-armed-conflict/index.html (accessed October 2, 2006).

The most vulnerable to these many health problems are children, especially the girl child.

Armed conflict results in the deterioration of the average level of health and nutrition. The myriad causes contributing to this include high levels of insecurity and displacement from jobs and farms, making procurement of food supplies difficult; lack of clean drinking water; and the disruption of vital preventive health care programs, including the provision of vaccinations. In the Darfur region of the Sudan, for example, though the country was free of polio from 2001 until 2004, civil conflict stopped children from receiving desperately needed vaccinations, and polio cases have been on the rise since 2004.[190]

At times when medical care is most urgently needed, medical services are often destroyed or forced to shut down. Girls, often enduring rape with a resulting pregnancy, are particularly affected because reproductive health care is not available for pre- and post-natal care, rape injuries, AIDS and other STDs, forced abortions, or infections. This causes infant and maternal mortality rates to soar during times of conflict.

SUMMARY

The girl child is confronted with many gender-related health problems. A world of discrimination is a challenging place for her to develop and grow in normal, healthy ways. The girl child so often exists simply in 'survival mode.' To leave this mode and enjoy fullness of life, it is crucial that girl child health issues have a central place in our interventions in girl child programs.

---

190   UNICEF, "Spread of Wild Polio Battled in Sudan with Additional Immunization Campaigns," UNICEF, http://www.unicef.org/media/media_23547.html.

Prevention and health needs of the girl child include the following:

- more female health workers and doctors;
- an understanding of her specific developmental needs, concerns, and outcomes;
- health clinics closer to home;
- emotional and mental health care;
- subsidized health care to encourage poor families to meet their daughters' needs;
- special care with nutrition and health needs addressed before and during adolescence;
- research conducted to show differences between girls' and boys' health and nutrition; and
- to be seen as equally valuable as their brothers—by families and societies.

Health issues must also be included in advocacy programs aimed at ending gender discrimination. The Church and society must understand the impact this has on the health, well-being, and survival of the girl child. Investments in better health care, safe motherhood, and improved education for girls and women have the potential to significantly improve the well-being of present and future generations of mothers and their children. Such investments will provide girls with hopes of a brighter tomorrow where their growth and development will not be impeded by unnecessary medical problems and disabilities.

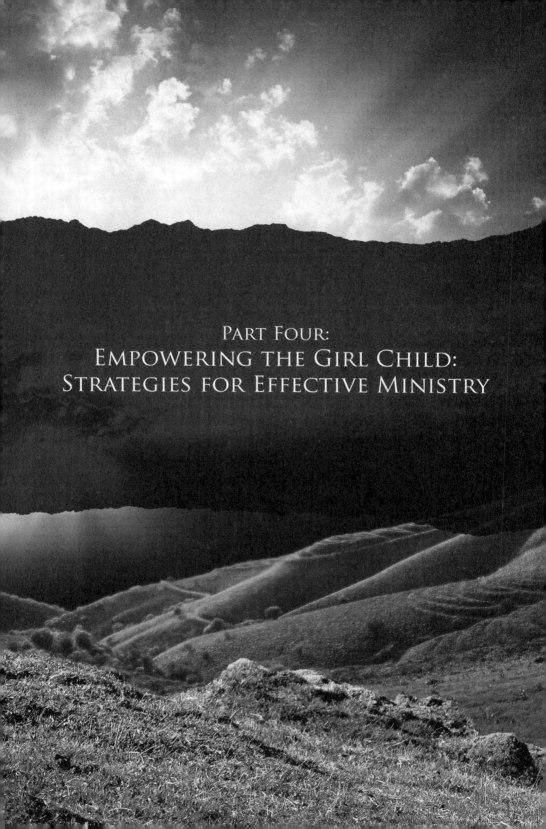

PART FOUR:
EMPOWERING THE GIRL CHILD:
STRATEGIES FOR EFFECTIVE MINISTRY

The girl child has the birthright to be loved and nurtured, to learn, to play, and to discover her community and world, and her rights and responsibilities within. And above all, she has the right to grow into her unique and full human potential, free from coercion, exploitation and abuse.

WORLD VISION CANADA, *GIRLS! STORIES WORTH TELLING*, 9

CHAPTER 10

AN OVERVIEW OF EFFECTIVE GIRL CHILD STRATEGIES

Desiree Segura-April

When I first began to research issues affecting the girl child, I was overwhelmed by the breadth of challenges girls face. How could we ever begin to address all of these issues? And yet, as Christians we are called to both become aware of the trials of "the least of these," *and* to do something to respond. We must go beyond our feelings of helplessness and seek to find ways to meet the needs of girls around the world, so that they might fulfill their God-given potential. In order for this to happen, we need to learn from those who are working directly with girl children, both in secular and Christian organizations. What are some strategies that are working? How can the Church implement and build upon these strategies? How can everyday people, like you and me, in local churches around the world begin to make a difference for the girls in their communities? These are the questions we will explore in this chapter.

THE GOAL OF ALL STRATEGIES

First of all, however, we must articulate the foundational vision or goal of all strategies for ministry with girl children. The Association of Women in Development (AWID) met in 1993 to discuss strategies for change that women have been using around the world in community development projects. Nearly 1,200 participants from almost every continent gathered to share their stories and compile suggestions for future work on behalf of women and girls. The United Nations Children's Fund (UNICEF) published the results of their gathering and stated, "Our vision for girl children is to free their bodies, so they are healthier, free their minds, so they can be productive economic players, and free their time, so they can be children."[191] This is the goal of all the strategies they suggest.

As Christians, we must add a spiritual dimension to this vision. The Gospel expands upon this by emphasizing the importance of freeing girls to become all that God has created them to be. The goal is that all girls might participate fully in the family of God and be free to use their unique God-given gifts, talents, and abilities in order to participate in building the kingdom of God. In 1992, World Vision affirmed this in their statement addressing the needs of girl children, stating that they seek to be an organization "that releases the girl child from all bondages that deprive her of her rightful place and potential in the world."[192] This vision or goal must be at the core of all of our strategies for ministry with girl children.

PRINCIPLES FROM EFFECTIVE STRATEGIES

With this as our foundation, let's now examine some of the general principles of effective strategies that emerge from most strategies for ministry with girl children.

---

[191] Kathleen M. Kurz and Cynthia J. Prather, *Improving the Quality of Life of Girls* (New York: United Nations Children's Fund, 1995), 9.

[192] World Vision quoted by Elnora Avarientos, "Today's Girl Is Tomorrow's Woman," *Together*, no. 49 (1996): 2.

INVOLVING GIRLS, FAMILIES, & COMMUNITY LEADERS

First and foremost, the girls themselves must be included in the development, implementation, and evaluation of the strategy. In 1998, World Vision Canada sponsored a conference called "Girls! Stories Worth Telling." This event brought together girls and practitioners from all over the world to share their stories and work together to develop an action plan on behalf of girls. Save the Children—Canada presented a workshop entitled "Child Focused Development" and described how girls (and boys) in a project in Bolivia played a very important role in contributing to their community's well-being.[193] In Colombia, three girls have been major leaders in a movement for peace in their country. They were actually nominated for the Nobel Peace Prize for their efforts![194] Obviously, they were much more than simply recipients of aid. They were vital actors in the transformation of their own lives, their entire community, and their nation. We must not simply attempt to design strategies for girls, but instead focus on working with girls.

We must not simply attempt to design strategies for girls, but instead focus on working with girls.

Not only must we involve the girls, but we must also involve their parents in our strategies. This is another principle emphasized by practitioners. Many development workers start with programs for educating mothers because mothers nurture children and pass along what they have learned. They are also identified as the most important agents of change for transforming customs and traditions in a community. Janet Museveni, the first lady of Uganda, describes mothers

---

193   World Vision Canada, *Girls! Stories Worth Telling: Report and Conference Manual* (Toronto: World Vision Canada, 1998), 23.

194   Pablo Carrillo, "Girls Lead Peace Effort in Colombia," *Together*, no. 58 (1998): 20-23; Dave Toycen, "Is Child-Focused Development Real Development?," *Together*, no. 65 (2000): 17.

as the "first line of defense for the child, especially the girl child."[195] She explains that in order to reach girls, we must plan strategies that teach mothers to value the life of girls differently and provide economic empowerment for families. Radha Paul, as director of gender and development for World Vision International, emphasized that education programs for mothers must go beyond literacy training and include well-planned educational strategies that seek to completely transform the way that women view girl children so that the way they treat them also changes.[196]

Along with mothers, we must also seek to educate fathers and other men in the community because they are often key decision-makers. This is where the Church has a unique opportunity. If the Gospel is truly "good news," then it should have the ability to completely transform a person's worldview and a community's value system. Secular development agencies agree that men must be involved in the process of change, and their views of women and girls must be transformed. However, full transformation can take place only as the Gospel is embraced and the Holy Spirit convicts people of the sinfulness of some of their beliefs and practices. Ultimately, if long-lasting change is to occur, there must be a partnership between men and women and the support of men in all gender issues.

A third related principle is that our strategies must also seek to transform the socialization and worldview of boys within communities. Since worldview is developed at a very young age through a process of socialization, it is logical that one way to change how men view women in a society is to transform what they are taught as boys. Therefore, our strategies must include interventions that challenge the way in which boys are socialized, and educate boys about the issues that girls face so that they too can be agents of change in their society.

Having said that boys must be included in our strategies, a somewhat paradoxical principle that practitioners stress is the importance of

---

195 Janet K. Museveni, "Cultural, Political and Social Empowerment of Girl Children," in *The Girl Child: Enhancing Life, Sustaining Hope 1998 Washington Forum*, ed. The Institute for Global Engagement (Federal Way, WA: The Institute for Global Engagement; World Vision Inc., 1998), 24.

196 Radha Paul, "What About the Girl Child?," *Together*, no. 65 (2000): 13–14.

specifically targeting girls in programs offered for all children. Although most community development or church programs are offered to both boys and girls, in some settings, the programs are underused by girls due to cultural biases. Where this is true, we must intentionally design strategies to meet the special needs of girls and encourage and enable girls to participate.

UNDERSTANDING CULTURAL CONTEXTS

Another important general principle is the need to understand the particular culture within which one is ministering with girls. Every strategy must be adapted to the cultural context, and some strategies may not be feasible in certain settings. A thorough understanding of the social, cultural, and religious situation related to girls within each particular culture is necessary before attempting to design a strategy for ministry.

In order for any strategy to bring about lasting change, it must eventually address the root causes of the obstacles that girls face. As was mentioned above, a society's beliefs about the status and role of women are passed on through the socialization process and the formation of worldview among its members. Thus, an effective strategy must at some level address the worldview of people and seek to bring about a transformation within it. Changing laws and policies is not enough: attitudes and behaviors must also be changed, which necessitates a worldview change among members of a community. A careful understanding of the cultural context is necessary for this to occur.

Since this transformation of worldview involves the entire community, our strategies must have a communal component, especially within community/family-centered cultures, which is another prevailing principle found within effective strategies. Helping individual girls will not provide sustainable, systemic change; we must seek the transformation of whole communities. Our strategies must help people build relationships and foster a sense of community among girls and within the wider circles of a society. At the same time, we must recognize that each individual girl is important and worthy of our efforts and whole communities can be changed one life at a time. Nevertheless, the whole community should participate in the process of change.

This leads to the idea that a goal within all strategies must be to persuade families, communities, and nations that fulfilling the potential of girls is a wise investment. Unfortunately, in many societies, this is not believed to be true. As mentioned in previous chapters, girls are often seen as an economic liability, especially in cultures where bride price, dowry, and ancestor veneration are practiced. However, development experts say that female literacy is a determining factor for how quickly a country is able to "move up" on the "national curve of transformation and sustainability. [In fact], how a nation treats, honors and respects the girl child will determine whether that nation gets on the curve at all."[197] All strategies must include a component that changes peoples' perception at all levels, such that girls are seen as contributing to the national economic welfare, rather than hindering it.

BOTH ADVOCACY & PROGRAMMING

In order to change this perception, strategies will need to include both advocacy and program elements. Much of what is needed to bring about changes for girls must be done by advocates for them at a variety of levels within each society and worldwide. Girls need us to be a voice for them and to help them find their voices at the family, community, and national levels. This will include being advocates among their parents and extended family, especially in family-centered cultures; among community leaders, including religious leaders; and with policy-makers at different governmental levels.

However, changing policies and speaking out on behalf of girls must go hand-in-hand with developing programs designed to specifically

---

[197] Robert A. Seiple, "A Rent in the Garment," in *The Girl Child: Enhancing Life, Sustaining Hope 1998 Washington Forum*, ed. The Institute for Global Engagement (Federal Way, WA: The Institute for Global Engagement, World Vision Inc., 1998), 14.

meet their needs and empower them to fulfill their potential. Within each culture, these programs and projects will look different, but it is clear that we must be intentional in providing a wide range of special services in order to bring about long-term, sustainable change.

As we seek to advocate and design effective programs, we as individuals and as Christian groups desiring to develop ministry strategies must be willing to first analyze our own attitudes, behaviors, and teachings. Again, these will be widely varied based on our own cultural background, but if we are to be successful in designing programs that challenge the "status quo," we must understand how we contribute to and participate in the very structures we are trying to change. This is especially important in regard to our doctrines, teachings, and practices within the Christian Church. Unfortunately, these have often contributed to the obstacles girls face, rather than challenging them. Thus, we must seek to understand our own beliefs and claim the power of the Holy Spirit for transformation. We must ask in what way we contribute to the stereotypes and gender biases in our homes, schools, communities, churches, vocations, and so on.

THEOLOGICAL COMMITMENTS

As we begin to understand our own biases, we must agree to certain biblical and theological understandings if we are to work together on behalf of girls around the world and in our local communities.[198] While Christian beliefs about the place and roles of women and children may vary, we must come to a fundamental understanding that views all human beings as created in the image of God and of equal value in God's sight. We must agree that girls in every society, albeit in different ways and to varying degrees of severity, are hindered from developing fully the gifts that God has given them. Our common goal for all strategies must be to seek ways by which we can help girls to develop these gifts in order to serve God and society, and to participate fully in the kingdom of God.

---

[198] For more on this topic, please refer to the second chapter in this volume.

Along with these theological understandings, another general principle is that our strategies must be transformational in nature. The Christian Gospel offers a unique power for transformation within society, and it is only through abiding in and proclaiming the name of Jesus that any strategy for change in the lives of girls will bring hope to them. Christ truly provides hope for the hopeless, and this must be at the core of all our strategies.

Finally, we must recognize that any strategy we develop will contain an element of risk and danger because it is inherently going to challenge the "status quo" and power structures within the society. Thus, there will likely be opposition to our efforts. Anyone desiring to develop a ministry with girl children must be aware of this risk. As Christians, we are called, I believe, to take this chance on behalf of those who have been oppressed and treated unjustly. Yet, we must never enter into this task lightly, or without a great deal of spiritual discernment, prayer, and the empowerment of the Holy Spirit.

SEVERAL EFFECTIVE STRATEGIES

With these general principles for all strategies in mind, we can now begin to look at some specific strategies that could be put into action by Christians around the world. Just as the obstacles and challenges that girls face are varied, so must the strategies be. The complexities of dealing with cultural issues and the interwoven nature of the problems make it such that to suggest that all strategies will work in all contexts would be presumptuous. It bears repeating that we must always be sensitive to the specific culture, tradition, value system, and other contexts of the girls with whom we are ministering. As well, certain strategies will apply at particular stages in a girl's life, while in other stages, different strategies will be more appropriate and effective. Therefore, as we look at a compilation of strategies, we must always remember that not all strategies are needed or even appropriate for all settings. The goal of the remainder of this chapter, then, is simply to provide some examples of strategies and suggest ways in which local churches might learn from and build upon these examples.

RESEARCH & EVALUATION

First, let's explore some general strategies suggested by those who work specifically with ministries and programs directed at girl children. At the research level, it is crucial that we advocate for researchers to gather and analyze data separately for boys and girls and for different ages of females. Historically, girl children have tended to be lumped together either with boys under the category "children" or with adult females under the category "women." This has contributed to the invisibility of the girl child because there is a relative lack of information specifically about her. Therefore, one strategy would be to participate in and advocate for research that is very intentional about gathering data about gender and age. This type of research lays the foundation for more specific strategies.

Another issue related to research is the lack of measures for evaluating the effectiveness of programs and projects for girl children. Both World Vision and UNICEF in a variety of sources mentioned that while the strategies and effective practices they described seemed to be improving the lives of girls, none had been adequately evaluated to determine actual success rates.[199] Therefore, another step in developing strategies for ministry with girls would be to incorporate evaluation measures to determine what practices are successful and what improvements are needed. As well, resources and personnel could be provided for research that would evaluate the effectiveness of existing programs and projects for girls to provide information for those seeking to develop further strategies for ministry.

RAISING CONSCIOUSNESS

Another general strategy focuses on raising consciousness about the issues that girls are facing. When I tell people that I'm studying "the girl child," I always have to explain what I mean by that and

---

[199] Kurz and Prather, *Improving the Quality of Life of Girls*; World Vision Canada, *Girls! Stories Worth Telling*; World Vision, ed. *The Girl Child: Enhancing Life Sustaining Hope* 1998 Washington Forum (Federal Way, WA: The Institute for Global Engagement, World Vision, Inc., 1998).

why it is an important area of study because most people have never considered girls as having unique issues and challenges, let alone as a "topic of study." I must first raise consciousness before I can even begin to delve deeper into the issues. This strategy is seemingly simple, yet profoundly important, because every person in every local church can work toward making the situation of girls more visible. As was mentioned above, the situation of girls is often invisible in statistical data and children's ministries. In order to spur people on to work for a cause, they must first be made aware of the cause.

World Vision Canada has produced an excellent resource for making presentations that can help educate people about the issues girls face and promote discussions leading to action. The kit includes three short video clips, overheads, handouts, commonly asked questions, presentations, resource lists, suggested solutions, basic background information about the issues, and ideas for discussion-starters.[200] They have also produced two other longer video resources that would be helpful in presentations, workshops, classes, or discussions.[201] We should seek to develop more resources like these to help raise awareness among the general public in our churches and communities.

TAKING ACTION

While research and consciousness-raising are important first steps, we must always seek to move beyond discussion and into action. Let's now explore some of the strategies that have been put into practice in a variety of places in the world. Again, the issues girls face are varied and complex depending on the specific culture, time, and place in which the girl child is raised. Thus, the specific strategies are equally varied and have different layers of complexity. For purposes of clarity, we'll discuss several strategies within each of the four general categories identified at the "Girls! Stories Worth Telling" conference mentioned

---

200 World Vision Canada, *Children at Risk Tool-Kit: Girl Children: The Potential Is Powerful* (Mississauga, ON: World Vision Canada, 1996). Available upon request from info@worldvision.ca.

201 Meta Media Productions and World Vision Canada, *Evening the Odds: The Story of the Girl Child* (Mississauga, ON: Meta Media Productions and World Vision Canada, 1996), video recording; World Vision Canada, et al., *Girls! Stories Worth Telling Video* (Toronto: World Vision Canada, March 2–6, 1998), video recording.

above. These categories include Education, Health and Nutrition, Exploitation, and Violence. We must always keep in mind, however, that many of the issues overlap within these categories, and thus the strategies will also. Therefore, we must seek to approach any strategy wholistically and be careful to assess how it fits into the larger picture of helping girls fulfill all of their God-given potential.

EDUCATION

Let's look first at the category of "Education." This is the area that currently presents the most hope for change; education is widely accepted to be the key to human progress. If prosperity is measured by economics, "economists and development experts now recognize that there are no prosperous nations that have a large segment of a population that is illiterate, and there are no illiterate nations where there is any form of sustainable prosperity."[202] Therefore, educating more girls would contribute substantially to lowering illiteracy rates, which in turn would help nations become more prosperous.

Action & Evaluation of Secular Educational Settings

As countries begin to understand the benefits of educating girls, the Church has a great opportunity to respond in this area. One vital role that churches can take is in educating parents about the value of educating their girls. We can also work with local Christians to encourage laws that require equal access for girls to compulsory, high-quality, relevant education. Where this is not feasible, churches could provide educational opportunities, ministries, and programs for girls, just as Sunday School was originally started for poor children who had to work and couldn't attend school during the week.

Many organizations offer Christians the opportunity to sponsor children and help provide the necessary funding for their education. World Vision is dedicated to sponsoring both girls and boys, even in communities where culture and tradition discourage the education of

---

[202] Seiple, "A Rent in the Garment," 11.

girls. Churches and community members could intentionally choose to sponsor girls and to assure that the sponsorship agency chosen is being intentional about programs with girls.

We could also help to provide financial support to families and specifically to girls with household responsibilities. Educational opportunities in developing countries must be designed to enable girls to perform their household duties *and* attend school. One way to do this is to help build schools in rural areas so girls can continue with their household expectations, but still be educated. Christians should also challenge societies to widen their perception of education to include academic, life skills, and vocational skills training and to recognize the learning that takes place in non-formal and informal settings.

As well, churches can encourage schools and teachers to be sensitized to the way in which boys and girls are treated differently and seek to treat them equally. Educational materials must be analyzed for gender stereotyping and sensitivity. In countries like the United States, we must challenge our school systems to consider gender biases and stereotyping in their classrooms. While it is perhaps more subtle, there is still a great deal that goes on in "developed" countries' classrooms to contribute to a devaluing of girls. Christians must speak out against this and seek strategies for educational reforms.

Finally, girls should be included in decision-making related to education, and the Church could encourage and help provide for girls a variety of mentors and role models, including female educators who have the same status and opportunities as male educators.

Action & Evaluation in Christian Education & Church Settings

As we advocate for the education of girls, we must also remember that faith development goes hand-in-hand with physical, emotional, and cognitive development. The Church must also seek to work with families to provide biblical education and spiritual nurture. The Church may have the unique opportunity to provide education through Bible teaching for girls who may not have that chance elsewhere.

Christian educators should also be very sensitive to the materials they use to ensure that they are gender inclusive. Since children think concretely,

> *When they hear man or the pronouns he or his, girls know that those words exclude them. They cannot comprehend man as a generic word. By the time they have the cognitive skills to deal with this concept, many of their expectations and beliefs are already established. Because we have used male words and masculine images for God so extensively, we have conveyed an incomplete image of God that children carry into adulthood.*[203]

It is crucial that educators in the Church consider this and make an effort to use inclusive language, both for humans and for God. Vogel suggests some good questions churches can ask themselves to measure how they may be unintentionally teaching children gender stereotypes. These include the following: Do men teach young children? Do women teach adults? Do both men and women help take the offering, serve communion, lead in worship, preach, and serve in the kitchen? In Sunday school curricula, are the stories about biblical women included? Do the contemporary applications of biblical truths portray men and women inclusively and in a wide variety of roles? Do we model equality in the classrooms by asking girls and boys to do the same tasks? Part of helping girls overcome their obstacles in the area of education includes the Church intentionally seeking to educate girls and boys in an inclusive way and not to perpetuate gender stereotypes.

---

[203]   Linda J. Vogel, "Teach These Words to Your Children," *Daughters of Sarah* 16, no. 5 (1990): 10.

Educating Families & Communities

Not only must we seek strategies for educating girls, but we must also consider within this category the importance of educating others in their lives. We've already discussed the vital role of mothers, fathers, and other community leaders in making changes for girls. Education is one of the key ways by which these people can be reached. It is especially important that non-formal educational strategies be developed by which women can learn new ways of valuing their girls, along with skills that can help to empower them economically. As well, parents need to be educated about the promotion of the acceptance of girl babies, appropriate stimulation and early childhood education, alternative rites of passage where female genital mutilation is practiced, and the benefits of postponing early marriages in cultures where this is prevalent.

Through informal modes of communication, such as workshops, seminars, or community gatherings, the Church can participate in this educational process. Once again, it bears mentioning that cultural sensitivity is extremely important when designing any curriculum, and yet the Christian Gospel must be brought to bear on these cultural practices. Sunday school classes may also be a place where people can grapple with the issues and explore what the Bible says about the value of girls and the way they should be treated.

HEALTH & NUTRITION

Let us now turn our attention to the next general category of "Health and Nutrition" and some strategies that we can implement to combat obstacles girls face in this area. If the Gospel is truly good news, should it not speak to the whole being, including the physical needs? These needs are at the basic level of survival for girls, and the Church can work with communities to ensure that girls have access to adequate food, shelter, and health care. UNICEF suggests that strategies in this area are especially important at the birth, infancy, and adolescent stages of a girl's life.[204]

---

[204] Kurz and Prather, *Improving the Quality of Life of Girls.*

Health Education, Advocacy, & Services

The Church must speak out against cultural practices such as selective abortions of female fetuses and female infanticide. Christians could develop an intentional strategy of adopting female babies from countries where these practices still occur. Cultural traditions of feeding girls last with the least nutritious food must be challenged in a culturally sensitive and appropriate manner. Churches could also provide nutrition education and supplementation to combat malnutrition among girls. Parents must be encouraged to utilize health programs, such as immunizations, equally for both boys and girls.

We must seek ways to provide adolescent girls with education about preventing sexually transmitted diseases and unwanted pregnancy. Churches could establish support ministries for pregnant teenagers and mothers, including education about prenatal care and birth spacing. Local Christians should advocate for the abolition of the unhealthy practice of genital mutilation in countries where this is practiced. Alternative ceremonies should be developed and practiced.[205] We must challenge unhealthy images of sexuality and female bodies portrayed in the media, while encouraging the nurture of girls' self-esteem and positive body images. A biblical response to all issues of health includes lifting up the value of life—all stages of life—because everyone is made in God's image.

Spiritual Well-being Equally Important

Along with meeting physical needs, Christians must also be concerned about the spiritual health of girls. "Definite theological concepts do not appear to develop until later in childhood. However, *impressions* and *awareness* early in childhood are very influential in forming the foundation for theological concepts later on."[206] Girls who are not cared for appropriately, especially as infants and in early childhood, will likely have a strong need to be valued and loved.

---

205 This concept will be discussed in further detail later in this chapter. For more on FGM, please see the third, seventh, and ninth chapters in this volume.

206 Robert E. Clark, et al., *Childhood Education in the Church*, rev. ed. (Chicago: The Moody Bible Institute, 1986), 349.

Their faith development may be significantly hampered by the lack of love and positive caretakers. The Church must recognize this and seek to minister to girls wholistically.

EXPLOITATION

Just as girls are often neglected physically and spiritually, they are also often exploited physically and sexually. This leads us to an exploration of strategies related to our next general category: "Exploitation." In this arena, girl children seem to have a sort of "double jeopardy" due to both their age and their gender being devalued in many societies. Girls tend to be one of the most vulnerable populations in the world for exploitation; in fact, some would argue, they are *the most* vulnerable. While boys are also exploited in factories, workshops, and other public-sector arenas, the exploitation of girls takes place in the private-sector workplace as well. Sexual exploitation is also much more likely to involve girls than boys.

Raising Public Awareness

How can Christians respond to the devastating exploitation of girls? The first step is to recognize that there is a problem. Although some governments are taking action, officials often look the other way. Christians must become advocates for exploited children so that governments will take notice of the problem, especially in the arena of sexual exploitation where they often won't admit it occurs. We must seek to raise public awareness about the risks and degradation of the commercial sex trade, as well as other exploitative labor practices.

As advocates, Christians must be willing to challenge multinational corporations to be responsible in their labor practices and working conditions. As well, we can advocate for independent monitoring of working conditions, age limits, wage equity among girls and boys, and flexible hours for children in order to allow for education and other activities. Often, girls have actually been sold into slavery or bonded labor. In those cases, we can raise funds to buy them back from slavery or partner with families to repay their loans to release bonded children from labor. It is crucial that along with this we help girls and families find alternative income sources so that they don't seek income in even more destructive trades, such as prostitution.

We must also challenge societies (including our own) to recognize the achievements of girls and women in non-traditional jobs, recognize that housework is everyone's responsibility, and insist that work at home be shared by both sexes. Finally, we must humbly ask the Holy Spirit to convict of the sinfulness of these exploitative practices and to lead us into action to prevent them from continuing.

Sexual Exploitation & Empowerment Girls

At the "Girls! Stories Worth Telling" conference mentioned above, several effective practices for dealing with sexual exploitation and the empowerment of girls were presented.[207] One presentation discussed the strategy of extending micro-business loans to marginalized young women and girls. Churches can help to provide small enterprise development and revolving loan programs, which have proved very successful, especially among young women. Another suggestion includes providing shelter, education, and skills training for street children and vulnerable girls to keep them from resorting to the streets and/or prostitution.

A video presentation about young girls involved in prostitution suggested that education is a key strategy for helping girls come out of this destructive lifestyle. Another presentation on the trafficking of girls in Nepal demonstrated that although there are legal sanctions against it, the practice is actually increasing. In order to combat this, strategists must understand the cycle of poverty and seek interventions that address the economics of this problem. Girls Clubs in schools were another effective practice that showed how providing a space for girls to come together to share ideas, build their self-esteem, and receive training can help to combat the likelihood of them falling into the exploitation trap.

---

[207] Clark, et al., *Childhood Education in the Church*, B-iv.

VIOLENCE

Finally, an arena closely related and often overlapping with exploitation is violence committed against girls, our last category. "The major and most devastating consequences of female gender-directed violence are borne by girls. [In the U.S.] 'one out of three girls is molested before the age of 18 as compared to one out of ten boys.'"[208] The types of violence are varied, ranging from emotional, physical, and sexual abuse to harmful cultural practices. Female genital mutilation, forced early marriage, foot binding, rape, sexual harassment, dowry customs, the *sati* (burning widows with their husbands at the funeral pyre), and other traditional practices are among these forms of violence against girls. Other indirect areas of violence include street gang involvement, drug-related abuse, female infanticide, and selective abortion based on gender. "From birth to the grave, throughout much of our allegedly 'modern' world, violence marks the lives of those born girls. We should not be surprised when girls are used, at best, as human workhouses, and, at worst, as human shields in time of war."[209]

Alternative Ceremonies & Practices

Certainly one must be very careful in passing immediate judgment about some of these customs because they are often an integral part of cultural traditions within these societies. It is important that Christians consider the role and function fulfilled by these practices, such as serving as a rite of passage from girlhood to adulthood. Our strategies must attempt to rescue as much of the cultural meanings as possible, while seeking to transform the harmful nature of the practices. Alternative ceremonies and practices can maintain much from the traditional practices without perpetuating the violence of these customs.

---

[208] Neera Kuckreja Sohoni, *The Burden of Girlhood: A Global Inquiry into the Status of Girls* (Oakland, CA: Third Party Publishing Co., 1995), 134.

[209] Seiple, "A Rent in the Garment," 9.

Save the Children worked with some local women in a village in Kenya to develop an alternative ceremony to female genital mutilation for girls at puberty.[210] Through many discussions and gatherings, they gained the approval of the male leaders as well. Some of those men worked with the women and girls to develop the alternative rite of passage. They maintained many of the elements of the tradition, such as education about womanhood, seclusion, gift giving, feasting, dancing, and so on. The new practice is now widely accepted in the village and has even spread to some of the surrounding areas. As Christians, we should seek to develop rites of passage where Christian values for sexuality can be passed on, while still respecting those cultural traditions not harmful to girls.

Advocacy, Support, & Healing

Along with seeking transformed ceremonies and practices, Christians must become stronger advocates for girls in order to combat violence. They must challenge governments to establish and enforce laws that protect girls (and all people) against violence of all types. Raising consciousness about the harmful effects of these practices on girls and teaching about them is another important role the church can play. As well, schools and communities must be encouraged to create safe environments for children.

Churches can also provide support groups and healing programs for girls who experience violence, along with support programs for abusers. Since the girl's "lesser status within the family and society... accounts for her greater abuse, it is vital that a new order of family functioning be devised enabling equality between the sexes. The myths and values which support a dominator and dominated inter-personal and global world need to be discarded in favor of equitable domestic and societal relationships."[211] The Gospel, as a transformer of myths and values, has the power to help the world to move toward this goal. The Church must preach this Gospel as one that speaks against the

---

210 World Vision Canada, *Girls! Stories Worth Telling*, 24.
211 Sohoni, *The Burden of Girlhood*, 165.

abuse of power that results in violence. Finally, through relationships and teaching, we must seek to help girls see themselves not as victims but rather as persons with great potential to have significance in life, despite what has happened to them.

THE CHALLENGE TO THE CHURCH

As you can see, there are so many strategies to explore, and in this short chapter, we have not been able to go into depth about them all. It is important to note, however, that the challenges girls face related to gender stereotyping in schools and media, eating disorders, and so on are seemingly more subtle and perhaps less problematic than others, such as selective abortion, unequal access to education, early marriage, or female genital mutilation. Yet, we must always keep in mind that many of these practices are based on cultural traditions that we may not understand. What may seem abhorrent in one culture may be perfectly acceptable in another, at least according to tradition and custom, and vice versa.

This is where I believe that Scripture and the Gospel must be allowed to transform a culture. As Christians, we believe there are some moral absolutes, but we have to be very careful to allow these to be biblically based and not culturally biased. All cultures have areas that need to be redeemed by Christ and transformed by the Holy Spirit. Obviously, I believe that the obstacles for girls described herein are areas in need of transformation in the cultures in which they occur. However, I also must recognize that it is only through the power of the Holy Spirit empowering the Church in each of these communities, and through truly biblical, contextual responses that this transformation should and will happen.

These suggestions provide some small and other rather large steps Christians could take toward helping girls overcome the obstacles they often face simply because they were born female. Unfortunately, until the Church recognizes that these problems exist, I fear that very few steps at all will be taken. The task seems overwhelming, and yet, when one considers that these issues face one-fifth of the population of the world, the issues cannot simply be ignored. Even if girls did not make up that much of the total population, they are still God's creations, and thus, every single one is precious in God's sight. It is time for the Church to become aware of the obstacles they face, and to respond, not only for the sake of the future women the girls will become, but also for the sake of the precious human beings they now are.

> *It is time for the Church to become aware of the obstacles they face, and to respond, not only for the sake of the future women the girls will become, but also for the sake of the precious human beings they now are.*

Who will accept the challenge? The Church can no longer leave this task only to those who work in the development field, such as World Vision and UNICEF. Bob Seiple, former president of World Vision, in reflecting on a visit to the Sudan where he found not a single little girl left in one village, remarked:

> *Wherever little girls are left behind, the world is less than whole. Indeed, the world is put at risk. I firmly believe this sorrow causes our Lord to weep. Who will be the world's conscience on behalf of the girl child? Who will hold us accountable? Who will cry for those who no longer have a voice?*[212]

With fear and trepidation, I pray that many will answer with me, "I will, Lord. I will cry out for girls." I have chosen this response not only because I once was a little girl, but also because I firmly believe that

---

[212] Seiple, "A Rent in the Garment," 15.

they are being overlooked, and they are precious in God's sight. May God give all of us the wisdom, stamina, and courage needed to put into action some of these strategies on behalf of the girls in our local communities and around the world.

Educate every child. All girls and boys must have access to and complete primary education that is free, compulsory and of good quality as a cornerstone of an inclusive basic education. Gender disparities in primary and secondary education must be eliminated.

UNITED NATIONS, *A WORLD FIT FOR CHILDREN*

CHAPTER 11

EMPOWERING THROUGH EDUCATION

Phyllis Kilbourn

Eight-year-old Muniamma blows on the kindling to help it catch fire, screwing up her eyes as the smoke billows toward her. She puts the pot of rice on to boil, hoists her two-year-old brother onto her hip, and sets off with her empty pitcher.

On her way back from the well, she collects her six-year-old brother from school and gives him lunch. Shouldn't she herself be at school?

Her mother arrives home from working in the fields, and says to herself, what would Muniamma learn in school? Here at home she is learning all she needs to know: a woman's work. Besides, who else could look after the young children in the day?[213]

---

[213] UNICEF, *The Lesser Child: The Girl in India* (UNICEF/Government of India, 1989), 3.

According to the United Nations, education is a basic human right, not a luxury for the rich. Education is an essential hope-offering intervention strategy due to its lifelong impact on the quality of life. World Vision states, "Formal education is recognized as a major tool in developing human capabilities, transmitting knowledge and cultural heritage and improving the quality of life."[214] Yet poverty and traditional values and customs keep millions of girls from receiving the education that is necessary to equip them to raise healthy families and participate in community development. Lack of opportunity for an education is a key factor in loss of hope for girl children such as Muniamma.

GENDER EQUITY

Fennema defines gender equity as the set of behaviors and knowledge that permits educators to recognize inequality in educational opportunities, to carry out specific interventions that constitute equal education treatment, and to ensure equal educational outcomes.[215] By this definition, educational equity for girls means equity for everyone.

By following gender equity guidelines to improve education, it is improved for boys as well as for girls. The goal of better serving girls does not entail neglecting or suppressing boys. By putting boys and girls on an equal plane, the relatively increased valuing of girls will also benefit boys by informing them of the strengths, capabilities, and contributions of girls and women. This, in turn, may help decrease the pressure many boys feel to conform to traditional roles, behaviors, and ways of thinking. Eventually, the stereotypes may be counteracted and eliminated so education may begin to be more gender-balanced.

---

214   World Vision, ed., *The Girl Child: Enhancing Life Sustaining Hope 1998 Washington Forum* (Federal Way, WA: The Institute for Global Engagement, World Vision, Inc., 1998), 7.

215   Elizabeth Fennema, "Justice, Equity, and Mathematics Education," in *Mathematics and Gender*, eds. Elizabeth Fennema and Gilah C. Leder (Baltimore: The John Hopkins University Press, 1990), 1–9.

OBSTACLES TO GIRLS' EDUCATION

In almost every region of the world, gender discrimination is all-encompassing and unrelenting, affecting all aspects of a girl's life. The powerful nature of this discrimination becomes evident when a family or a society determines whether or not to send girls to school, and even girls who are allowed to attend school are still not free of gender discrimination. To this day, two-thirds of all people across the globe who cannot read are female.[216] Girl children daily face obstacles that prevent them from fully participating in the educational process or cause them to drop out altogether.

The barriers to girls' education stem from complex cultural and economic practices that favor boys over girls along with a host of other complicating factors. The following are but a few of the multifaceted obstacles that hinder a girl's education.[217]

POVERTY

In poor areas, both boys and girls may miss out on opportunities for schooling. Sometimes, schools are too far away for children to attend. Other times, parents struggle to provide food and shelter for their families, and they simply cannot afford to pay for the required school fees and uniforms. They also frequently feel pressure to keep children home to work for them.

In western nations, poverty also affects the quality of education children receive, especially from lack of home encouragement and enrichment experiences that would help them achieve their educational goals. For many, college is not an option. In Illinois (USA), for example, approximately 46 percent of the single mothers have incomes that are at or below the poverty level and another 12 percent are near the poverty level. Women's low earnings have a direct impact on the number of

---

216   Astrida Neimanis and Arkadi Tortisyn, *Gender Thematic Guidance Note*, National Human Development Report Series (UNDP Human Development Report Office, July 2003), 6.

217   For more on this topic, please refer to chapter 3 of this volume.

children living in poverty in Illinois, currently one in five.[218] Women continue to be over-represented in the lowest-paid, lowest opportunity jobs in the economy. Money for school lunches, clothing, and materials puts a drain on already sparse funds.

COMMUNITY ATTITUDES & VALUES

In situations of poverty, girls are more likely to miss out on education because of community attitudes and values. Those who are pregnant or young mothers are often excluded from classroom attendance. A foundational principle of educational systems is the promotion of equality of access, participation, and benefit for all children. Nevertheless, research into community practices often demonstrates real discrimination against girls when it comes to education. Children living in poverty often have fewer educational opportunities, and discrimination, preferential attitudes toward boys, and rejecting attitudes toward girls cause girls to have even fewer educational opportunities. Societies do not realize that they are not just harming the children but also the future of their community and nation.

Preferential Treatment of Boys

Teachers as well as parents often give preferential treatment to boys. Greater value is placed on the boy because daughters are expected to marry young, have children, and run a household. Therefore, in some countries, a boy's education is considered a better investment since one day he will be the one to earn a living and care for his aging parents. Thus, boys are given the "first in line" privilege when educational opportunities are passed around. As a result, they are more apt to make a higher salary than girls.

On the other hand, an educational investment in a girl will never be recouped because one day she will belong to her husband's family. And sometimes it is the potential husband, especially from rural areas, who

---

218 Gender Equity Advisory Committee, *Ensuring Equal Opportunity for All Youth and Adults in the Education and Workforce Preparation System* (Springfield, IL: Illinois State Board of Education, 2002), 1, http://www.isbe.net/career/pdf/perkins_equity.pdf.

fears marrying a girl who is 'too educated.' An educated girl expressing her own ideas and opinions is a perceived threat that he might not want to risk encountering.

Role of the Girl Child

The girl child's role is seen as caregiver for younger children, cooking, working in the fields, carrying water, doing housework, or performing other domestic duties. Some parents do not feel that girls have the capacity for studies. And since it is assumed they will not work in the future, parents do not see a need to educate the girls. A proverb in one Southeast Asian country states, "A woman's brain cannot perceive anything further than the handle of a spoon."[219]

> *A proverb in one Southeast Asian country states, "A woman's brain cannot perceive anything further than the handle of a spoon."*

CULTURAL & PARENTAL BELIEFS

Education is perceived as a threat to traditional cultures; society fears that education will result in a girl becoming immoral, perhaps even a prostitute, and failing to uphold traditional thought. She will no longer be respectful to her elders and will become uncontrollable. In the worst-case scenario, an educated girl might even change and challenge the culture and tradition.

Parents fear that education will ruin their daughters' marriage prospects, and that it will make them reject the traditional roles of the submissive wife, mother, and homemaker. She will have an opportunity to work, become financially independent, and have a choice of whom she will marry. In addition, the more educated a girl is, the higher her dowry or bride price becomes, thus giving her fewer opportunities for marriage.

---

[219] World Vision Australia, *Education for All* (Compiled by Information Services, World Vision Australia, 1993), 3.

To avoid these traditional threats, girls are denied an education and kept under the control of their fathers, husbands, and brothers. Society and parental attitudes are summed up in the words of an African educator, "No man wants a well-educated wife. Women who talk back to men stay unmarried."[220]

SCHOOL-BASED FACTORS

After their struggles to reach the classroom, girls often find they are still denied a fulfilling educational experience. They soon discover that the school system itself plays a significant role in creating and maintaining gender differences. A girl's learning and self-esteem soon are undermined by lessons and textbooks full of messages suggesting that girls are less important than boys or are not as capable to learn. Various studies, including a major one conducted in Zambia,[221] reveal several school-based factors that affect girls' participation and performance at school.

School Location

Long walking distances to school affect school attendance in rural and many urban areas. Often, girls are too tired to concentrate on schoolwork after the long walk. Also, they are less able to cope with the physical hazards such as flooded rivers, rocky escarpments, or wild animals that they may encounter en route. Parents often weigh up the value of the time the girl spends walking to school against the workload she could undertake if the same time were spent at home. Parents are also concerned lest girls who take the same long route to and from school every day may be sexually molested.

School Infrastructure

Many girls state that the school facilities and infrastructures available to them do little to attract them to attend school but rather dissuade

---

220   UNICEF, *Education of the Girl Child: Her Right, Society's Gain* (UNICEF, 1992).
221   Ministry of Education Lusaka, *Girls' Education: A Situational Analysis at the Provincial level of Girl Child Education in Zambia* (Lusaka, Zambia: Programme for the Advancement of Girls' Education, 1999).

them. Instead of school officials addressing girls' special concerns such as having adequate sanitation facilities, sufficient supplies of clean water, and adequate school facilities, the needs expressed by the boys—such as sport equipment and facilities—are given priority. Even the few desks that may be available in the classroom are usually first assigned to boys, requiring the girls to either sit on the floor or to crowd into the few remaining seats.

Quality of Schooling

Low levels of real learning achievement discourage girls from spending time and effort that, in their estimation, will not help them better their lot in life. Along with poor facilities and learning resources, often too much time is spent on manual work such as working on their teacher's farm or involvement in school or community cleanup projects, leaving little learning time in the classroom. A girl's responsibilities to help in the home also leave little time for completing homework assignments outside the classroom.

Sometimes, the curriculum is not relevant to the girls' needs and is gender-biased. Many of the books and illustrations portray women and girls in subordinate, unchallenging, "helpless" roles whereas they portray men and boys as being leaders. Often, the teaching is in English, a language that few encounter outside the school setting.

Life skills and practical subjects that would interest girls in the learning process and provide them with vital hands-on learning experiences in their homes and community generally are missing from teaching methods and school curricula. While girls tend to succeed in learning through active discovery teaching methods, boys tend to focus their learning on passive acquisition of knowledge where teaching is principally directed toward memorization of knowledge that will help them pass their exams. Rote learning strategies put less emphasis on a personal incorporation of understanding, values, and attitudes. Subsequently, girls who are taught with passive learning styles are demoralized, feeling they are not succeeding or relating to what goes on in school because it has little application to their home and community life.

School Culture Does Not Manifest Gender Neutrality

Traditional teacher training tends to cater to boys' interests and behaviors as a means of keeping classroom order. Boys generally act out their frustrations in a manner often disruptive to the classroom. In contrast, girls predominantly repress their frustrations by withdrawing. Teachers' methods of controlling boys also include making them contribute often. Thus, teachers inadvertently favor boys to girls in the traditional classroom setting.

As a result of cultural biases, adults' expectations vary with respect to boys and girls. Many teachers testify to a difference in potential between boys and girls, especially in technical areas. In problem situations where students appear stumped, adults tend to rescue girls by giving them either easy clues or by blatantly revealing the answer. With boys, however, the general practice is to force them to figure it out themselves. Research shows that this kind of "help" undermines girls' confidence in their abilities.

Because of different self-esteem levels, boys and girls come to very different conclusions about themselves, even when the data on which they base their decisions are the same. Often, boys accept success and take credit for their accomplishments more readily than girls. The combination of the facts that girls are given fewer chances to solve problems independently, and that girls are harsher in judging their own achievements, has serious effects on the self-confidence of girls. Thus, any differences in achievement may be rooted in these culturally different expectations.

Girls in Zambia have described several ways they observe gender inequality being exhibited in the classroom:

1. The distribution of school chores tends to replicate the gender-based distribution of household chores: leadership positions and challenging tasks are assigned mostly to boys while girls do the practical work.

2. Stereotyped reactions are made to pupils' contributions. For example, a boy's mistake is taken as his own whereas a girl's is said to be typical of all girls.

3. A girl's contribution may be treated with neglect or ridicule while that of a boy receives courtesy, attention, and praise.

4. The actual teaching is directed more to the needs and interests of boys, with insufficient attention being paid to what is important to girls.

5. Teachers and school authorities show strong expectations that girls will adopt a submissive, docile attitude.

6. Certain subjects are traditionally regarded as easy and suitable for girls, others as difficult and suitable for boys.

7. School is a place where boys regularly overshadow girls. Boys constantly dominate in the classroom, in school activities, and on the sports-field.

8. Teachers, boys, and many girls themselves have low expectations that girls can produce good academic work, especially in mathematics and science.[222]

The ideas that men excel in mathematics, science, and technology and that women excel in the arts are two of many beliefs and cultural influences that are passed down through generations. Subtle and unintended messages can create the idea among girls and boys that there are fields they cannot be successful in because of their sex. Children reflect and reinforce this attitude through their peer interactions.

If girls continue to be bypassed when considering technical work, women will never have a stronghold in the technical fields and the traditional views will never be changed. In order to rectify this cycle, societies can reevaluate stereotypical roles, and girls can be encouraged to pursue more technical careers.

---

[222] Ministry of Education Lusaka, *Girls' Education*, 5.

School Personnel

Most schools have a higher proportion of male than female teachers, especially in positions of responsibility and in rural schools. In some societies, there are cultural barriers against males teaching girls. Girls need female teachers to provide counseling and to serve as inspirational models to raise the girls' aspirations and confidence levels. Female teachers can also reassure parents that the education of their children is in good, safe, and understanding hands.

Personal Embarrassment

Many situations cause girls such acute personal embarrassment that they would prefer to stay away from school rather than experience the consequences. Such situations include not having a school uniform, having to attend class in a worn-out dress, having to leave school to find fees, being teased or harassed by the older boys, or being solicited by teachers.

In summary, girls assume from the never-ending suggestions and insinuations coming from books, the orientation of the curriculum, and the remarks of teachers and fellow pupils that a girl is less than a boy, that she is knocking at the door of a man's world, that she is in school only to suffer, and that therefore, her proper place is in the home and the kitchen.

EDUCATION AS EMPOWERMENT

There is a growing consensus that education is the single most vital element in combating poverty and empowering women. Thus, targeting more equitable education techniques will not only improve the lives of individual women, but will also advance the community as a whole through having that many more worthwhile contributors.

The United Nations Development Programme points out that nearly a billion people, two thirds of them women, are unable to read a book or sign their names—much less operate a computer or understand a simple application form.[223] They will live, as now, in more

---

[223] Neimanis and Tortisyn, *Gender Thematic Guidance Note*, 6.

desperate poverty and poorer health than most of those who can. They are the world's functional illiterates, and their numbers are growing.

The consequences of illiteracy are profound, even potentially life-threatening. They stem from the denial of a fundamental human right: the right to education.[224] Yet, according to UNICEF's *State of the World's Children 2007*, more than 61 million school-aged girls in developing countries are growing up without access to basic education. Even though school attendance is compulsory in most countries, there are 115 girls for every 100 boys out of school.[225] Millions of others struggle in sub-standard learning situations where little learning takes place.

Focusing on girls' educational achievements and career aspirations allows society to ensure women economic security, a better quality of life, and more career choices. As a result, the need for social welfare will decrease, since women with inadequate education head most families in poverty. Thus, targeting more equitable education techniques will not only improve the lives of individual women, but will also advance the community as a whole by empowering more women to become worthwhile contributors.

Girls have a fundamental right to a high-quality education that serves their needs. They require an education that will equip them for the future. They ought to have help in knowing which subjects will help them find good jobs and to be given the chance to study these. Without an education, girls are less able to prepare for productive work, provide health care for themselves or their children, sustain or protect themselves and their families, or have a fulfilling life. Illiteracy makes it difficult to interact or participate in a meaningful way in the decision-making processes of community and society.

Parent Involvement

Given poverty and cultural biases, it is not easy to persuade parents to send their daughters to school. It can be done if a concerted, deliberate effort to involve parents and to create learning environments

---

[224] United Nations, "Convention on the Rights of the Child," Geneva: Office of the High Commissioner for Human Rights, 1989. Article 28.

[225] UNICEF, *State of the World's Children 2007: The Double Dividend of Gender Equality* (New York: UNICEF, 2006), 4, 7.

and curriculum that are culturally appropriate and acceptable to the community are in place. If children know that their parents are concerned about education, they most likely will be concerned, too. The most successful way to get parents concerned is for the community to give them a voice in the educational process. Parental involvement in vital decision-making, curriculum choice, and scheduling encourages and informs parents, helping them to value education even for their girl children.

Creative Program Planning

Girls often have special needs that prevent them from accessing available education. Some may be homeless, disabled, survivors of abuse, or part of a minority group. Young mothers also may discontinue their education, even if they want to keep on learning. Children with special needs do not always fit into traditional moulds for education. Rather, these children require creative program planning that overcomes the barriers to their education. Programs that provide flexibility include part-time studies, evening, mobile or home classes, special school terms for farming children; mentoring programs such as older girls mentoring younger ones; and provision of childcare when the mother has to work.

In Bangladesh, where formerly only one in ten girls from poor villages enrolled in school, the Bangladesh Rural Advancement Committee is making a big difference. To start with, classes are free. Families choose teachers, and about 80 percent are women; this encourages girls to enroll, and gives role models to other women. A maximum of thirty students per teacher ensures that teachers have more time for each student. Since children cannot get help at home, no homework is given. Classes are negotiated with parents; usually the classes run two to three hours per day with no long holidays in the school year so that children can work in the fields or at home if necessary.

The results? According to the Bangladesh Rural Advancement Committee (BRAC),

> *BRAC began its Non-Formal Primary Education Programme in 1985 with 22 one-room schools and by 2003 it was operating more than 34,000 schools...These schools account for about 11% of the primary school children. The BRAC schools teach the same competencies as the government schools; however, they enroll and retain a higher proportion of hard-to-reach children, such as girls, who make up 65% of the student body. BEP has been particularly successful in persuading conservative communities in remote rural areas to send their girls to school.*[226]

Due to the work of BRAC and other groups, the primary school enrollment ratio in Bangladesh is now 111 girls for every 107 boys.[227]

PRINCIPLES OF EMPOWERING EDUCATIONAL PRACTICES

What children learn at school should be relevant to their everyday lives. Since home management and childcare will be at the top of girl children's job description, courses concerning their role in the family and home are invaluable: nutrition, health education, hygiene, financial management and budgeting, and tasks of motherhood. Since many girls also need employment, courses in vocational training, marketing, and skills can help them to prepare for meaningful employment.

> *Principles of Empowering Educational Practices:*
> *Relevance*
> *Sensitivity*
> *Holism*

---

[226] BRAC Bangladesh, "Education," BRAC, http://www.brac.net/education.htm.
[227] UNICEF, *State of the World's Children 2007*, 118.

Educators also need to be sensitive to children's home situations, considering the girls' role in the home along with their ensuing schedule of cleaning, cooking, drawing water, and/or childcare. Children from poor families may struggle to do homework, particularly if their parents have not been educated, or if their home is noisy, crowded, or poorly lit. Children who also have to work in the home or in the fields may have little time for study.

Perhaps for these children, skills such as sewing or vegetable marketing could be used both in the home and as a money-generating project.

Education must be holistic, addressing a child's cognitive, physical, social, emotional, moral, and spiritual development. Education so conceptualized unfolds from the child's perspective and addresses each child's unique capacities and needs. The vision of educational quality must also extend to issues of gender equality and equity, health and nutrition, parent and community involvement, and management of the educational system itself.

BENEFITS OF GIRLS' EDUCATION

Education is a right of all children, and a necessity for their families and communities. Societies benefit economically and socially when their girls are educated. Education of girls, therefore, is one of the best investments a society can make. An educated woman has the skills, information, and self-confidence she needs to be a better parent, worker, and citizen. Laurence H. Summers, then vice president and chief economist of the World Bank, argued that "investment in the education of girls may well be the highest-return investment available in the developing world."[228]

UNICEF emphasizes that educating girls can help eradicate poverty and promote peace.[229] Education decreases social burdens on governments, increases family incomes, and produces a larger and better-prepared workforce. At the same time, broadened educational

---

[228] Beth Fellows, "The World Bank and Girls' Education 1999," *Together* (January–March 2000).

[229] UNICEF, *State of the World's Children 2007*, 4.

opportunity for all is thought to be the most effective means to reduce the misunderstanding, intolerance, and lack of respect that are at the core of disputes between communities, groups, and countries.

Enriching Choices & Experiences

Education empowers girls by broadening their choices and experiences, thus giving them a more fulfilling and productive life. An educated woman tends to make more independent personal, political, and economic decisions. Basic education is considered the single most important factor in protecting children from exploitative child labor and sexual exploitation. The World Bank reported in 1999 that educating girls "raises economic productivity, lowers maternal and infant mortality, reduces fertility rates, improves the health, well-being and educational prospects of the next generation, promotes sounder management of environmental resources and reduces poverty."[230] It has also been described as the single most important factor contributing to national economic growth.

Later Marriages

Women who are educated tend to marry later and choose to have fewer children. Such marriages result in better maternal and child health; the mother's risk of developing infection and dying during childbirth is greatly reduced. She is also more likely to breastfeed her children, and her babies are more likely to survive the first year of life. Because educated women know more about the value and necessity of good nutrition, they tend to be healthier and to raise a healthier family. Their children are more likely to be immunized and better nourished.[231]

She is more likely to stand up for herself, such as by protecting herself from HIV and AIDS. She also encourages her children to become educated. Research also demonstrates that better-educated girls who marry later have children who are more likely to thrive, and command better wages with each year of schooling.

---

230   Fellows, "The World Bank and Girls' Education 1999."
231   UNICEF, *State of the World's Children 2007*, 2, 4.

Yet today, some 115 million primary school-age children in developing countries still do not attend school, and more than half of these are girls.[232]

PROMOTING GIRLS' EDUCATION

Some educators argue that single-sex schools where girls are not intimidated by or pressured to defer to boys would allow girls to participate more fully. It would also allow teachers to use materials that are more relevant to the needs and learning situations of the girls. Others believe that co-education better prepares girls for the obstacles they will face in the working world.

Key measures that UNICEF has proved effective in promoting girls' schooling, and has enhanced the quality of the school experience for all children, include the following:

- offering a learning experience that is child-centered, relevant, and conducted in the local language;
- recruiting and training teachers to be more sensitive to gender and child rights issues;
- locating schools closer to children's homes;
- ensuring that schools are places of safety, with an adequate supply of safe water and latrines;
- rooting out gender bias from textbooks and materials.[233]

Words are powerful and can influence a girl's attitudes and performance in school and at home. Parents, teachers, and community leaders need to be instructed in how to offer words of encouragement. Stereotypes are powerful, too. Girls need to be encouraged to question and challenge them, not just accepting the answers they are given. Girls must be encouraged to take risks and challenges to effect needed change.

---

232 UNICEF, *State of the World's Children 2007*, 7.
233 Charlotta Sterky, "BRAC Reaches Girls with Primary Education in Bangladesh," *E'Dev News*, UNICEF (December 1991), 6.

BRIDGING THE GENDER GAP

The most urgent priority for girls is to ensure access to, and improve the quality of, education for girls. This will entail a commitment to educate the community on the value of the girl child. Radha Paul states, "The attitude toward, and treatment of, the girl child is perhaps the most glaring example of a circular analysis that attributes the effect to the cause and the cause to the effect. Because she is of no value, she is a burden to the family; and because she is a burden, she is of no value."[234]

To bridge the gender gap and ensure access to and quality of education, the following factors are vital:

- including the most vulnerable children;
- advocating for national educational policies to eliminate gender bias and discrimination at all levels of education;
- gaining an understanding of the specific reasons why girls do not enroll and why they sometimes do not succeed in school as well as boys;
- striving for quality educational programs;
- utilizing alternative education programs to meet specific cultural or other needs;
- being willing to work around a flexible schedule;
- educating all teachers, principals, supervisors, and other administrators to be sensitive to gender issues and aware of children's rights;
- encouraging more female role models both in the educational systems and the work force;
- ensuring that learning environments are safe and healthy for girls;
- making all studies and extra-curricular activities available to girls;

---

[234] Radha Paul, "What About the Girl Child?" *Together* (January–March 2000): 13.

- commencing early childhood programs;
- providing community-based childcare centers;
- enlisting parent and community involvement;
- providing measurable progress indicators;
- eliminating negative cultural attitudes and practices against girls.

Without access to education, girls will continue to be denied the knowledge and skills needed to advance their status. Societies and families also will continue to suffer adversely when girls are not educated. Recent studies make a strong case that an investment made today in girls and young women will pay off not only in their own lives but also in the lives of their children—tomorrow's mothers. The task may be difficult, but it is certainly not impossible.

Speak up for those who cannot speak for themselves, for the rights of all who are destitute. Speak up and judge fairly; defend the rights of the poor and needy.

PROVERBS 31:8–9

States Parties shall respect and ensure the rights set forth in the present Convention to each child within their jurisdiction without discrimination of any kind, irrespective of the child's or his or her parent's or legal guardian's race, colour, sex, language, religion, political or other opinion, national, ethnic or social origin, property, disability, birth or other status.

UNITED NATIONS, "CONVENTION ON THE RIGHTS OF THE CHILD," ARTICLE 2

CHAPTER 12

ADVOCACY: CHAMPIONING THE RIGHTS OF THE GIRL CHILD

Phyllis Kilbourn

The Masai warriors in Kenya have a traditional greeting they use when meeting one another. Translated into English, it means, "Are the children well?" If the answer is, "Yes," then all of the society is well. If the answer is, "No," then no one in the society is well. The Masai's tradition models the *State of the World's Children* declaration that "The true test of a civilization is how well it protects its vulnerable and how well it safeguards its children's future; children are both its vulnerable and its future."[235] Advocacy is an effective strategy in both prevention and intervention to safeguard our children's rights and future.

---

[235] UNICEF, *The World Declaration on the Survival, Protection, and Development of Children* (UNICEF, 1992).

DEFINING ADVOCACY

An advocate pleads the cause of another or stands up for some person or cause. An advocate has a two-pronged task: to act on behalf of others to do for them what they cannot do for themselves and to work alongside others to empower them in what they are trying to accomplish. Advocacy also is a biblical and moral responsibility based on justice. The biblical principle of justice for all people is rooted in the recognition that all people are created in the image of God and subsequently have a unique relationship with God (Genesis 1:27).[236] The words justice and righteousness are used more than 600 times in the Old Testament and 200 times in the New Testament. Justice primarily is the right use of power or authority. In the Old Testament, the words justice and righteousness are almost interchangeable, both indicating a conformity to God's standard of holiness.

We serve as advocates because God has commanded that we seek justice: "Learn to do right! Seek justice, encourage the oppressed. Defend the cause of the fatherless," the prophet declares (Isaiah 1:17). In very few places is justice (and therefore the character of God) more trampled underfoot than with girl child issues. Belief in the value of boy children over girl children discredits the biblical affirmation that God in his justice has created all people equal. As advocates of justice, we must challenge cultures and policies that disrespect the inherent value and dignity of persons. A just and righteous perspective starts by asking how we can provide opportunities for the girl child, equally as to the boy child, to develop her full God-given potential and become all God intended her to be.

Gary Haugen reminds us that the struggle for justice is not fought on the battlefield of power, truth, or even righteousness, but ultimately the battle against oppression stands or falls on the battlefield of hope.[237] One of the primary reasons why advocacy is ineffective and weak is

---

236   For more on this topic, see McConnell, Orona, and Stockley, eds. *Understanding God's Heart for Children: Toward a Biblical Framework* (Colorado Springs, CO: Authentic, 2007).

237   Gary Haugen, *Good News about Injustice* (Downers Grove, IL: InterVarsity Press, 1999), 67–68.

because advocates have lost hope that they can make a difference. God not only calls us to seek justice, he also equips us for that task. As he teaches us, we will learn how to be a voice against those customs, traditions, or people who oppress the girl child. For effective advocacy, we must find hope to seek justice.

WHY ADVOCACY IS VITAL

Often, children cannot protect themselves; they are vulnerable to many forms of exploitation. The girl child is often among those who have no voice; she needs someone to speak up for her. We already have recounted many instances of the global, rampant discrimination against the girl child, who often is unwanted simply because of her gender. For example, midwives in Africa and Asia get paid less for delivering a girl; and boy babies often are greeted with celebrations while girl babies are greeted with tears. In many countries, preference for a son means that infant girls die from neglect, abandonment, or infanticide. For those who survive, they soon discover that to be girl children means receiving less food and health care, having more violence unleashed against them, and rapidly becoming ensnared in unfair labor practices.

Yet every child has a right to protection, love, parental nurture, fair treatment, education, and security. When greed, ignorance, poverty, or harmful traditions take precedence, the girl child becomes especially vulnerable to losing her rights. Without an advocate to take up her cause, the girl child has few, if any, options open to her to speak out against these injustices.

Girl children will be shaped by the kind of care and respect that they receive. If current trends continue, they will be followed by another generation of children who likewise will have no voice in the kind of care society shows them. Advocacy must promote and protect the rights of the girl child and increase awareness of her needs and potential. The girl child must also receive her own unique voice as her awareness of and participation in social, economic, and political life is achieved.

WHOSE RESPONSIBILITY?

Whose responsibility is it to be an advocate for the children when the Masai declare that, "No," things are not well within the society, there are problems with the children, they are not well? Or when a society does not fulfill its obligation to protect the children? Are we to simply relegate the role of caring for children to government forces and social agencies? Even if governments have the means and knowledge to protect girl children from abuse and exploitation, doing so may not be a high priority on their agendas. According to Proverbs 31:8–9 (and other similar Scriptures), the Church has a special mandate to be that voice, protecting every child's right to grow up free from abuse and exploitation, free to develop into the person God designed him or her to be.

Perhaps our initial reactions to speaking up on behalf of the girl child are feelings of helplessness and being overwhelmed at the scope of the challenges confronting her, especially in light of our own feelings of inadequacy. Moses felt the same way when God asked him to go to Pharaoh, demanding deliverance of God's people from his repressive regime. Moses implored Aaron to be his spokesperson—his advocate. And, yes, their first efforts were rather a dismal failure considering that things only got worse; under the wrath of Pharaoh, the oppression of the people only increased.

Yet God has mandated his body to respond to the injustices of each generation. Again and again, with dogged persistence, Moses and Aaron went before the Pharaoh with God's message, "Let my people go." And finally, their voices were heard; the people were set free. Likewise, as we speak out for the girl child, she, too, can experience true liberation.

And advocacy by those who are compassionate about acting in their best interests, seeking to change laws and attitudes that strike against them, is the first step to empowering the girl child. The global Church needs to become a united voice that forcefully reminds governments, communities, and local churches about their responsibilities for the welfare of the world's children. The Church needs to stir the world's conscience. Sojourner Truth, a woman who could neither read nor write, points the way for us: She never gave up talking or fighting against slavery and mistreatment of women, not even against odds far worse than we and our children face today. Once, a man from northern Ohio rudely confronted her, asking, "Old woman, do you think that your talk about slavery does any good? Why I don't care any more about your talk than I do the bite of a flea." "Perhaps not, but the Lord willing, I'll keep you scratching," Sojourner replied.[238]

Advocacy is a life-changing role that, in some measure, we can all be engaged in, keeping oppressors of the girl child 'scratching' until we get results.

UPHOLDING THE RIGHTS OF GIRL CHILDREN

Raising consciousness about children's rights must come through action. To provide an effective voice for girl children, we must be aware of the rights accorded them by local governments and the international community. International documents on the rights of the child, most notably the United Nations *Convention on the Rights of the Child* (1989), can become powerful weapons for advocacy. The perception of child rights must include basic needs for survival, love, care, education, and restoration of the child into the mainstream of society and, if possible, with the family.

We also must be aware that governments who have signed declarations on the rights of the children are often caught violating the very rights they have promised to uphold. Signing a law and implementing a law are two quite different things. Children protesting these acts of injustice usually have their voices quickly silenced. When governments fail to protect the children, their only hope is for a more powerful person or group to become a voice on their behalf.

---

[238] Marian Wright Edelman, *Families in Peril: An Agenda for Social Change* (Cambridge: Harvard University Press, 1987), 112.

CONFRONTING INJUSTICES

Through previous chapters, we have been made aware of the many injustices confronting the girl child that need to be rectified. These injustices include child marriages, preferential treatment for boy children, harmful traditional practices, and violence and exploitation. We must always be sensitive to cultural issues behind certain actions and rituals. For example, in the case of harmful traditional practices, before advocating for the nullification of the practice, one must first investigate the reasoning behind it. Often, a less harmful and more meaningful ritual to replace a harmful current practice can become the focal point of advocacy.

To advocate for the empowerment of the girl child, we must advocate for the elimination of:

- all forms of discrimination against the girl child;
- negative cultural attitudes and practices;
- prejudice against girls in education, literacy, skill development, and training;
- discrimination against girls in health and nutrition;
- economic exploitation of child labor and unfair labor practices;
- all forms of violence against girls;
- the gender gap, which causes inequality between boys and girls;
- the commercial sex trade; and
- the lack of enforcement or failure to honor conventions and laws ratified for the girl child's protection.

Advocacy must also address the need for strengthening the family and community to bring about a change in attitudes that result in a difference in the way the girl child is treated, allowing her to be accepted without discrimination. Only then will her status be elevated and the next generation of girl children be impacted. When mothers have been liberated and empowered to break the traditions surrounding gender-based discrimination, they can support their daughters in assuming positive attitudes toward their significance, roles, and potential.

ADVOCACY STRATEGIES

How do we respond to the painful stories of so many young girls in both developed and developing nations? The journey from childhood to adulthood is never easy, but rather is fraught with difficulties, dangers, and discrimination. Though the experiences of girl children are expressed in different ways in various cultures, each girl experiences pain when she is humiliated and rejected. Our conviction for advocacy must not only be based on God's command to be a voice for the voiceless, but also on the conviction that every girl child is a precious God-given gift. We first need to check our own beliefs and attitudes toward the girl child! Are there areas of gender discrimination lurking in hidden recesses of our minds?

We must align our personal valuing of the girl child with the value God places on her. This is what will:

- govern the way we personally treat her;
- fire our appeals as an advocate;
- strengthen our supplications to God on her behalf; and
- enable us to teach her how her heavenly Father views her, giving his promised hope for her future (Jeremiah 29:11).

INGREDIENTS OF ADVOCACY

A group of researchers studied different child advocacy efforts to find the ingredients of those efforts that achieved their goals. The group found that successful advocates share four characteristics:

1. they propose solutions to the problems being addressed;
2. the solutions they offer empower children and families to make decisions about their own lives;
3. they develop partnerships with concerned people inside government agencies; and
4. they use more than one approach.[239]

Problems are only the beginning point. In order to respond to the needs of the girl child, we must be confident that there are solutions. Effective advocacy moves from problem to solution; it shows people that they can make a difference. This provides a way to deal with the feelings stirred up by anger over issues of injustice and the ensuing feelings of helplessness and guilt. It also provides an answer to the question, "What can I do?"

The solutions we propose, however, need to be carefully thought through for the impact they will have on the children, the family, and the community. The goal is to find solutions that result in empowerment, allowing the girl child to have a voice in the affairs of her life. To accomplish empowerment, solutions should result in a change of attitudes, values, and practices for families and communities, changes that ultimately will liberate the girl child.

Having partners inside child welfare agencies, social service structures, and government policy-making groups is essential to bring about change. Often, social workers, public school officials, government employers, and policy-makers will share a common concern with you over issues touching the lives of the girl child. If their motivation is low, you can be a stimulus to their involvement in protective solutions.

---

239   Sheryl Dicker, *Successful Advocacy for Children* (New York: The Foundation for Child Development, 1990), 7.

No one solution will address all the ills of the girl child; the root causes of discrimination are too numerous to address single-handedly. Nor is there a magic or quick cure. Our strategies must embrace a variety of approaches, tools, and methods.

ADVOCATING FOR HOPE

The PHULNA Project (Primary Health and Uplift Network Alliance) in India has high hopes for India's girl children. Their "wish list" is full of hope-filled desires:

- We hope she will read and write.
- We hope she will sign her name instead of a thumb impression.
- We hope she will get married only after twenty.
- We hope she will not be numbered with maternal deaths.
- We hope she will rejoice at the birth of her own girl baby.
- We hope she will not lose any of the children to whom she gives birth.
- We hope she will learn to stand on her own feet.[240]

India in the post-independence era made an unequivocal expression of the commitment of the government to the cause of children through constitutional provisions, policies, programs, and legislation. The government today, however, recognizes that traditions, customs, and social practices that place greater value on sons than on daughters or that view the girl child as an economic burden still hinder the girl child from being able to achieve her full potential.

---

[240] Shalini Shah, "Evangelical Perspectives on Mission and Ethics," *Drishtikone* (May 1, 1996): 19–21.

FAMILY & COMMUNITY ATTITUDES

To achieve long-lasting changes for girls, advocacy must involve being a voice that radically changes family and community perceptions, attitudes, and practices toward the girl child. Any rational analysis of girl child issues demonstrates that cultural beliefs and practices are at the root of discrimination against the girl child. We must promote the concept that being born female is a privilege, a responsibility, and a challenge, not a curse of the gods or fate, or the result of evil in one's previous life.

Changing attitudes and value systems is the most difficult task of advocacy. Yet we must promote change if we are to successfully address issues that deprive the girl child of holistic and healthy childhood development. Current research affirms the truth that harmful practices stem not so much from poverty, but from a preferential attitude toward boys and a rejecting attitude toward girls.

There are many ways to voice our concerns for the girl child and to bring about constructive changes for her in the present and the future. The following are several successful methods:

1. conducting community education programs, including raising community awareness of girl child issues through such means as posters, educative methods, rallies, peaceful demonstrations, mobile theater, or dramas;
2. providing constructive, culturally sensitive debates and discussion through the media (radio, television, newspapers, videos, posters);
3. campaigning for needed policy changes to eliminate discrimination against the girl child at all levels of her life;
4. working with decision-making bodies to influence their actions that affect the girl child;
5. creating public dialogue to monitor enforcement of laws for children's rights;

6. engaging the local churches in addressing harmful cultural practices and attitudes with a bias against the girl child and discovering significant alternative practices.

Be sure you include girls' participation in these events, sharing their concerns and feelings. Girls can be a powerful voice in bringing their situations before the public. Precautions, however, must be taken to ensure that the child will not suffer adversely, or suffer reprisals, from speaking out against culturally or politically sensitive issues. Coming at it in a positive light may require suggesting alternatives that will improve the quality of life for both girls and boys.

EMPOWERING GIRLS TO BE A VOICE

Many cultures make it difficult to even speak to the women of a community, let alone have it deemed acceptable to promote the suppressed voice of women and children. Some societies have established accessible and strong women's networks, campaigning to improve the status and opportunities of women. Ultimately, for long-term benefits and change in deeply entrenched cultural attitudes and traditions, girls must join together in speaking out against those issues that hold back their healthy development.

The author had the privilege of visiting leaders of a girl child's advocacy group in Zimbabwe. The Girl Child Network started as an informal discussion group with ten sixth-grade girls and a female teacher at Zengeza High School. They met to discuss various gender issues that impinged on their daily lives. Realizing the need to represent the girls' voices and redress the gender imbalance prevalent in various aspects of the socioeconomic, religious, and political life, the Girl Child Network (GCN) was birthed in 1999.

Generally in Zimbabwe, the boy child is given priority in all aspects of life. This gender bias has resulted in the escalation of homelessness for girls, early unplanned marriages and pregnancies, and challenges to the health and education of the girl child. This is a major concern because in

Zimbabwe, 180,000 people have already died of AIDS. Approximately 1.3 million children have been orphaned, and "women and girls are twice as affected by HIV, compared with the general population."[241] These figures do not include the countless unreported cases of HIV and AIDS. The aim of the Girl Child Network is to highlight the plight of the girl child and to redress gender imbalances in society through various activities. The Network's main objectives are to:

1. sensitize, conscientize, and educate society about various forms of child sexual abuse;
2. adequately empower young girls to resist various forms of sexual abuse through networking, workshops, and campaigns;
3. devise realistic ways to curb sexual abuse;
4. improve the self-image of girls by discouraging promiscuity and economic dependence on men;
5. network and document information of girls' club activities and produce a magazine or newsletter on a quarterly basis;
6. ensure that the girls actively participate in gender sensitization programs at an early age so as to prepare them to fully lead other women in the future;
7. enable girls to easily access information on opportunities available to them through a defined channel such as clubs in schools, colleges, and universities and to communicate with one another;
8. instill a sense of confidence in the girls, enabling them to assume leadership positions in all spheres of home, community, and work.[242]

---

[241] Joint United Nations Programme on HIV/AIDS, "Zimbabwe," UNAIDS, http://www.unaids.org/en/CountryResponses/Countries/zimbabwe.asp.

[242] The Girl Child Network Zimbabwe, unpublished project brochure.

The Network soon became a platform to highlight sensitive issues like rape, forced marriages, and HIV and AIDS. It also provides a safe environment where girls can share their successes and failures without fear of reprisals or being dishonored.

Currently, the Network has more than sixteen clubs and 1,500 members in Zimbabwe. GCN's varied activities focus on the following basic concerns that also provide countless opportunities for children to "speak up for themselves" and empower them to do so:

- advocacy and lobbying (child sexual abuse, reproductive health, HIV and AIDS, children's rights);
- sports development program;
- arts development program (theater, music, dance, creative writing, film, drum majorettes);
- education and training programs
    - women as role model scholarships
    - job attachments and placements
    - vocational training
    - applications to international and national universities
    - high achievers awards;
- research and policy formulation;
- counseling rehabilitation and monitoring;
- fundraising activities;
- networking with other organizations.

The Girl Child Network is concerned that the issues swirling around the girl child be addressed while the girls are still young. To facilitate addressing these issues earlier, the Network provides a "safe house" for emergency cases of rape, sexual abuse, or physical abuse. The safe house provides a confidential environment for counseling and training.

FRUITS OF ADVOCACY

The Prayas Institute of Juvenile Justice, one of India's largest child rights organizations, combines advocacy for child rights with practical assistance. A sewing and tailoring workshop is available for girls who have been trafficked into sexual or domestic violence. The floor above the workshop is a night shelter for girls who were once left alone on the streets or exploited by traffickers. The third floor is made up entirely of dorms for the girls and includes a counseling center, health clinic, a library, and classrooms.[243]

Prayas' activities include HIV and AIDS education workshops for children and child rights activists in disadvantaged communities as well as in government schools. The organization also runs a medical clinic for street and slum children in New Delhi, operates two mobile health vans for poor and working children throughout the capital, and runs a toll-free phone service to rescue children in distress. Vocational training is another key component of the Prayas model. Prayas runs non-formal educational and vocational training centers in slum communities. At the centers, lessons on sanitation, health care, and child rights are held alongside classes in math, Hindi, and history. The school curriculum is tailored for specific communities.

Before these amenities could be provided for the girls, much advocacy for legal changes had to occur. At the request of Prayas, the national government amended the country's 1986 Juvenile Justice Act (JJA) to conform to the Convention on the Rights of the Child that India signed in 1992. As a result, the legal definition of a child has been raised from fourteen for a boy and sixteen for a girl to include any child below the age of eighteen.

The amended JJA also includes provisions for the reintegration of disadvantaged children into society and new requirements for child participation in the workings of the government. While the JJA used to simply be a tool for victimizing children, it has now been turned into an advocacy tool meant to ensure the welfare of children.

---

[243] NGO Committee on UNICEF, *Putting Child Rights Into Action* (UNICEF, n.d.), 1–4.

Members of Prayas are aware that the battle to make India's governmental policies on both local and national levels more child-friendly is ongoing. India's national budget reflects this: sixteen percent of the budget is spent on defense, and only 2 percent is spent on programs for women and children. "Prayas" is a Hindi word meaning "attempt"; the name is a poignant reminder of the changes that still need to be inaugurated for children.

HOPE

This chapter has attempted to portray not only the severity of the girl child situation that is so pervasive in societies around the globe, but also to paint pictures of hope through significant advocacy strategies and projects that have been launched to enhance hope for the girl child. This hope has been promised to her as part of her spiritual birthright:

> *For I know the plans I have for you declares the Lord,*
> *plans to prosper you and not to harm you, plans to give you*
> *hope and a future.*
>
> *Jeremiah 29:11*

A God-directed future will meet the deepest longings of the girl child, challenging her capacities and giving her purpose and meaning in life. Though the girl child has been trapped in a destructive cycle of harmful practices, poverty, exploitation, and injustice, through becoming her advocate, we can witness the joy of seeing the cycle broken. Yes, we truly can celebrate hope for the girl child—a hope that redefines and challenges the lies that have successfully kept her on the margins of society.

Hope springs from the twin goals of empowerment for girls: 1) being able to challenge their past heritage of discrimination and devaluation, and 2) knowing their true identity as children who have been created in God's own image. These goals fuel the hope that girls can implement changes needed to develop to the fullest their God-given potential. God is involved in their lives! With his help, they can have a fresh sense of identity and self-worth. They are free to emerge from the cocoons that discrimination has so tightly wound around them, being transformed as beautiful butterflies that are enabled to soar with their own dreams and aspirations.

So God created human beings in his own image,
in the image of God he created them;
male and female he created them.

GENESIS 1:27

So in Christ Jesus you are all children of God through faith.
There is neither Jew nor Gentile, neither slave nor free, neither
male nor female, for you are all one in Christ Jesus.

GALATIANS 3:26, 28

CHAPTER 13

SPIRITUAL HEALING: RESTORED TO HIS IMAGE

Snowden Albright Howe

This is what the healing ministry is all about. It is to bring lost and foundering souls into wholeness in Christ. It is to see the wrecked and splintered pieces of the foundered ship not only repaired, but made for the first time truly seaworthy with Another at the helm.[244]

The girl child indeed has been wounded by the poisonous darts of discrimination. Not only her body, but more importantly, her soul, has taken the brunt of the pain. Often, her wounds have been hidden and covered over so that the infection increased and spread instead of healing. How can we who love the girl child and hurt for her wounds bring healing to her *soul*? Better still, how can we be channels through which God, the Healer, can minister his healing balm to his beloved children?

This chapter concerns emotional healing or what has sometimes been called *healing of memories* or *inner healing*. Inner healing is not an exact science with concrete steps and certain results. This chapter will, however, offer methods used by clergy and counselors to minister healing to the deeper soul wounds that have been buried in memory and emotion.

---

244   Leanne Payne, *Healing Presence* (Westchester, IL: Crossway Books, 1989), xv.

David Seamands wrote pioneering books on the subject of inner healing in the 1980s. In *Healing for Damaged Emotions*, Seamands wrote:

Letters and testimonies have confirmed my belief that there is another realm of problems, which requires a special kind of prayer and a deeper level of healing by the Spirit. Somewhere between our sins, on the one hand, and our sickness, on the other, lies an area the Scripture calls "infirmities."

We can explain this by an illustration from nature. If you visit the far West [USA], you will see those beautiful giant sequoia and redwood trees. In most of the parks the naturalists can show you a cross section of a great tree they have cut, and point out that the rings of the tree reveal the developmental history, year by year. Here's a ring that represents a year when there was a terrible drought. Here's where the tree was struck by lightning. Here are some normal years of growth. This ring shows a forest fire that almost destroyed the tree. Here's another of savage blight and disease. All of this lies embedded in the heart of the tree, representing the autobiography of its growth.

And that's the way it is with us. Just a few minutes beneath the protective bark, the concealing, protective mask, are the recorded rings of our lives. Here is the discoloration of a tragic stain that muddied all of life...as years ago behind the barn, or in the haystack, or out in the woods, a big brother took a little sister and introduced her into the mysteries— no, the miseries of sex.

> *Such scars have been buried in pain for so long that they are causing hurt and rage that are inexplicable. In the rings of our thoughts and emotions, the record is there; the memories are recorded, and all are alive. And they directly and deeply affect our concepts, our feelings, and our relationships. They affect the way we look at life and God, at others and ourselves.*[245]

These painful memories, as Seamands reminds us, are not automatically transformed by a spiritual experience. In fact, these memories are often great hindrances to spiritual growth. And, until the girl child receives deliverance from childhood wounds, she cannot really mature. It is as if part of her is frozen in time. She is still a little girl, locked into that stage of life. Seamands highlights the difficulties in healing:

> *Unfortunately, these memories do not seem to be reached by our ordinary levels of prayer. Sometimes prayer seems to make the pain even worse. You feel you are in quicksand: the more you fight and struggle, the deeper you sink. I believe this situation calls for a special kind of shared praying and healing.*[246]

This chapter will explore that "special kind of shared praying and healing." First, it is imperative to always remember that God is the Healer, and we are the helpers. We can be channels for His healing grace, but that is the *most* we can be, channels through which God can work. In that process, however, it is up to us to be the most effective channels we can be.

---

[245] David Seamands, *Healing for Damaged Emotions* (St. Paul, MN: Victor Books, 1981), 19.

[246] David Seamands, *Putting Away Childish Things* (Wheaton, IL: Victory Books, 1993), 34.

Agnes Sanford wrote one of the first books of the twentieth century on Christian healing. In this book, Sanford compares praying to using an electric iron, explaining that "while the whole world is full of that mysterious power we call electricity, only the amount that flows through the wiring of the iron will make the iron work for us."[247] The same principle is true of the creative energy of God. The whole universe is full of it, but only the amount of it that flows through our own beings will work for us. We are the electric light bulbs through whom the light of God reaches the world!

The question, then, is: How can we be effective channels for God's healing to others? How can we, so to speak, check our wiring and wattage, or unclog our channels, so that God's love can reach most effectively through us to others? The first step, naturally, lies in our own relationship with our Lord; we cannot give to others what we do not have ourselves.

This chapter will suggest special methods of prayer for those who have been wounded, but these methods rely on an intimacy with God and an expectation that God will speak and act as we connect with Him. We can be most helpful to others as we cultivate for ourselves a deep relationship with and reliance on our Lord. In addition, we must explore blocks to healing such as the need to forgive or be forgiven, and we must explore these blocks within ourselves as well as for others. Remember that our healing Lord loves the little ones to whom you minister even more than you love them.

---

[247] Agnes Sanford, *The Healing Light* (St. Paul, MN: Macalester Park Publishing Company, 1947), 17, 33.

In the words of Paul to the Ephesians:

> *Since, then, I heard of this faith of yours in the Lord Jesus and the practical way in which you are expressing it toward fellow Christians, I thank God continually for you and I never give up praying for you; and this is my prayer. That God, the God of our Lord Jesus Christ and the all-glorious Father, will give you spiritual wisdom and the insight to know more of him: that you may receive that inner illumination of the spirit which will make you realise how great is the hope to which he is calling you—the magnificence and splendour of the inheritance promised to Christians—and how tremendous is the power available to us who believe in God.*
>
> *Ephesians 1:15–19 (JB Phillips)*

ESTABLISHING A RELATIONSHIP

David Seamands observes, "We are broken in the context of relationship; and we are also healed within the scope of relationships."[248] How true this is of the girl child who, within relationships, has suffered rejection, abandonment, exploitation, and abuse. These experiences may or may not have physical repercussions, but they invariably cause emotional wounds, especially when the rejection or abuse was perpetrated by those who should have loved and protected the child. In these cases, immense damage is done to the child's ability to trust others and to have a positive sense of self-worth. This damage will certainly affect her relationships with others and with God. In *The Sacred Romance*, these hurtful experiences are compared to arrows that strike the heart:

> *However, [the arrows] come to us, whether through a loss we experience as abandonment or some deep violation we feel as abuse, their message is always the same: kill your heart. Divorce it, neglect it, run from it, or indulge it with some anesthetic (our various addictions).*[249]

The first step for Christian caregivers is to establish a relationship with the hurting girl in which trust and caring can grow. This process may be slow and difficult, but it is essential for the wounded girl to feel truly valued by another and safe enough to risk trusting that other. Dr. Tim Clinton, therapist and president of the American Association of Christian Counselors (AACC), has stated that in his work with clients who have had "painful pasts," as many as five or six of the initial therapy sessions may need to be directed primarily toward building trust![250] Developing a relationship is the first step to healing, the step that makes all other steps possible.

---

248 Seamands, *Healing for Damaged Emotions*, 13.
249 Brent Curtis and John Eldredge, *The Sacred Romance* (Nashville, TN: Thomas Nelson, Inc., 1997), 27.
250 Tim Clinton, audiotape of lecture by Tim Clinton presented at American Association of Christian Counselors, n.d.

THE PROCESS OF INNER HEALING

As we examine the process of inner healing, let's also follow one girl child's journey through each of the phases. We will call her Janie.

Janie is an adult who is especially perceptive and wonderfully creative. I have chosen to share part of Janie's journey toward healing because it illustrates several important concepts, and because, as I worked with Janie, it became apparent to me that she and God were doing the therapy; I was merely the facilitator. My hope is that as you read about Janie, you will be encouraged that you also can be a facilitator for God's spiritual healing of his hurting children.

Janie sought counseling because, while on a business trip, she experienced profound sadness and a strong temptation to use alcohol to reduce that sadness. Both the emotion and the temptation were familiar; Janie had spent five weeks in an alcohol treatment center as a college student. After her treatment, however, she had remained sober and had entered into a life-changing relationship with the Lord Jesus Christ. She had spent her last fifteen years in a productive career with increasing ministry opportunities in her church. She knew she had some struggles, but life seemed manageable.

Then on a visit to her childhood home, uncomfortable memories and emotions began surfacing. These experiences culminated several months later on the business trip that scared her enough to bring her into counseling. With her permission, let me share here some of her journal entries after she began coming to me as her counselor.

April 4: Questions...

Father, in early February, You told me— "I know you have questions—I have the answers, if you put your focus on me." So, here I am Lord—I have a list of questions...

As I see that picture of me in the desert right now, as a small, frightened, vulnerable child, standing on the edge of the desert, why do I only see You on the edge, but distant? I asked You to take my hand and to put Your arm around me and go with me. But, I just see You on the edge of the desert as well, not even near me—expressionless, cold, uninvolved, non-responsive, just watching.

Why? I know in my head that this is not true. I felt so angry about that this week—I don't see You in the desert, just like I don't see You in my painful time during high school. S. said to meditate on the fact that You know my struggles—but it seems like you were not there—except as a spectator—why? Also, why was I in such deep pain in high school? Who is this frightened child inside? I didn't even know she was there. All I have are questions and pieces of memories...

Why do I deep-down crave—like a starving person— understanding and love when I know Your son Jesus—I have experienced His presence, joy, and life within me? Why am I so deeply starving? When I am in the here and now, I feel Your presence and comfort. But during this journey back in time, I cannot feel, see, hear, or accept Your love and comfort. I revert to the fearful feeling of emptiness, hopelessness, and isolation, and the tears flow. And, Lord, how did I get here, anyway? One year ago, I was blossoming in ministry and leadership and filled with passion and joy for giving my life away. Today, I am barely functioning—curling up in a ball and crying, afraid. Is this the frightened child that has been in hiding, running all of these years? Please come in and heal these broken places deep within me.

April 7: Searching for the Truth...

Lord, I thought I knew You—experienced You walking and talking with me—maybe it has not gone much below my head. So, I thought that I would look and see what Jesus' image of You was in His darkest hour (in Gethsemane)—I looked in the gospel of Mark—I gasped as I saw that He called You 'Abba'—a term of endearment—I gasped because my picture of You is dark and cold—I would call you 'Darth Vader.' Who is this person that I think is You? My picture does not line up with Your Word. I never knew this before. So all of these months that I have been wrestling with the issue of intimacy with You have been futile because, though my head says to run to You, and that You are my all in all, I have not budged—why would I run to the lap of a Darth Vader-type person?

No wonder I keep searching—longing, starving for love and understanding. Where were You? I was just a child! I still feel angry.

Father, about eight years ago, walking along the beach, I looked down to see that the waves washed away enough sand to reveal the very top of a big, beautiful sand dollar. I felt like You told me that this is me—there is a treasure within me that my husband will be able to see. I thought You meant buried within an unattractive person—the old 'beauty is on the inside' thing. But, I wonder if You meant that there is treasure buried in there with the pain—behind that nailed shut door. S. said there may be joy and blessings in there—maybe there is a treasure as well. Maybe when I nailed shut a door in my life—lots of stuff got buried—treasure and pain. Lord, is that what You meant?

CONFRONTING THE PAIN

The next step in healing is more problematic because it is more painful. In Seamands' words, "For many of us...healing begins at the point of pain."[251] Just as a deep physical wound would need to have the bandages unwrapped, the wound cleaned and anointed with salve in order to heal, so, too, do emotional wounds need to be cleansed and healed. The "covering" created by ignoring, denying, suppressing, or repressing the pain has been a defense mechanism; removing that defensive covering in order to re-experience the pain will *not* feel like healing at first! The same would be true with a physical wound. Think of a time when, perhaps, you were slicing vegetables and sliced a finger by mistake. Didn't you instinctively cover the finger with the other hand in an attempt to stop the bleeding and the pain? And wasn't it *scary* then to uncover the cut, acknowledge the pain, and see how bad the damage was? Would the cut have healed, however, if you had never uncovered it, cleaned it, or applied ointment or stitches? A foundational step in healing is to face our problem head-on.

Edward Smith writes, "if I refuse to feel, I cannot heal,"[252] suggesting that current emotions can serve as a pathway or "open window" to the wounds of the past. When emotions surface that seem extreme for present circumstances, those strong emotions have often been unburied from the past by a trigger in the present. In his method of Theophostic counseling, Smith encourages his clients to focus on the present strong emotions (not the causative factors for them) and then to "drift" with those emotions to the past, to find a memory in which those same feelings were experienced. That memory may reveal some of the causes of the deeper pain.

---

251 Seamands, *Healing for Damaged Emotions*, 20.
252 Edward Smith, *Genuine Recovery* (Campbellsville, KY: Family Care Publishing, 1996), 61.

Other methods of reconnecting with painful past events could include *telling* the story, *drawing* the story, or, especially with younger children, *dramatizing* the story through play.[253] In any case, according to Smith, "If I choose to look through the window I will confront my wound face-to-face and feel its fresh fury again."[254] *Then* it is possible to find healing.

Painful emotions and memories are often buried internally as a means of self-protection. But as Dr. Sandra Wilson states in the AACC audio cassette, *Helping People with Painful Pasts,* defense mechanisms that worked as childhood solutions (defense mechanisms) often become adult problems when maintained into adulthood. In her words, "Too often people try to put the past *behind* themselves without first putting the past *before* themselves." She also refers to Nehemiah 2:13–17, a passage in which Nehemiah inspects the walls of Jerusalem for damage before rebuilding. She says that it is important to "review" the past, to see the childhood experiences with adult eyes, before building for the future. Often, childish conclusions ("I was the cause of this bad event") and the mis-beliefs they have fostered ("I must therefore be a very bad person") can be changed in adulthood if they are unburied and examined. Confronting the pain is a difficult but essential step toward healing.

April 10: The Voice Who Sings to You...

Father, S. said that I should take your hand in this desert, because of what I do know of You. So, on Friday afternoon, I told You that I will take Your hand and trust You in this desert—I said that I feel small and weak. I asked You to show me what You really looked like and were. Words cannot describe the depth of Your answer to me on Friday night. The phrase from the Michael W. Smith song, "I

---

253 For more on play therapy for children, please refer to the other books in Smith's recovery series.
254 Smith, *Genuine Recovery,* 13.

Know Your Name" that has been resonating in my mind for the last week is, "the voice who sings to you." Driving uptown, I plopped the CD in and during the symphonic overture of the first song, I heard Your answer. You sang to me—You sang to that little person behind the nailed shut door. You sang to me through the music of Beethoven, Handel, Tchaikovsky, Brittain. As I sang in choruses, played the piano and listened to these composers, You were whispering Your love and comfort to the little me behind that door, because music seemed to reach in deeper than people, words or anything else could. I remember crying deeply whenever I played "O Holy Night" on the piano. And in the Michael W. Smith song, "I Know Your Name." It says, "yes, I know your name, I'm the one that brought you to this place, the voice who sings to you, the hand that clings to you." So, You sang to me all of those years. Oh, Lord, what a dramatic contrast to my picture of You. You knew that I could not see You—I could not see You in the people around me—but, I could hear You. Music seemed to reach down to the core of me and comfort me like a warm, familiar blanket.

April 20: It Sure Feels Strange, but Good, to Talk About This Stuff

Lord, I have never had a safe place or person with whom to share this stuff. It is scary, but, oh, how I have needed a safe place! I have always been the safe place for others. It is almost like I never felt like I should or could discuss this stuff. I have always felt like I am different—like I should not or do not have the same longings or feelings that other people do—I just felt different.

Lord, I want to fly—I have had clipped wings; I have been in chains; I feel frozen and unable to move. Father, I am so afraid. Is my memory blocked by the condemnation

I feel and hold and live enslaved to? I nurse it, protect it, and use it to continue to hammer nails into that door. It seems like there are so many ways that I continue to hammer that door shut. Who is that child there? I don't feel like I know her. Help me to open that door and reach her—so that she can fly. So that she can draw, create, sing, write, and pour her life into others, pointing them to you. But as little corners creak open through this process with S., the tears flow. It feels like such deep pain sometimes. Oh, I am so afraid. But, I need to be here [in counseling]. I am grateful to be here. You have brought me to this place—to this desert and to S. It is scary and also such a relief. I do not want to leave this desert until all of my stuff has been exposed to the light of truth and to the healing hand of your Son, Jesus...Please free me.

May 1: Shame...

Father, last Friday (Good Friday), I heard You clearly tell me that I must tell S. of those things that fill me with shame—that which I am in bondage to. Today (Monday), I asked You— "did you really tell me that I have to tell S. that stuff?" I immediately knew the answer because that question sounded too familiar. Something like, "did God really tell you not to eat of the fruit of that tree?" Lord, give me the courage. Lord, I will be real with S. I will obey You because You have guided me through this process so far—giving me pieces of memories, pictures in my head and words through my pen or keyboard. I will trust You. I am still waiting for a new picture, but I will trust You. Are all of these things feeding that same insatiable hunger or unsatisfied beast within me: food, substance abuse, busyness, rescuing people, being in controlling relationships, keeping people at a distance or hiding even though I desperately want to be known and understood, cranking up the volume of music to quiet the pain.

But, Lord, in this process over the last month or two, I see what I have never seen before. A child that was in so much pain—she learned very early that it was not safe to be real or to have or show feelings. She had to rock herself and talk to herself. She learned to stuff her tears and never share herself with anyone. She was afraid and confused and felt ugly, bad, and different. She grew to believe that she deserved to be treated as less of a person than others.

Lord, on Tuesday, I was crying—so filled with sadness. Then, I saw Your hand reach down to me—to where I sat in such overwhelming sadness. I reached up to You and felt Your comfort. Father, in the past I saw Your hand—but I always pushed it away. This time it seemed different—full of love—strong and gentle. This is the hand that clings to me, isn't it?

HEALING PRAYER

In an atmosphere of trust and caring, when the old memories and accompanying emotions have been accessed, then it is possible to invite the Lord Jesus to come into the memory. Simply say to Jesus, "Lord Jesus, I invite you to come and stand in my memory for I need to hear your truth."

When you either see or sense Jesus' presence, go back to the memory picture and 'stir it up' again. Allow the intensity of the emotion to increase as much as you can. In the midst of the darkness, look over at the Lord and listen for his words. Watch him and observe his behavior. He will often act out the truth for you to see. If he opens his arms to you, walk into them. Whatever you hear him say, confess it out loud. Receive his healing.[255]

---

255 Smith, *Genuine Recovery*, 18.

David Seamands expresses a similar concept concerning healing prayer:

> *Often what is required in situations of this kind is prayer for the healing of memories—the healing of that little child or teenager who underwent certain experiences which made him stop growing, experiences which imprisoned him, froze him at one stage in his growth. All those memories need to be offered to God in a prayer for healing, so that the person can be freed from his pain and compulsion.*
>
> *You may ask, 'What happens then? Will he no longer remember? Will the memories be erased?' Certainly not! But the power of the emotions which surround those memories—the sting, the pain, the fear, the hate, the hurt, the lust—will be broken. They will be devitalized, no longer effective and operative.*[256]

The memory itself doesn't change after healing prayer; instead, the emotions surrounding the memory change. Some believe that this occurs because each painful memory contains a lie "which was planted in one's mind during the time of the trauma."[257] These lies are statements such as, "I am worthless," or "No one will ever love me." The wounded person may understand *logically* that such statements are not true, but the statements *feel* true.

When the lie within the memory picture is recognized and acknowledged, Jesus can then be invited to come and bring his truth and light. The lie and the darkness cannot then remain. The awesome power of the lie is in its ability to produce actual consequences in my life. If I believe the lie, it will work itself out in my life and produce the

---

256 Seamands, *Putting Away Childish Things*, 36
257 Smith, *Genuine Recovery*, 18.

same consequences as if it were true. If I believe I am powerless in a relationship, I will allow myself to be dominated and controlled. If I believe I was guilty for the abuse I received as a child, I will live a life crippled by false shame. A lie is a deception. Yet it is only a deception for as long as a person believes it. Once the truth is embraced, "the lie loses its power. Knowing the truth is more than logically knowing it—it is knowing it in your heart as well as your head. Most people already logically know more truth than they will ever 'know.' Once you 'know' the truth, the truth does indeed set you free."[258]

Seamands and Smith both recommend a quiet, relaxed time of prayer in which the guidance of the Holy Spirit can be sought and the presence of Jesus acknowledged. Both authors describe a sort of three-way conversation between the wounded one, the caregiver, and Jesus.

May 5: I Will Open Up My Heart & Let the Healer Set Me Free

Dear Lord Jesus, I left my appointment with S. filled with hope and peace, thank You. I prayed that I could reconnect with You—the real You—not that angry-looking person or the shark lurking in the dark roaring waves below me, but the You that sang to me and the hand that clings to me. You reminded me of how You not only held me close through music, You gave me hope. As I listened to music, You gave me glimpses of who You created me to be—who I could be if I were not paralyzed by fear and shame.

Is it consistent with Scripture to invite Jesus in this way to go back into memories of the past? Why would it not be? Hebrews 13:8 explains, "Jesus Christ is the same yesterday and today and forever" (cf. Psalm 90:2, 4; John 1:15; 8:57–58).

---

258 Smith, *Genuine Recovery*, 19.

Richard Foster gives an example of his experience with healing prayer that seems especially relevant for those who love and work with children:

I was once called to a home to pray for a seriously ill baby. Her four-year-old brother was in the room, and so I told him I needed his help in praying for his baby sister. He was delighted to help, and I was delighted to have him, for I know that children can often pray with unusual effectiveness.

He climbed up into the chair beside me. "Let's play a little game," I suggested. "Since we know that Jesus is always with us, let's suppose that he is sitting over in that chair across from us. He is waiting patiently for us to focus our attention on Him. When we see Him and the love in His eyes, we start thinking more about His love than about how sick Julie is. He smiles, gets up, and comes over to us. When that happens, we both put our hands on Julie, and as we do, Jesus puts his hands right on top of ours. He releases His healing light right into your little sister sort of like a whole bunch of soldiers who go in and fight the bad germs until they are all gone. Okay?"

Seriously the boy nodded. Together we prayed just as I had described it to him, and then we thanked God that this was the way it was going to be. Amen. While we prayed, I sensed that my small prayer partner had exercised unusual faith.

The next morning Julie was perfectly well. Now, I cannot prove to you that our little prayer game made Julie well. All I know is that Julie was healed, and that was all I needed to know. ✱

✱ Richard Foster, *Prayer: Finding the Heart's True Home* (San Francisco: Harper Collins Publishing, 1992), 209–210.

Francis MacNutt, a Roman Catholic priest who has also written and experienced much in the area of spiritual healing, summarized healing prayer this way:

> *The idea behind inner healing is simply that we can ask Jesus Christ to walk back to the time we were hurt and to free us from the effects of that wound in the present. This involves two things then:*
>
> 1. *Bringing to light the things that have hurt us. Usually this is best done with another person; even the talking out of the problem is in itself a healing process.*
> 2. *Praying the Lord to heal the binding effects of the hurtful incidents of the past.*[259]

I have found by experience that this kind of prayer is *usually perceptibly answered.* At times, the healing is progressive and takes several sessions, but I believe that it is always God's desire to heal us of those psychological hurts that are unredemptive and that prevent us from living with the inner freedom that belongs to the children of God. When this kind of prayer is seemingly not answered, I assume that we simply have not yet gotten to the bottom of the matter, either because:

1. There is a need for repentance, usually a need for the person to forgive someone who has hurt him or her.
2. There is a deeper, more basic hurt we have not yet discovered or reached.
3. There is a need for deliverance.

---

[259] Francis MacNutt, *Healing* (Notre Dame, IN: Ave Maria Press, 1974), 183.

After the prayer for the healing of the hurt (the negative part, as it were), we can pray for Jesus to fill up in a positive way whatever is missing in the person's life. Since we have such a basic need for love, the conclusion of a prayer for inner healing usually involves a filling with God's love of all the empty places in our heart.

ROOTS...

"And I pray that you, being rooted and established in love may have power, together with all the saints, to grasp how wide and long and high and deep is the love of Christ" (Ephesians 3:17–18). "Remain in me, and I will remain in you...If you remain in me and my words remain in you...As the Father has loved me, so have I loved you...remain in my love" (John 15: 4, 7, 9, NIV). If I remain rooted in Jesus and allow His words to nourish me, His words will become my words spoken to me. No longer, 'I am bad,' but 'I am a treasure.' As His words become my words, I will have a heart like His. I will be what He created me to be. Lies and shame kept me from being who He created me to be. Lord, speak the truth to me—pull the weeds and set me free.

May 8

Lord, this weekend, I told you that I felt like I have two people inside me. Today I read the parable of the weeds. The owner told the servants to allow the weeds to grow with the wheat and to pull the weeds at harvest time. I asked you what this meant. You showed me. The parable speaks of an enemy planting weeds just after good seed was planted. Early in my life the enemy planted weeds in me—lies and shame. They have been allowed to grow within me until now. But, at the same time, over the last fifteen years, the good seed has been growing as well. To pull the weeds early would have hurt the good seed. But, it is harvest time now—this process of healing is painful—pulling out the weeds to be burned—but you waited until the good seed had good root. You waited until I grew to some level of intimacy with You—at least where I knew Your voice (Matthew 13: 24–30):

- You are bad.
- *You are gifted in leadership.*
- You are dirty.
- *Encouragement.*
- You are undeserving.
- *You are loveable.*
- You are ugly.
- *You have potential.*
- You are nasty.
- *I (God) have plans for you.*
- You are shameful.

Lord, you clearly showed me this weekend that I can no longer hide or bury my feelings, or ignore them or run from them, or go to sleep to forget them, or stay busy to ignore them.

CONCLUSION

Like many girl children around the world, Janie is still in the process of healing. But these selected entries from Janie's journal seem to reflect the method outlined above in spiritual healing. As children begin to feel safe with their counselors, they will begin to talk (and write and draw) about the pain in their past. As little by little the girls open themselves up to that pain and invite the Lord's healing, truth will become clearer to them—the truth of their pain, the truth of God's love, the lies that have held them captive, and the positive reality that they can choose instead. As is evident from Janie's journal entries, the healing process does not necessarily occur neatly, in orderly stages—

but that is true for most of life! As wounded children return again and again to those steps of trust building, facing the past, and seeking the healing touch of Jesus, hope and freedom will become increasingly evident in their lives.

CONCLUDING REFLECTION

*Naaman went to his master and told him
what the girl from Israel had said.*

2 KINGS 5:4

*What is a girl? Property? Unpaid labor? A sex object? A
lineage connector? A social stabilizer? A dangerous pollutant?
Or a human being, created in the image of God, liberated by
the life, death and resurrection of Jesus, empowered by the
Holy Spirit, commissioned for creative service in God's world?*

MIRIAM ADENEY, "CLEAR OUT! THIS GIRL ISN'T DEAD!" *TOGETHER* 49: 5

CHAPTER 14

NAAMAN'S SLAVE GIRL: A GLANCE AT THE SOIL OF YHWH[260]

Renita Boyle

> *Now Naaman was commander of the army of the king of Aram. He was a great man in the sight of his master and highly regarded, because through him the LORD had given victory to Aram. He was a valiant soldier, but he had leprosy.*
>
> *Now bands of raiders from Aram had gone out and had taken captive a young girl from Israel, and she served Naaman's wife. She said to her mistress, "If only my master would see the prophet who is in Samaria! He would cure him of his leprosy."*
>
> *Naaman went to his master and told him what the girl from Israel had said.*
>
> *2 Kings 5:1–4*

---

260 Or Yahweh, the Old Testament name for the LORD God.

So begins the story of one of the most visible miracles in the Old Testament. The great Commander Naaman is healed of his leprosy and becomes the first non-Israelite to believe in and worship YHWH in a foreign land. Though the focus of the account is Naaman, the invisible miracle of another speaks most to my heart: that of the forgiveness and grace displayed by the unnamed slave girl. Everything we know of her is found in these verses, and yet, what we must speculate about her life is what makes her brief testimony all the more powerful.

Consider the following possible scenes from her life.

SCENE 1

Syria and Israel are at it again. The two nations are in constant conflict, especially along the border. A girl on the verge of womanhood is wakened from her sleep by the thundering sound of horses' hooves, the shouts of men, and the frightened screams of women and children. Though this is her first experience with war, her community has been aware of Syria's imminent threat for months. Mothers watch at their windows; children must not stray too far; fathers and brothers leave their crops for combat. Many never return, and those who do repeat the same story, defeat after defeat. Syria has won another victory by the hand of Naaman, and YHWH has handed them over to him.

The weary echoes of a besieged nation reverberate in the girl's heart even as quickly approaching footsteps pound in her ears. The thin mattress rustles beneath her; her family has gone, taking their body heat with them. She clambers to her feet, a chill of terror surging up her spine. The warm goat's hair quilt crumples like confusion around her. She searches the shadows. Is that her mother frantically rocking the baby "shush, shush?" Is that her sister dragging her curious brother away from the window? Are those her grandparents cowering together in the corner? Is that her father drawing near, kneeling low and gripping her shoulders in his strong hands? "Bolt the door behind me," he commands. "Then hide! Hide!"

She is rigid with fear, but her father's voice stirs her to action. She follows him down the wooden ladder to the near-empty stable and tool room. The panicked pet lamb bleats and darts around her legs. Her father reaches for his spear, unlatches the door, and is gone. There is a scuffle outside, the clash of weapons, the sickening sound of metal meeting flesh. The door is closed, but even its thick fir beams cannot stifle death. She is suddenly aware of unfamiliar voices. The language is unknown, but the tone is unmistakable. She must hurry, must act to protect her family! Her fingers tremble as she fumbles for the bolt, clacking it into place. Her head is reeling, her body spinning, her pulse racing. "Hide! Hide!" It is too late. Heavy footsteps, two loud thuds; the door is burst from its hinges. Her scream shatters the sunrise. Shards of light pierce her scampering eyes. A soldier stands in the doorway, bronzed armor gleaming like a serpent's skin.

SCENE 2

It is a long journey from the hills of Gilead to the city of Damascus. Long enough for early summer drought to tighten its grip over late spring rains. Long enough for the sun's razored whip to sear parched lips thirsting for plundered wine and a cool breeze. Long enough for looted goats, sheep, and oxen to grow thin on the changing terrain. Long enough for the near exhaustion of pillaged grain and travel-weary captives. With each trudging step, the swift blow of numbing shock yields to harsh new realities. Rebellious prisoners are taught their first lessons in brutality, servitude, and bludgeoned dignity. Roped wrists and ankles welt up like tears. Bodies wilt, heads droop, spirits sag like possession-burdened donkeys forced to serve new masters. The girl's sandaled feet begin to callous but she is raw, her ragged, sweat-soaked tunic clinging like grief from her neck to her ankles. Darkly circled eyes betray a longing for rest, but sleep, when it comes, has joined forces with the oppressor. Desolation inhabits her dreams even as it does her days.

The girl has long since searched the faces of the living chain for those most familiar to her. Her sister and brother keep pace some distance behind, and her mother, too. But there is little comfort in their presence. Even when they are allowed to speak, there are no words to express the loss of her father and the rape of her mother, an act so unspeakable that each elusive glance becomes an inaudible whisper of shame. Though she wants to hope for those missing, her grandparents and infant sister among them, little can remain of the village and the prospect of survival.

Most of the men lay dead or dying in pools of earth-soaked blood. What the soldiers had not pillaged for use or sale was broken or set ablaze. Ransacked cups and bowls hurled against walls fell in jagged pieces to dusty floors. Abandoned rattles and dolls, severed handles, and chipped spouts decorated chaotic mounds of growing rubble. Fractured earthenware jars and pitchers hemorrhaged wine, water, and dyes. Dried beans and lentils, flour, and salt spilled from overturned pots; sticky wild honey and sweet perfume from prized jugs. Devastation was relentless in every detail. Winter cloaks heaved from alcoves were thrust on deserted bedding, soaked with oil, and torched. Prayer caps and intricate *tallith* shawls stoked the burgeoning vision of hell. Dangling weights on wooden looms were strewn like marbles on flame-fraying threads. Waiting spindles nestled in baskets of freshly combed wool fuelled the blaze. Reed instruments whistled laments; horns and stringed lutes were silenced forever. On the surrounding terraces, rampant flames devoured the stubbled remains of newly harvested barley and maturing wheat. Pre-pruned grape vines and olive trees crackled, ripening figs popped, rooftops crumbled, spilling vine-twined trellises. The hillside farmers had survived drought many times, protected crops from mildew and scorching winds, and fended off swarms of ravaging locusts, but this enemy they could not survive. The dying village collapsed breathless, smoke-choked lungs gasping for air, coughing up ashen fumes to the heavens.

The ruined village lay far behind the captives now, out of sight but ever smoldering in their memories. Damascus rose before them, imposing its might, dominating the landscape and their uncertain future.

SCENE 3

"Make way! Make way!" The train of the conqueror approaches the city gate. "Syria is victorious! Long live King Benhadad!" Naaman's foot soldiers, archers, axe-men, and sling-men advance with renewed purpose, backs straighter, heads higher, each stride more ardent than the last, each chant louder. "Naaman is victorious! Long live Naaman!" Cavalrymen gallop up and down the line cracking their whips, and horses' manes and tails wave like victory banners. "Praise be to Rimmon, god of thunder!" Officers hungry for home and glory flex their pride astride chestnut steeds and command the entrance to the city.

Beggars stop crying for alms, peddlers and water-carriers stop shouting their wares, traders stop bargaining, laborers stop their work, children stop playing, singers and storytellers yield their audience. Shrill trumpet blasts, cheering crowds, billowing streamers. All ears heed the crescendo of victory; all eyes witness the parade; all but those who are unwilling participants in it. The girl's eyes are swelling with fear; her heart is screaming but unheard; her every nerve tingles with apprehension.

The procession advances past market stalls and barrows laden with the exotic, past shops and stables attending to the necessary, past inns caring for the weary, past the temple ministering to Rimmon's servants. Naaman's troops are brought to a halt in the palace courtyard, rhythmic marching ceasing in precision. The captives are ordered into rank and file, and the girl is jostled into the center of the front row. Children younger and older are crying, seeking comfort on either side. Her searching senses scan those around. She can see her brother thrashing against a soldier, hear her sister weeping to her left, but her mother is out of eyesight, out of earshot, out of reach.

The commanding officer bids silence. She suppresses the emotional revolt rising up within her, blinking back a few rogue tears. There is a rippling stillness among the captives and gathered crowd. The clattering rattle of chariot wheels on cobbled stones and the stately stepping of a military mount magnify the silence. King Benhadad is making his way from the palace, General Naaman flanking his right. A royal fanfare heralds their arrival. All eyes turn their attention to the king then quickly dart away. The congregation bows in reverence; the captives cower in fear; the girl stands humiliated.

The captives have never seen General Naaman, but there is no mistaking him. The king lifts his scepter, the congregation rises, and the commander leads the troop in a deafening unified salute. Soldiers present arms, javelins, spears, swords, and shields snap to attention, feet thunder in single-stanced conformity, voices boom. The general's dancing stallion rears back, nostrils flaring, muscles rippling, front hooves pawing the air, his striking persona an extension of the general himself. Naaman sits high in the saddle with leather reins in one hand, gleaming sword unsheathed like glory in the other. His ornate ceremonial armor reflects his favor with the king and his reputation in battle helmet, coat of mail, belt buckle, shield, and dagger glistening like victory in the sun. Audible gasps escape from among the assembly. He is dazzling to behold. The king nods to him. He rides forward to meet his commanding officer and inspect the spoils of war.

The girl cannot take her eyes from the great general, cannot stop the feeling of awe even as her heart seethes with rage against him. The great Naaman who ordered the siege of her village, who stands as an enemy of YHWH but is blessed by him, is speaking with his men, taking pride in his troop's success, taking pleasure from her people's pain. He ambles along, body swaying in calm repose to the stallion's gentle gait. He is inspecting the front row. The girl's eyes follow him making an inspection of their own. She strains for the tone of his voice, peers to see the size of his hands, notes the repulsive flaking of his skin. Sometimes nodding, sometimes stopping, always menacing, Naaman moves closer to the girl one captive at a time.

All at once the girl is roused from her obsession. Naaman is almost upon her! Rage is overcome by fear, blind panic wells up inside. She does not now dare to look. She is not able to run. He is a horse length away. She hastily bends her head, dark disheveled hair falling forward to camouflage her fleeing face. The stallion's gallant steps get louder.

Naaman is close at hand! Her stomach churns, thoughts collide. "Ride past, ride past!" she begs in a frantic prayer to YHWH. The stallion stops. There is a pause. Leather squeaks, armor jangles, the stallion snorts. Naaman dismounts, throwing his full weight to one side, feet thudding to the ground. The girl can feel him drawing close, hear him breathing, smell his sweating body. She opens her eyes and braces herself against the rough grip of his hand on her chin, his fingers digging into her cheeks. He jerks her head from left to right then left again now to center. He commands the attention of her eyes in his and releases her small body with such force that she topples unbalanced to the ground.

No one dares to help. The girl weeps. Naaman nods to his officer, points to the girl, remounts his stallion, and rides on.

SCENE 4

Naaman's slave girl sits silently at the open window of her shared quarters and looks out into the night. The plush fields and orchards on the foothills of Mount Herman are no longer visible beyond the city wall. Damascus has gone to bed for the night, the nearby Abana river lulling it to sleep. There is a hint of freshly baked bread in the air, with cumin, mint, and dill. With her eyes closed, she can almost imagine herself back at home, but the blended aroma of cherries, pomegranates, peculiar flowers, and rare spices mingle up from the garden below and root her to the present.

"Naaman has everything," her mistress had said to a friend, tears streaming, "except the cure for his leprosy." Naaman's slave girl is sleepy, but her thoughts are restless. She cannot stop thinking about the overheard conversation. She cannot stop thinking of Naaman. She cannot stop thinking of the past.

Years have gone since her march from freedom and family into slavery and strangers. Time may have healed the chafing of her wrists and ankles, but little can heal the chafing of her heart. She has learned survival, adjusted to her circumstances, and can even find moments of joy in the present. The past, however, is never far away, reclaiming hard-fought ground and constantly presenting new challenges to her fragile forgiveness.

Memories of invasion invade her again tonight. Her mother's wailing pleas for mercy drowning in shrill trumpet blasts. Her father's streaming blood curling around her bare feet. Her grandparents beaten, her infant sister abandoned, her village destroyed, and all the while the victory chant, "Naaman is victorious!"

She is overcome by a wrenching throb. A silent sob escapes on her breath. Hot tears find familiar paths down her cheeks. She cups her face in her hands and gives way once more to violent grief, shoulders shuddering. How she longs for her mother's touch, her father's voice. She can just recall the fading images that bring eventual calm. Tears come more gently now until they do not come at all. Pining gives way to the dull thud of reality. The past can never be changed no matter how much she wishes it or how often she mourns. She will never see her family again. No. This is her life now. The same stars might be shining over Israel, but she is in Damascus, Yhwh the only remnant she has of home.

Yhwh's presence had been so woven into her daily life that she could not, even now, comprehend a life without him. She had heard the history of her people many times. How the Lord had chosen them and called them out of slavery in Egypt. How he guided them through the wilderness to the Promised Land, bestowing love, provision, and protection through many amazing miracles. How the Lord had given the commands to Moses and remained faithful to his people even through their continuous disobedience. Grandfather had told her many stories about David, the brave shepherd boy who killed the mighty Goliath and became a king after God's own heart. "That is what we want Yhwh to say about us," he had said. "He does not wish to become angry with us for turning to idols like King Solomon."

Her great-grandfather had been alive during the peace, when Israel was a united kingdom, but she had never known anything but conflict. She prayed for lasting peace to come. She had heard the command of the Lord so often that it had become part of her. "Hear, O Israel:

The LORD our God, the LORD is one. Love the LORD your God with all your heart and with all your soul and with all your strength" (Deuteronomy 6:4–5). The faith of her people had become her own. She knew the one true God, and he knew and cared for her.

The girl shivers. An intense sense of peace overcomes her doubt. "Yhwh is the creator of these stars. He is the master of everything that happens under them." She prays. "Please help me to love you with my whole heart and to be devoted to you in this place, in this household."

She had known from the first day that her master was sick. His skin was blotchy, puffy, and white. His leprosy was not yet so severe as to keep him from his duties, but it was painful to him and might one day cost his life. At one time, his suffering brought her a perverse sense of comfort. Anger, grief, and despair had turned her heart relentlessly toward revenge.

Gradually, however, the one true, forgiving, and compassionate God had softened her heart toward Naaman. As she had once longed for his death, she now longed for his life. So did everyone who loved him. Naaman had paid physicians for every possible cure but to no avail. He secretly suspected that he was being punished by Rimmon and often joined the king to worship Rimmon and make sacrifice in an attempt to appease him. This was also unsuccessful. With each failure came greater disappointment and less hope. It seemed that Namaan had exhausted every option.

Naaman's slave girl slips quietly from the window into bed. The conversation rings in her ears as she closes her eyes. "Naaman has everything, except the cure for his leprosy." She begins to wonder again if there is anything she can do for him, any way that she can help beyond her prayers. She hates his futile devotion to Rimmon and longs for him to know the one true God. She rolls onto her right side, drawing the covers close up under her chin. She sighs, trying to shake Naaman out of her mind, but it is no use. "If only Yhwh's prophet were near at hand." Though she has never met him or witnessed the miracles Yhwh has performed through him, she knows his reputation.

The prophet Elisha saw Elijah being taken to heaven in a flaming chariot, healed the water making good out of bad, and turned a little oil into abundance. Yes, and she had heard a new slave from Samaria sharing about how he had brought a dead boy back to life. "What an incredible thing to do." She begins to stir with excitement. "If Elisha can defeat death," her eyes pop open, "can bring a boy back to life, maybe, no surely, he can heal my master!" Naaman's slave girl is overcome by the excitement of miraculous possibility. She wants to run and tell her mistress, wake her in the dead of night, act without the restraint of her position, but wisdom constrains her. "What ifs" begin to crowd her enthusiasm. What if they won't listen to her—a young, foreign, female slave? What if they won't believe her—she can give no proof of what she offers and indeed, no leper has been healed in Israel during Elisha's time. What if they suspect her motives, question her loyalty, and punish her for her boldness? The girl is aware of the mounting obstacles, but knows the faith growing in her heart will be rewarded. A soft and gentle peace settles on her as she prays for the courage she will need in the morning.

THINGS TO THINK ABOUT

It is impossible, of course, to know what really happened to the unnamed slave girl, but I believe with all my heart that the emotional truth of her life is echoed in the historical fiction above. We know from the account in 2 Kings 5 that she was young when captured and bold when necessary. She was a victim of war, but an apostle of peace. She was enslaved to her enemy, but served her God. She had every right to hate, but found healing. She had most reason to question but more faith to believe. She could not change the past, but she changed history. She was unidentified, but not insignificant.

Naaman's slave girl was not a superficial character playing a bit part in the healing of another. Like so many of the girls who are mentioned in these pages, she was a flesh and blood person in need of a miracle of her own. The internal and invisible seed of forgiveness at work in her blossomed into a full-blown act of grace. Naaman listened to his slave girl and was healed not only physically, but also spiritually.

Naaman's touching response to Elisha is evidence of the seed of God's forgiveness and grace in his own life:

> *Now I know that there is no God in all the world except in Israel. So please accept a gift from your servant...please let me, your servant, be given as much earth as a pair of mules can carry, for your servant will never again make burnt offerings and sacrifices to any other god but the LORD. But may the LORD forgive your servant for this one thing: When my master enters the temple of Rimmon to bow down and he is leaning on my arm and I have to bow there also—when I bow down in the temple of Rimmon, may the LORD forgive your servant for this.*
>
> *2 Kings 5:15, 17, 18*

Naaman's affirmation of YHWH's power and mercy in front of all of his men was, in itself, a genuine act of worship. His sincere plea for forgiveness when, in returning home, he would have to accompany the king to Rimmon's temple was a genuine act of repentance. His request for the soil of Israel was a visible sign of all that had occurred, and was a genuine act of testimony to his changed life. To all of these, Elisha responded, "Go in peace" (2 Kings 5:19).

I often wonder how the slave girl felt when Naaman returned not only healed but also changed. Did she steal a glance at the soil of YHWH? Did he thank her? Did he turn to her for instruction on faith? What effects did Naaman's conversion have on him, his marriage, his household, his job, and his country? The girl's act of forgiveness and grace changed history. We are reminded again that there is only one God in the world, that God alone can save and forgive, that the Lord is free to work where he wills and that the Lord is merciful and will forgive anyone who turns to him, whatever their nationality or background. In fact, the account of Naaman's healing is so important in emphasizing these things that Jesus referred to it at the start of his public ministry. Knowing that his own people would reject him, he suggested that the Gospel be given to others. There had been many lepers in Israel at the time of Naaman, but only Naaman had been healed. So, too, the Gospel would be offered elsewhere. God was sovereign and would show mercy where he willed. The crowd was furious when they heard this and showed their rejection of Jesus and his message by trying to kill him (cf. Luke 4:24–30).

Naaman's slave girl was a captive, an exile among the enemies of her God and nation. She had been forcibly abducted from country and home, made a slave to her captor, and subjected to all the indignities of her position. The inner reconciliation she achieved is a miracle in itself, but she abounded in grace at some risk to herself by voluntarily helping those who detained her. She took a giant step emotionally. Physically, she did a small thing that yielded great rewards. The fact that Naaman acted on her advice demonstrates her proven character. She spoke of the prophet of the Lord in Samaria. For Christians in ministry today, we can recommend a Savior. Indeed, for many of the girls we have read about, we are like modern-day Elishas, offering hope where little has existed before.

Some have become known to us throughout these pages, by name and history: Sabita (Nepal), uneducated family breadwinner; Mulugojam (Ethiopia), wife at age nine and mother at thirteen; Grace (Uganda), abducted into marriage and forced to fight in war with her baby on her back; Cham (Cambodia), electrically shocked into "hosting" five to ten men each day as a prostitute; Undina, laborer in the fields by day, surrogate parent to her siblings at night.

Most of the girls we have met throughout these pages, however, remain faceless, hidden under a dark veil of gruesome statistics. En masse, they are known to us as "The Girl Child," at risk from such stomach-churning neglect, violence, and abuse as to make her "the most disposable of human commodities." She is aborted, poisoned, drowned, strangled, or starved. She is malnourished, drug addicted, infected with HIV and AIDS. She is given, sold, or stolen into marriage, domestic labor, and prostitution. She is mutilated by circumcision, anorexia, or bulimia. She is intelligent but illiterate.

There has never been a time in history with so many children in terms of number and percentage of the population. There have never been such a high proportion of children at risk. The scale of current need is overwhelming and escalating. In 2005, there were nearly 2.2 billion children globally. Already vulnerable, more than 90 percent of them live in the world's neediest areas.[261]

Jesus had the harshest words for those who failed to meet the needs of the vulnerable, particularly the needs of widows, orphans, and children. There can be no denying the great physical and spiritual need of the world's smallest people. Whatever you do for a child today, you do for God. Are God's priorities your priorities?

God dignified humanity not by becoming a grown man, but by becoming a fetus in the womb. He went through every age and stage of childhood. In so doing, he showed that being fully human does not mean being an adult. Children are not half-human because they are small. They have a Savior with whom they can identify because he identified himself with them. Whatever you do for a child in the name of Christ today, you reaffirm God's dignity in that child. How will you be like the Savior today?

Children make up the largest unreached people group in the world, but receive the least attention in terms of mission and mission training.[262] When you share the Gospel with a child today, you give him or her the best hope for the future. Have we made children a focus of the great commission, or are they the great omission?

Not everyone can or should work with children. Children need well-trained workers armed with the love of God, the Gospel, and

---

261 UNICEF, *State of the World's Children 2007: The Double Dividend of Gender Equality* (New York: UNICEF, 2006), 125.
262 See, Dan Brewster and Patrick McDonald, *Children—The Great Omission?* (Oxford, UK: Viva Network, 2004), 2–3.

a call. Children's workers must have access to training that focuses specifically on the developmental needs of the child mentally, physically, emotionally, and spiritually. What we believe has a profound effect on how we act. When you train someone to work with children today, you teach a child in the way he or she should go (cf. Prov. 22:6). How will you improve your practice today?

Those of us privileged enough to volunteer our voices to the pages of this book, want nothing more than to inform, educate, and encourage the work of Jesus Christ with "The Girl Child" wherever she is found and in whatever situation. The task at hand is certainly overwhelming, often discouraging, and seldom "successful" in the world's eyes. However, Naaman's slave girl is an example of what heaven proves over and over again: that rejoicing is the reward of each single soul saved. Let us pray together that more and more of them belong to little girls.

BIBLIOGRAPHY

Adeney, Miriam. "Clear Out! This Girl Isn't Dead!" *Together,* no. 49: 4–6.

Africa News Service Files. "Child Labour: A Blight in Cote D'Ivoire." Africa News Service, January 16, 2001.

Ahuja, Ram. *The Indian Social System.* New Delhi: Ravat Publications, 1997.

American Association of University Women. *Gender Gaps: Where Schools Still Fail Our Children.* New York: Marlowe & Company, 1999.

-------. *How Schools Shortchange Girls: The AAUW Report.* New York: Marlowe & Company, 1995.

Ammo, Joseph. "The World According to Adolescents." South Asia Forum, 2001. http://www.hsph.harvard.edu.

Anirban, Roy. "Indian Religious Seers Call to End Female Foeticide." Reuters News Service, June 24, 2001, New Delhi.

Asian Development Bank. "Indonesia: Supporting Girl Street Children." *Seagen Waves* 1, no. 1 (August 2007). http://www.adb.org/Documents/Periodicals/SEA-GEN/vol01-01/ino-girl-street-children.asp.

Avarientos, Elnora. "Today's Girl Is Tomorrow's Woman." *Together,* no. 49 (1996).

Bales, Kevin. "Slavery Today." Free the Slaves. http://www.freetheslaves.net/NETCOMMUNITY/Page.aspx?pid=301&srcid=208.

-------. *Understanding Global Slavery: A Reader.* Berkeley, CA: University of California Press, 2005.

"Bartered, Battered, Burned." *The Telegraph,* March 31, 2001. http://www.telegraph.co.uk/arts/main.jhtml;jsessionid=C4AKL02E1THRDQFIQMGSFF4AVCBQWIV0?xml=/arts/2001/03/31/bofir31.xml (accessed December 21, 2007).

Beausay, William and Kathryn Beausay. *Girls! Helping Your Little Girl Become an Extraordinary Woman.* Grand Rapids, MI: Fleming H. Revell, 1996.

Bilezikian, Gilbert. *Beyond Sex Roles.* Grand Rapids: Baker Book House Company, 1985.

Bloem, Renate. "Child Labour: A Gender Perspective." *Women's Watch,* United Nations. November 16, 1999.

BRAC Bangladesh. "Education." BRAC. http://www.brac.net/education.htm.

Bradshaw, Bruce. "Preventing Child Exploitation through Community Survival Strategies." *Together* (April–June 1990): 1.

Brewster, Dan, and Patrick McDonald. *Children—The Great Omission?* Oxford, UK: Viva Network, 2004.

Brink, Paul. "Debating International Human Rights: The 'Middle Ground' for Religious Participants." *The Brandywine Review of Faith and International Affairs* (Fall 2003).

Brown, Lyn Mikel, and Carol Gilligan. *Meeting at the Crossroads: Women's Psychology and Girls' Development.* Cambridge, MA: Harvard University Press, 1992.

Burns, John F. "Child Marriages, Though Illegal, Persist in India." *The New York Times*, May 11, 1998. http://www.ishipress.com/indiamar.htm (accessed December 21, 2007).

Carrillo, Pablo. "Girls Lead Peace Effort in Colombia." *Together*, no. 58 (1998): 20–23.

Cedar, Paul. "Where Is Hope?" *Pursuit* 1, no. 4 (1993): 1.

Center for Reproductive Rights. "Female Genital Mutilation (FGM): Legal Prohibitions Worldwide." February 2005. http://www.crlp.org/pub_fac_fgmicpd.html.

Child Health and Development. "Child Survival in the South-East Asia Region." World Health Organization. http://www.searo.who.int/EN/Section13/Section37/Section135.htm.

Clark, Robert E., Joanne Brubaker, and Roy B. Zuck. *Childhood Education in the Church.* Rev. ed. Chicago: The Moody Bible Institute, 1986.

Cleland, J.G., and J. K. Van Ginneken. "Maternal Education and Child Survival in Developing Countries: The Search for Pathways of Influence." *Social Science and Medicine* 27, no. 12 (1988): 1357–68.

Clinton, Tim. Audiotape of lecture by Tim Clinton presented at American Association of Christian Counselors, n.d.

Cohn, D'Vera. "The Campaign Against Female Genital Cutting: New Hope, New Challenges." Population Reference Bureau. http://www.prb.org/Articles/2007/CampaignAgainstFemaleGenitalCutting.aspx.

Commission on Human Rights. "Report of the Special Rapporteur on the Sale of Children, Child Prostitution and Child Pornography, Ms. Ofelia Calcetas-Santos." Human Rights Internet. http://www.hri.ca/fortherecord1999/documentation/commission/e-cn4-1999-71.htm#chii.

Constitution of the World Health Organization as adopted by the International Health Conference. New York, June 19–22, 1946. Signed on July 22, 1946 by the representatives of 61 States. Official Records of the World Health Organization, no. 2, p. 100 and entered into force on April 7, 1948.

Curtis, Brent, and John Eldredge. *The Sacred Romance*. Nashville, TN: Thomas Nelson, Inc., 1997.

Dareer, Asma El. *Women, Why Do You Weep? Circumcision and Its Consequences*. London: Zed Press, 1982.

De Sarkar, Bishakha. "Killing Daughters to Avoid Watering Your Neighbour's Plant." *The Telegraph*, Lucknow, India, n.d.

Delgado-Schenk, Renata. "Children's Rights in Chile: Alternative Report on the Implementation of the Convention on the Rights of the Child by Chile." World Organization Against Torture. Geneva: United Nations, 2007. http://www.undp.org/rblac/gender/itsourright.htm.

Department of Gender, Women and Health. "Gender in Tuberculosis Research." WHO 2004. http://www.who.int/gender/documents/en/tuberculosislow.pdf.

Dicker, Sheryl. *Successful Advocacy for Children*. New York: The Foundation for Child Development, 1990.

Dorkenoo, Efua. *Cutting the Rose: Female Genital Mutilation—The Practice and its Prevention*. London: Minority Rights Group Publications, 1995.

Dorman, Linda. "Trafficking Women and Girls in Asia." *Together* (April–June 2000): 7.

Dudones, Jill. "Unkindest Cut." *Ms. Magazine*, March 29, 2007.

Edelman, Marian Wright. *Families in Peril: An Agenda for Social Change*. Cambridge: Harvard University Press, 1987.

Eke, N., and K.E.O. Nkanginieme. "Female Genital Mutilation and Obstetric Outcome." *The Lancet* 367, no. 9525 (June 3, 2006): 1799–1800. http://www.proquest.com/ (accessed January 8, 2008).

Ennew, Judith, and Paul Stephenson, eds. *Questioning the Basis of Our Work: Christianity, Children's Rights, and Development*. London: Tearfund, 2004.

Evans, Tony. *Human Rights Fifty Years On: A Reappraisal*. Manchester, UK: Manchester University Press, 1998.

Evusa, Juliet. "A Change of Attitude: A Thematic and Critical Analysis of Female Genital Mutilation Debates Across the Media from 1986 to 2001." Presented at "The Children of the World: Risk and Hope" conference, Ohio University, Ohio, April 5–7, 2001.

Family Planning Association of Pakistan. "India: Seminar on Adolescent Girl's Health." *Women's International Network News* 28 (Autumn 1992): 25.

Fellows, Beth. "The World Bank and Girls' Education 1999." *Together* (January–March 2000).

Fennema, Elizabeth. "Justice, Equity, and Mathematics Education." In *Mathematics and Gender*, edited by Elizabeth Fennema and Gilah C. Leder. Baltimore: The John Hopkins University Press, 1990.

Foster, Richard. *Prayer: Finding the Heart's True Home.* San Francisco: Harper Collins Publishing, 1992.

Gender Equity Advisory Committee. *Ensuring Equal Opportunity for All Youth and Adults in the Education and Workforce Preparation System.* Springfield, IL: Illinois State Board of Education, 2002. http://www.isbe.net/career/pdf/perkins_equity.pdf.

Gettis, A., J. Getis, and J.D. Fellmann. *Introduction to Geography.* 9th ed. New York: McGraw-Hill, 2004.

Goodkind, Daniel. "Should Prenatal Sex Selection Be Restricted? Ethical Questions and Their Implications for Research and Policy." *Population Studies* 53, no. 1 (1999): 49–61. http://links.jstor.org/sici?sici=0032-28(199903)53%3A1%3C49%3ASPSSBR%3E2.0.CO%3B2-D.

Gopalan, Sarala, and Vijay Bhaskar. "Response of the Government to the Girl Child." Paper written for the South Asia Forum, 2001. http://www.hsph.harvard.edu/grhf/SAsia/forums/girlchild/response.

Gow, Melanie. "Assisting Children in Especially Difficult Circumstances." *Together*, no. 42 (January–March 2000): 4.

Haag, Pamela, and American Association of University Women Educational Foundation. *Voices of a Generation: Teenage Girls Report About Their Lives Today.* New York: Marlowe & Company, 2000.

Halloran, Richard. "The Rising East: Millions Victimized by Modern-Day Slavery." *The Honolulu Advertiser*, November 19, 2002.

Harris, Bruce. "Casa Alianza." http://www.casa-alianza.org/es/news.php (accessed August 18, 2002).

Haugen, Gary. *Good News about Injustice.* Downers Grove, IL: InterVarsity Press, 1999.

Hawkins, Linda. "Because They Are Girls." In *A Safe World for Children*, edited by Melanie Gow. Monrovia, CA: World Vision International, 2001.

Hosken, Fran P. *The Hosken Report: Genital and Sexual Mutilation of Females.* 4th rev. ed. Lexington, MA: WIN News, 2002.

Human Rights Watch. "Jordan: Victims Jailed in 'Honor' Crime Cases." *Human Rights News.* http://hrw.org/english/docs/2004/04/16/jordan8465.htm.

Husseini, Rana. Interview by Diane Sawyer. *20/20*, PBS. 1998.

Ignatieff, Michael. *Human Rights as Politics and Idolatry.* Princeton: Princeton University Press, 2001.

-------. *The Rights Revolution: The 2000 Massey Lectures.* Toronto: House of Anansi, 2000.

ILO-IPEC. "Combat the Trafficking of Children." International Labour Office, 2002. http://www.ilo.org/ipecinfo/product/viewProduct.do?productId=767.

-------. "Multilateral Programme of Technical Cooperation." International Labour Organization. http://white.oit.org.pe/ipec/documentos/docproying.pdf.

ILO-IPEC Geneva. *Hazardous Child Domestic Work: A Briefing Sheet.* Geneva: International Labour Office, 2007.

International Labour Organization. "Provisional Record, Ninety-Sixth Session, Geneva, 2007." Report of the fifth sitting of the International Labour Conference, June 8, 2007. http://www.adb.org/Documents/Periodicals/ADB_Review/2001/vol33_1/street_girls.asp?p=gender.

International Programme on the Elimination of Child Labour. "Armed Conflict (Child Soldiers)." International Labour Organization. http://www.ilo.org/ipec/areas/Armedconflict/lang--en/index.htm.

Irvine, Graeme. "Taking the Child Seriously." *Together*, no. 42 (1994): 3.

Jamison, Laura. "Killing for 'Honor': Legalized Murder." Amnesty International USA. http://www.amnestyusa.org/amnestynow/legalizedmurder.html.

Joint United Nations Programme on HIV/AIDS. "Children and Orphans." UNAIDS. http://www.unaids.org/en/PolicyAndPractice/KeyPopulations/ChildAndOrphans/.

-------. "Women and Girls." UNAIDS. http://www.unaids.org/en/PolicyAndPractice/KeyPopulations/WomenGirls/.

-------. "Young People." UNAIDS. http://www.unaids.org/en/PolicyAndPractice/KeyPopulations/YoungPeople/.

-------. "Zimbabwe." UNAIDS. http://www.unaids.org/en/CountryResponses/Countries/zimbabwe.asp.

Khadka, Kanti. "Learning from Experience: Girls Rights." Presented at the Save the Children Listen to Girls Forum, December 1998.

Koso-Thomas, Olayinka. *The Circumcision of Women: A Strategy for Its Eradication*. London: Zed Press, 1987.

Kupp, David. "Growing Up a Girl: A Tough Life." *Voices*, no. 1 (1994): 3.

Kurz, Kathleen M., and Cynthia J. Prather. *Improving the Quality of Life of Girls*. New York: Association for Women in Development, 1995.

Levinson, F. James, and Lucy Bassett. "Malnutrition Is Still a Major Contributor to Child Deaths." Population Reference Bureau. http://www.prb.org/pdf07/Nutrition2007.pdf.

Mackoff, Barbara. *Growing a Girl: Seven Strategies for Raising a Strong, Spirited Daughter*. New York: Dell Publishing, 1996.

MacNutt, Francis. *Healing*. Notre Dame, IN: Ave Maria Press, 1974.

McConnell, Douglas, Jennifer Orona, and Paul Stockley, eds. *Understanding God's Heart for Children: Toward a Biblical Framework*. Colorado Springs, CO: Authentic, 2007.

McMinn, Lisa Graham. *Growing Strong Daughters*. Grand Rapids, MI: Baker Books, 2000.

Mehrotra, Aparna, and Rini Banerjee. "Life Without Violence: It's Our Right." UNDP. http://www.undp.org/rblac/gender/itsourright.htm.

Meta Media Productions and World Vision Canada. *Evening the Odds: The Story of the Girl Child*. Mississauga, ON: Meta Media Productions and World Vision Canada, 1996. Video recording.

Ministry of Education Lusaka. *Girls' Education: A Situational Analysis at the Provincial level of Girl Child Education in Zambia*. Lusaka, Zambia: Programme for the Advancement of Girls' Education, 1999.

Mocria, Ellene. *Child Brides*. London: Channel 4, 1999.

Morris, Kelly. "Feature: Issues on Female Genital Mutilation/Cutting—Progress and Parallels." *The Lancet: Medicine and Creativity* 368 (December 1, 2006): S64–S67. http://www.proquest.com/ (accessed January 8, 2008).

Mother Teresa. *My Life for the Poor*. New York: HarperCollins, 2005.

Museveni, Janet K. "Cultural, Political and Social Empowerment of Girl Children." In *The Girl Child: Enhancing Life Sustaining Hope 1998 Washington Forum*, edited by World Vision. Federal Way, WA: The Institute for Global Engagement, World Vision, Inc., 1998.

Nair, Omana. "Hope for Street Girls." *ADB Review 33*, no. 1 (2001). http://www.adb.org/Documents/Periodicals/ADB_Review/2001/vol33_1/street_girls.asp?p=gender.

National Crime Record Bureau. "Chapter 5—Crime Against Women." Crime in India—2005. http://ncrb.nic.in/crime2005/cii-2005/CHAP5.pdf, 242.

Ndungane, Njongonkulu. Media statement. Pan African News Agency. Cape Town, South Africa, November 2, 2000.

Neimanis, Astrida, and Arkadi Tortisyn. *Gender Thematic Guidance Note*. National Human Development Report Series. UNDP Human Development Report Office, July 2003.

NGO Committee on UNICEF. *Putting Child Rights Into Action*. UNICEF, n.d.

O'Grady, Ron. *The Child and the Tourist: The Story Behind the Escalation of Child Prostitution in Asia*. Bangkok: ECPAT, 1992.

Office of the Special Representative of the Secretary-General for Children and Armed Conflict. "Children Affected by Conflict." United Nations. http://www.un.org/special-rep/ children-armed-conflict/index.html (accessed October 2, 2006).

Orenstein, Peggy. *Schoolgirls: Young Women, Self-Esteem, and the Confidence Gap*. New York: Doubleday, 1994.

Paul, Radha. "What About the Girl Child?" *Together* (January–March 2000): 13–14.

Payne, Leanne. *Healing Presence*. Westchester, IL: Crossway Books, 1989.

Phillips, Lynn. *The Girls Report: What We Know & Need to Know About Growing Up Female*. New York: The National Council for Research on Women, 1998.

Piot, Peter. "Uniting the World against AIDS." Speech, Woodrow Wilson Center for International Scholars, Washington, DC, September 20, 2007.

Pipher, Mary. *Reviving Ophelia: Saving the Selves of Adolescent Girls*. New York: Ballantine Books, 1994.

Plan UK. *Because I Am a Girl: The State of the World's Girls 2007*. London: Plan International 2007. http://www.plan-uk.org/pdfs/plan_uk-girls_report2007.pdf.

Robin, Debra J. "Educating Against Gender-Based Violence." *WEEA Digest*, Women's Equity Publications.

Rutter, Virginia Beane. *Celebrating Girls: Nurturing and Empowering Our Daughters*. Berkeley, CA: Conari Press, 1996.

Sadker, Myra, and David Sadker. *Failing at Fairness: How Our Schools Cheat Girls*. New York: Touchstone, Simon & Schuster, 1994.

Sanford, Agnes. *The Healing Light*. St. Paul, MN: Macalester Park Publishing Company, 1947.

Scott, Dave. "Theological Dignity and Human Rights for Children." In *Understanding God's Heart for Children: Toward a Biblical Framework*, edited by Douglas McConnell, Jennifer Orona, and Paul Stockley, 23–31. Federal Way, WA: Authentic, 2007.

Seamands, David. *Healing for Damaged Emotions*. St. Paul, MN: Victor Books, 1981.

-------. *Putting Away Childish Things*. Wheaton, IL: Victory Books, 1993.

Seiple, Robert A. "A Rent in the Garment." In *The Girl Child: Enhancing Life, Sustaining Hope 1998 Washington Forum*, edited by World Vision, 9–15. Federal Way, WA: The Institute for Global Engagement, World Vision Inc., 1998.

Shah, Shalini. "Evangelical Perspectives on Mission and Ethics." *Drishtikone* (May 1, 1996): 19–21.

Shandler, Sara. *Ophelia Speaks: Adolescent Girls Write About Their Search for Self*. New York: Harper Perennial, 1999.

Smith, Edward. *Genuine Recovery*. Campbellsville, KY: Family Care Publishing, 1996.

Sohoni, Neera Kuckreja. *The Burden of Girlhood: A Global Inquiry into the Status of Girls*. Oakland, CA: Third Party Publishing Co., 1995.

Sommers, Christina Hoff. "The War Against Boys." *The Atlantic Monthly* (May 2000).

Steiner, Henry, and Philip Alston. *International Human Rights in Context: Law, Politics, Morals*. New York: Oxford University Press, 2000.

Sterky, Charlotta. "BRAC Reaches Girls with Primary Education in Bangladesh." *E'Dev News*, UNICEF (December 1991).

Tanaka, Janet. "Will Size 22 Fit Through the Pearly Gates?" *Daughters of Sarah* (September/October 1989): 16.

Thomas, Sue. "AIDS Myth Fuels S. Africa's Child-Rape Scourge." Reuters News Service, Johannesburg, November 5, 2002.

Toycen, Dave. "Is Child-Focused Development Real Development?" *Together*, no. 65 (2000): 17.

Tumlin, Karen C. "Trafficking in Children and Women: A Regional Overview." Paper presented at the Asian Regional High-Level Meeting on Child Labour, Jakarta, Indonesia, March 8–10, 2000. http://www.ilo.org/public/english/region/asro/bangkok/download/yr2000/child/trafficking.pdf.

UNAIDS. "Fact Sheet: Revised HIV Estimates." Joint United Nations Programme on HIV/AIDS. http://data.unaids.org/pub/EPISlides/2007/071118_epi_revisions_factsheet_en.pdf.

-------. "HIV/AIDS and Gender-Based Violence." UNAIDS 2003. http://data.unaids.org/Topics/Gender/genderbasedviolence_en.pdf.

UNESCO. *World Education Report.* New York: UNESCO, 1995.

UNICEF. "Child Marriage." Child Protection from Violence, Exploitation and Abuse. http://www.unicef.org/protection/index_earlymarriage.html.

-------. "Children in Unconditional Worst Forms of Child Labour and Exploitation." *State of the World's Children* 2006. http://www.unicef.org/sowc06/pdfs/figure3_7.pdf.

-------. "Sara...Daughter of a Lioness." Episode 3, Tape 367. VHS. UNICEF, 1998.

-------. "Domestic Violence against Women and Girls." *Innocenti Digest,* no. 6 (June 2000).

-------. *Early Marriage: A Harmful Traditional Practice, A Statistical Exploration.* New York: UNICEF, 2005. http://www.unicef.org/sowc06/pdfs/Early_Marriage_12.lo.pdf.

-------. "Early Marriage: Child Spouses." *Innocenti Digest,* no. 7 (March 2001).

-------. *Education of the Girl Child: Her Right, Society's Gain.* New York: UNICEF, 1992.

-------. *The Lesser Child: The Girl in India.* UNICEF/Government of India, 1989.

-------. "Life After Early Marriage." UNICEF Innocenti Research Centre. http://www.unicef-irc.org/presscentre/presskit/innocentidigest/storiesid7.pdf.

-------. "Rights of Girls." *UNICEF Staff Working Papers: Evaluation, Policy and Planning Series.* New York: UNICEF, 1999.

-------. *Sex Differences in Child Survival and Development.* Amman: UNICEF Regional Office for the Middle East and North Africa, 1990.

-------. "Spread of Wild Polio Battled in Sudan with Additional Immunization Campaigns." UNICEF. http://www.unicef.org/media/media_23547.html.

-------. *State of the World's Children 2007: The Double Dividend of Gender Equality.* New York: UNICEF, 2006.

-------. *The World Declaration on the Survival, Protection, and Development of Children.* New York: UNICEF, 1992.

United Nations. "Convention on the Rights of the Child." Geneva: Office of the High Commissioner for Human Rights, 1989.

-------. "Fact Sheet No. 23, Harmful Traditional Practices Affecting the Health of Women and Children." Office of the High Commissioner for Human Rights. http://www.unhchr.ch/html/menu6/2/fs23.htm.

-------. *Patterns of First Marriage: Timing and Prevalence*. New York: United Nations, 1990.

-------. *Too Young to Die: Genes or Gender?* New York: United Nations, 1998.

-------. "The United Nations Fourth World Conference on Women." Division for the Advancement of Women. http://www.un.org/womenwatch/daw/beijing/platform/girl.htm.

The United Nations Fourth World Conference on Women. "Beijing Declaration and Platform for Action." United Nations. http://www.un.org/womenwatch/daw/beijing/platform/violence.htm. Paragraph 112.

United Nations Population Fund. "Adolescents Fact Sheet." UNFPA. http://www.unfpa.org/swp/2005/presskit/factsheets/facts_adolescents.htm#ftn7.

-------. "Child Marriage Fact Sheet." UNFPA 2005. http://www.unfpa.org/swp/2005/presskit/factsheets/facts_child_marriage.htm (accessed January 8, 2008).

-------. "Ending Violence Against Women and Girls." In *The State of the World's Population 2000*, edited by UNFPA. New York: UNFPA, 2000. http://www.unfpa.org/swp/2000/english/ch03.html.

-------. "Frequently Asked Questions on Female Genital Mutilation/Cutting." UNFPA. http://www.unfpa.org/gender/practices2.htm#12.

-------. "Gender Inequality and Reproductive Health." UNFPA. http://www.unfpa.org/swp/2003/english/ch2/index.htm.

-------. "Involving Men in Promoting Gender Equality and Women's Reproductive Health." United Nations. http://www.unfpa.org/gender/men.htm.

Vogel, Linda J. "Teach These Words to Your Children." *Daughters of Sarah* 16, no. 5 (1990): 10.

Weber, Kristine. "Out in the Cold: The Street Children of Mongolia." People's News Agency. http://www.prout.org/pna/mongolian-street-children.html.

WHO Europe. "Young People's Health in Context: Selected Key Findings from the Health Behaviour in School Aged Children Study." Fact Sheet Euro 04/04. http://www.euro.who.int/document/mediacentre/fs0404e.pdf.

WHO Statistical Information System (WHOSIS). "Mortality Database, Table 1: 'Numbers of registered deaths,' Ecuador 2000, Peru 2000, El Salvador 1999, Mexico 2001, Uruguay 2000." http://www3.who.int/whosis/mort/table1.cfm?path=whosis,mort,mort_table1&language=english.

WiLDAF/FeDDAF—West Africa. "Female Genital Mutilation, a Daily Fight to Eradiquate [sic.] this practice in Guinea for the Rights of Women and Girls." Women, Law and Development in Africa. http://www.wildaf-ao.org/eng/article.php3?id_article=77.

World Health Organization. "Community-Based Management of Severe Acute Malnutrition." World Health Organization. http://www.who.int/child-adolescent-health/New_ Publications/CHILD_HEALTH/Severe_Acute_ Malnutrition_en.pdf.

-------. "Female Genital Mutilation." WHO June 2000. http://www.who.int/mediacentre/ factsheets/fs241/en/.

-------. "Tuberculosis." WHO March 2007. http://www.who.int/mediacentre/factsheets/fs104/ en/index.html.

World Vision. "The Effects of Armed Conflict on Girls." *World Vision* (July 1996).

-------. *Every Girl Counts: Development, Justice, and Gender*. Monrovia, CA: World Vision Canada, 2001.

World Vision, ed. *The Girl Child: Enhancing Life Sustaining Hope 1998 Washington Forum*. Federal Way, WA: The Institute for Global Engagement, World Vision, Inc., 1998.

World Vision Australia. *Education for All*. Compiled by Information Services, World Vision Australia, March 1993.

World Vision Canada. *Children at Risk Tool-Kit: Girl Children: The Potential Is Powerful*. Mississauga, ON: World Vision Canada, 1996.

-------. "The Girl Child—Background." In *Children at Risk Training Packet*. Canada: World Vision, n.d.

-------. *Girls! Stories Worth Telling: Report and Conference Manual*. Toronto: World Vision Canada, 1998.

World Vision Canada, Foster Parents Plan of Canada, Save the Children—Canada, and Christian Children's Fund of Canada. Girls! *Stories Worth Telling Video*. Toronto: World Vision Canada, March 2–6, 1998. Video recording.

"Young Women." World Vision Australia, 1992.

INDEX

K

Kenya
    alternatives to female genital mutilation, 203
    early marriage, 132–134
    female genital mutilation, 132–134
    Kwale, 174
    Masai, 132–134, 229, 232
    poverty, 174–175
Kilbourn, Phyllis, 121, 145, 209, 229
Kingdom of God, inclusion of females, 28
Kogoya, Lepinus, 14
Kogoya, Undina, 14, 282
Kony, Joseph, 11
Korea, sex selection, 124
Kupp, David D., 39
Kurz, Kathleen M., 62, 120

L

Laban, 31–32
LaDue, Nancy, 165
Lalela, a Romanian orphan, 112–113
Latin America
    Bolivia, 187
    child prostitution, 16
    Chile, 149
    Colombia, 187
    early marriage, 135
    Guatemala, 153–154, 166
    Nicaragua, 150
Laws. *See also* Legal issues
    The Child Marriage Restraint Act, 138–139
    Juvenile Justice Act, 242
    Pre-Natal Diagnostic Techniques Acts, 124
Legal issues
    advocacy for girls, 233
    female genital mutilation, 55, 132
    laws. *See* Laws
    roots of girl-boy disparity, 45
    strategies for girls, 189
    traditional cultural practices, 60
Leprosy. *See* Naaman's slave girl
Lineage, gender equality, 5
Literacy. *See* Education
Living environment, unhealthy conditions, 173–174

Wives. *See also* Marriage, early
   ideal wife mold, 6
   soldiers', 10–11, 151–152
   temple wives, 11
Work
   child labor. *See* Child labor
   exploitation at work, 13, 155–156, 200–201
   son preference, 52
   unhealthy environments, 174
World Bank, benefits of girls' education, 222, 223
World Health Organization
   body image issues, 102
   elimination of female genital mutilation, 64
   health, defined, 164, 165
   health as a right, 166
   tuberculosis, 176
World Vision
   education for girls, 195–196
   education for mothers, 188
   evaluation of program effectiveness, 193
   girls as gifts, 86
   "Girls! Stories Worth Telling." *See* "Girls! Stories Worth Telling"
   goal of strategies for girls, 186
   raising consciousness, 194
   rights of girls, 184

Y
Yahweh (YHWH), 271, 272, 277–279, 281
YHWH, 271, 272, 277–279, 281
Yogyakarta poverty reduction scheme, 154–155

Z
Zambia
   school gender inequality, 216–217
   school-based factors against girls, 214–218
   triplet girl starvation, 3
Zechariah, 32
Zelophehad, 30
Zengeza High School, Girl Child Network, 239
Zimbabwe, Girl Child Network, 239–241